THE PENNINE WAY

THE PATH, THE PEOPLE, THE JOURNEY

About the author

Andrew McCloy is a writer and journalist specialising in walking and the outdoors and has written or contributed to over 20 titles, from family and history rambles to exploring the British coast on foot. An experienced long-distance walker, he wrote the first ever guide to walking from Land's End to John o'Groats. He's a member of the Outdoor Writers and Photographers Guild, contributes to a variety of magazines and newspapers and is also a freelance access and recreation consultant. He was formerly Information Officer for the Ramblers' Association and has variously worked for the Youth Hostels Association and Community Transport. Andrew is married with two daughters and lives in Derbyshire, where he is presently an elected member of the Peak District National Park Authority.

THE PENNINE WAY

THE PATH, THE PEOPLE, THE JOURNEY

Andrew McCloy

CICERONE

2 Police Square, Milnthorpe, Cumbria LA7 7PY
www.cicerone.co.uk

© Andrew McCloy 2016
First edition 2016
ISBN: 978 1 85284 924 5

Printed and bound by KHL Printing, Singapore

A catalogue record for this book is available from the British Library.
Photographs are credited with the relevant image.

Front cover: Walker below Pen-y-ghent (© Jon Sparks)
Back cover: For many Pennine Way walkers, High Cup is one of the
highlights of the entire trail. (© Steve Westwood)

Contents

Acknowledgements

This book is dedicated to all those, past and present, connected with the Pennine Way Association, who since the late 1930s have championed this unique trail. In particular, thank you to Chris Sainty for unhindered access to his encyclopedic knowledge of the Pennine Way and for his enthusiastic support for this book, and to Mandy Sainty for also reading the manuscript. Peter Stott freely shared his passion for the path, and others such as Mike Imrie, Trevor Hardy and Ron Powell also lent their assistance.

Thanks to the present Pennine National Trails Partnership Manager, Heather Procter, for her support, and to Mike Rhodes and Martyn Sharp, who between them have done so much over so many years to improve the Pennine Way at its southern end. Chris Woodley-Stewart from the North Pennines Area of Outstanding Natural Beauty, Debra Wilson at the Moors for the Future Partnership and Kate Hilditch from the Yorkshire Dales National Park Authority also put up with numerous enquiries.

John Martin gave me invaluable assistance trawling the archives of the Youth Hostels Association; and the staff of London Metropolitan Archives guided me through boxes of historical documents relating to Tom Stephenson and the early years of the Ramblers' Association.

There were so many other people who happily gave up their time to talk about a long-distance path that evidently meant so much to them: Mary Jephcott, Joan Proctor, Alan Binns, Steve Westwood, John Manning, Colin Speakman, Keith Carter, Paddy Dillon and Gordon Miller. Thank you to Adrian Braddy at The Dalesman magazine and to the Bayes family of Horton's Pen-y-ghent Café; to Andrew Dalby for sharing his memories of working alongside Tom Stephenson; and to all the accommodation providers and publicans who I pestered with questions.

A special thank you to the other Pennine Wayfarers, not just those who shared their memories of past walks but also those who I met on the trail in the summer of 2015 and who chatted about their own journeys. I've changed some names, but I'm grateful for both their trust and their friendship on the trail.

I have tried to gain consent for all quotes and check references as thoroughly as possible, although some proved difficult, but if any mistakes have crept in they are all mine and I apologise in advance.

Personal thanks to Nicky Phillips for reading through the draft text and suggesting improvements. And last but certainly not least, thanks to Penny for putting up with my mild obsession about a footpath, her all-round support and for baking an industrial quantity of tasty flapjack for the walk itself; to Jenny for her encouragement; and to Caitlin, whose energy and enthusiasm may well one day see her lacing up her boots at Edale ...

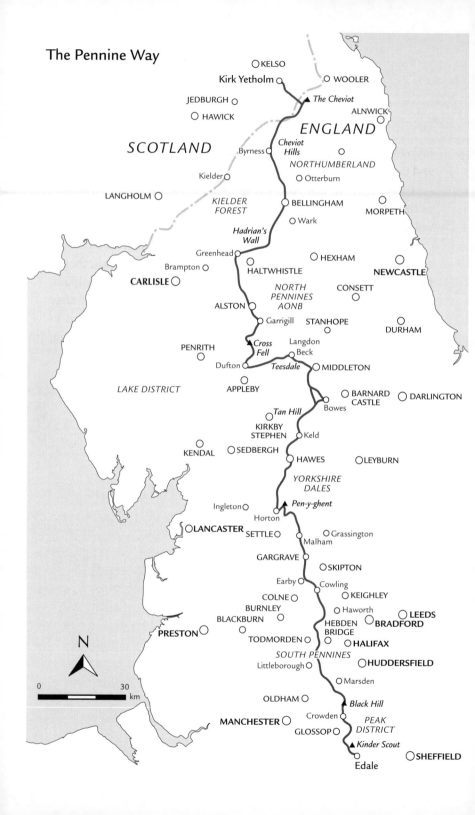

Introduction

The Pennine Way and I grew up together. I don't mean that it shared a room with me or was part of the family, but I was born within a year of it opening and I have always felt an attachment to the path. When I was young, our family holidays usually involved walking and the outdoors in some sort of way; and even growing up in suburban south London I was always aware of the Pennine Way. To my mind, it loosely shared the same company as a trek through the remote Himalayas or a walk from Land's End to John o'Groats – a fabled journey, an extreme physical challenge undertaken by a handful of really grown-up people. It seemed daunting and exciting in equal measure, with an ever so slightly mysterious air to it. John Noakes and his dog walked it for his TV programme *Go with Noakes*, which only added to the thrill factor. Over time, it became lodged in my consciousness, but I had never even stepped foot on it.

As a teenager, I bought a copy of Tom Stephenson's official guidebook to the Pennine Way. It had evocative photos of wild-looking hill country, dramatic scenes that seemed remote and detached from my day-to-day life. I followed the text across purple heather moors, over windswept hills and alongside the Roman Wall; I studied the map extracts carefully, following the red line as it wove its way amid often tightly packed black-and-white contours, page after page after page.

In my mid teens, I began long-distance walking and discovered the challenge, fun and adventure of exploring paths on my own and with others, but not yet the Pennine Way. It was an ambition, certainly, but still something I kept at arm's length. Perhaps I felt I wasn't ready for it, or maybe there was a growing awareness that this famous old path was in a spot of bother: overuse and erosion had given it an increasingly bad press, so that people shook their heads and said it wasn't worth walking any more.

However, over the years I explored short sections of the Pennine Way on foot and got to know some parts, like the Yorkshire Dales, quite well. I eventually moved to live near its southern end in the Peak District, but still it was there and still I hadn't walked it all.

As both the Pennine Way and I neared 50, I decided it was now or never. I hadn't really thought of it in any 'midlife' challenge or crisis sort of way, but clearly others had. A few months before I set off, I attended a small celebratory event in Edale organised by the Peak District National Park Authority, marking the Pennine Way's 50th birthday. Among the speakers was author and local resident Mark Wallington, whose light-hearted and enjoyable account of walking the Pennine Way with his dog was published in 1997. He outlined a theory as to why so many men of a certain middling age walk the Pennine Way (or at least try to), inviting the audience to imagine a typical young man's bucket list cataloguing all the things he might want to achieve or experience in life. It could include buying an expensive sports car, going out with a supermodel, skydiving, playing guitar in a rock group, scoring a winning goal in an FA Cup Final, 24-hour parties, walking the Pennine Way, and so on. However, as that young man gets older, more and more items on the wish list are crossed off as unobtainable, until he realises that he's reached the point where walking the Pennine Way is the only thing left that's even remotely feasible. Along with the rest of the audience, I laughed, but not quite as loudly as everyone else.

There's something genuinely fascinating about the Pennine Way. If a long-distance path could be said to work on different levels, then this is it. It was the first to be created in Britain and is arguably still the most famous. Damian Hall, author of the official National Trail Guide to the Pennine Way, introduces the path as 'the original, the classic, the daddy; it's the oldest, the roughest and toughest of them all.' The long and valiant fight to secure public access to the hills is bound up in its history, while its fluctuating fortunes mirror those of the youth hostels movement, whose assorted buildings still dot the Pennine hills. Our relationship with wild places, the growth of modern recreational trailwalking, the impact of our feet on the ground and pioneering moorland restoration work, stand-out characters like the dogged Stephenson and idiosyncratic Wainwright – all of this is part of the Pennine Way's rich and multilayered story.

And then there's that thing deep inside that makes some of us want to walk 268 miles across high and lonely moorland in the first place:

challenge, adventure, ambition, daring, purpose, single-mindedness, escapism, masochism, madness. The camaraderie of the trail and the solitude of the hills are both there, too, however incongruous that might seem. So why does this rugged, exhilarating and flawed upland footpath evoke such profound feelings? And would I be able to walk from one end to the other and work it all out?

I had all these thoughts swirling round in my mind as I packed my rucksack for the start of the walk at Edale in July 2015. I would walk continuously for 17 days from Derbyshire to the Scottish border, up the backbone of northern England, and try to understand the Pennine Way phenomenon – how it came into being, its evolution over five decades and why it has endured for so long, despite all its problems. I would talk to as many different people as I could about the path, especially those, like me, who were walking it in its 50th year, and would try to make some sense of why and how a mere walking trail could develop such an identity. This is the story of a most remarkable path.

1

EDALE – CROWDEN

'The cockpit of the battle for access'

It was a low-key beginning to the walk, which despite all the build-up felt appropriate now that the moment of departure had finally arrived. There was no great fanfare, no speeches, just a buzz of nervy anticipation at the prospect ahead and an eagerness to get away. I went through what would become the familiar routine of shouldering my pack, checking that nothing had been left behind and confirming which direction to set off in, then waving goodbye to anyone who happened to be standing nearby and looking in my direction. In this case it was my wife, since she had driven me to Edale.

I posed for a few photos by the smart new Pennine Way wall plaque and carved oak gate, which shows the route in a central panel. Both were specially installed in April 2015 by the Peak District National Park Ranger Service as part of the Pennine Way's 50th anniversary. Across the lane stood the Old Nags Head, a handsome and historic pub, long associated with both the trail and the rambling movement generally. So, too, is the aptly named Rambler Inn just down the road, once called the Church Hotel and also popular with Pennine Wayfarers. But 9.30 in the morning is too early to be in a pub, even if it happens to be open, and I had a long way to walk.

The weather seemed rather muted, too, with the leaden skies of north Derbyshire making for a grey and rather silent Edale valley. After leaving the village and crossing a couple of fields, I reached the top of a short slope and paused to take stock. I recall two thoughts quite clearly. First, after all the preparation and planning, I was actually walking the Pennine Way – it had begun, it was for real! Forget all the chatter, just get on and walk the damn thing. The second was that it wasn't raining. If this sounds pessimistic, it was largely because the forecast for the day was poor and I had set off in a heavy waterproof coat. But now, having plodded uphill, I was hot, so I peeled off an outer layer and immediately felt fresher and more alive to my surroundings.

I confidently resumed my stride across the hillside towards the head of the valley. I could really tackle just about anything now, I told myself. Within half an hour, it was raining.

To take my mind off the weather, I mused as I walked: why, I wondered, does the Pennine Way begin (or end) at Edale? Why not start it at nearby Castleton, larger and more accessible and overlooked by the shapely dome of Mam Tor? Or at a point further south in the limestone uplands of the Peak District, where arguably the Pennines as a continuous body of high ground (it's not really a proper chain of hills) really finish, eventually tapering off into the Trent valley? Over the years, Ashbourne, Leek and even Dovedale have been suggested as alternative start/finish points.

However, unlike Castleton or Ashbourne, where the streets tend to be thronged by tourists, Edale's clientele is dominated by more adventurous and hard-nosed outdoor types. Ever since Edale station was opened over a century ago, trains from Manchester and Sheffield have routinely disgorged crowds of ramblers every Saturday and Sunday; and long before the Pennine Way was opened, this otherwise small and unassuming village was where you headed if you were serious about walking in the Peak District.

Looking around the narrow valley, hemmed in by crags and ridges, it was also clear that Edale is where the really high stuff begins. It signals the start of the Dark Peak, named after the underlying millstone grit that forms the lofty moorlands covering the northern half of the national park. It's a sombre landscape of largely horizontal lines, bare and unpopulated, most of it above the 1500ft mark and with a peat overlay that can create boggy and uncompromising conditions. But rather than geology, I suspect that the Pennine Way's departure point owes more to the historical issue of public access, and in particular to the celebrated hill that loomed above me now – Kinder Scout.

It is hard for today's generation of walkers, including Pennine Way users like myself, to appreciate that within living memory you simply weren't allowed on over 50 square miles of Kinder Scout and Bleaklow (the next major moorland to the north). In the early decades of the last century, it was reckoned to be the largest area of privately owned land in England from which the general public were completely excluded. A small army of gamekeepers made sure, sometimes robustly, that it was kept that way, so that the heather moors remained the grouse-shooting preserve of the rich owners and their guests. Open access, national trails, definitive maps of public rights of way – there was none of this for ramblers back in the 1930s. The uplands had been effectively privatised following the Enclosure Acts of the 18th and 19th centuries, so that much of the high Pennines was acquired by a handful of wealthy owners who curtailed public access. As workers began to pour out of the burgeoning industrial cities either side of the Pennines every weekend looking for open-air recreation, the sense of injustice grew and ramblers became more militant. Nowhere in the Peak District embodied this sense of public exclusion more than Kinder Scout. Speaking many years after the Pennine Way was eventually opened, its creator, Tom Stephenson, described Kinder Scout as 'the cockpit of the battle for access' and, for him, the trail simply had to start here.

Indeed, if there's a hill in the South Pennines that matches the pre-eminence of the Pennine Way, then it's probably Kinder Scout. Like the Pennine Way, it has a distinctive character and a reputation all of its own, even a spiritual pull for some people. It isn't just that it's high (2000ft), but it also feels seriously big. The summit plateau stretches almost 15 square miles and is made up of giant mounds or waves of dark chocolate-coloured peat, known as hags, and patches of bog and rough vegetation. Dotted about are weirdly shaped tors and it is fringed by precipitous rock edges. On Kinder Scout, you know you're on something high and expansive that commands respect; but you also know that the Pennine Way goes across it.

Despite the unpromising weather, I made good progress along well-walked tracks to the head of the valley and within the hour I was puffing up a steep, stone-pitched pathway known as Jacob's Ladder, which was once a well-used packhorse route. It seemed to rise vertically above me onto the broad south-western flank of Kinder Scout and, although I knew the path quite well, I could tell that I hadn't walked it carrying a full backpack before. I paused at the top, gasping for breath, as the mist and rain enveloped me.

Visibility was down to just a few feet and it was cold, wet and hostile. And this was early July. I carefully followed the path past the trig point on Kinder Low and along the rocky edge of the summit plateau to Kinder Downfall. A couple of fellrunners appeared momentarily out of the gloom, then were instantly swallowed up by it once again. Soon I reached the Downfall, a narrow chasm where the Kinder river gurgles over a rocky shelf, tumbling down the steep rocky hillside far below. In really fierce conditions, the wind is funnelled up this defile and can blast the water high into the air in vertical plumes of spray; and in exceptionally cold winter conditions, the water freezes over the rocks in a white waterfall, providing ice climbing for the seriously intrepid.

When the Pennine Way was officially opened in 1965, the route from Edale to Kinder Downfall was not along the valley to Jacob's Ladder and around the outer edge of Kinder Scout, as it is now, but directly up the hillside and then across its boggy and featureless centre. From Edale village, walkers headed straight up the steep slopes of Grindsbrook Clough beyond the Old Nags Head – a 1750ft rocky scramble beside a lively stream. Just minutes from the start, this must have been a baptism of fire for most long-distance walkers carrying a full pack. If they managed it without mishap, the next challenge was negotiating the bog. There are plenty of hair-raising stories of walkers not just sinking into the oozing peat but getting totally disorientated by the myriad peat hags, especially when the weather closed in. And this was just the opening challenge on day 1 of the Pennine Way. It was as if it had been deliberately designed to weed out the ill-prepared and uncommitted. One experienced Pennine Way walker described this first stage to me as 'a real granny stopper'.

Even in the mist I had glimpsed patches of erosion around Kinder Low; but although the boots of Pennine Way walkers had certainly churned up the bare peat since the early days and the route across the middle had progressively worsened, Kinder Scout's environmental problems are much more complex. Ironically, the same hills that the factory workers from the early 20th century fought so hard to access bear the scars of 150 years of atmospheric pollution, as the toxic smoke from Manchester's coal-fired textile industry blew across the high ground of the Peak District and left a devastating legacy in the form of acid rain and heavy metals. It killed off most of the sphagnum moss that once covered the peat and acted like a giant protective sponge, and any remaining vegetation was further ravaged by the unchecked grazing of sheep and periodic fires. Ramblers' boots simply compounded the problem. The water table dropped, the bare peat dried out and either blew away or was carried off by water, and an ecological disaster unfolded. The most badly damaged peat had the same acidity as lemon juice and almost nothing was able to grow on it.

Writer and long-distance walker John Hillaby, who came through here on the Pennine Way in the 1960s, famously referred to the eroded top of Kinder Scout as an example of 'land at the end of its tether'. In his book *Journey Through Britain*, he described how all life had been drained out or burnt off, and how any green covering had all but disappeared so that just the exposed banks of dark-brown peat remained. 'Manure is the analogy that comes most readily to mind,' he observed. 'The top of Kinder Scout looks as if it's entirely covered in the droppings of dinosaurs.'

Although some professed to enjoy the so-called sport of 'bog trotting', the worsening conditions on the summit meant that the Jacob's Ladder path around Kinder's western edge, first identified as a wet-weather alternative, eventually became the officially recommended route. At the time, and when the new National Trail Guide that appeared in 1990 showed only the Jacob's Ladder route, there were protests from the Ramblers' Association and the Pennine Way Council, who claimed that the Countryside Commission was not following correct procedures for varying the route of a national trail and that both routes should still be shown. However, back in 1951, the year the Pennine Way was designated and over a decade before it was formally opened, the Sheffield and Peak District branch of the Council for the Preservation of Rural England held a Local Pennine Way Conference at Edale, where some speakers registered their unease that a waymarked path could be routed across the middle of Kinder Scout in the first place. Might it not compromise the mountain's wild spirit, some asked, or lead novice ramblers into difficulties?

In the end, of course, the Pennine Way did indeed go up Grindsbrook Clough and across the centre of Kinder Scout, without signposts or a prominent line of cairns; and despite it being switched to Jacob's Ladder, the original route is still a public right of way (and it's all designated open access land anyway) so you can still walk it if you choose. But, as I tried to shelter from the gusting rain to check the map, shivering slightly despite several layers of clothing, I couldn't help but think that the bigger challenge for the novice Pennine Way walker is simply getting over Kinder Scout in the first place.

There were some other ramblers dotted about the Downfall, huddling in slender rock crevices munching soggy sandwiches and looking stoical. I decided to power on through the murk and get off the summit. At the far north-western tip of Kinder Scout, the path descended steeply to Ashop Head and, all of a sudden, I dropped below the cloud line, the rain stopped and at last I could see. Below me, the Pennine Way veered right at Mill Hill on a long, slabbed path across Featherbed Moss. To the left, a path came up a small side valley called William Clough, on its way from distant Hayfield. It was along here, on Sunday 24 April 1932, that a group of ramblers answered a blast on a whistle by leaving the established right of way to scramble up the slopes in defiance of a line of gamekeepers. It was to become one of the most celebrated moments in the history of the outdoor access movement and, looking back now, was inextricably linked to the ensuing long fight to create the Pennine Way.

The story of the Kinder Scout Mass Trespass has been told many times and there's no need to repeat it in great detail here, except to underline how completely Kinder Scout was out of bounds to the general public. Access was restricted to a handful of relatively short and hard-won public rights of way, all of which kept off the really high ground. The actual trespass itself was relatively brief and by all accounts the group from Hayfield didn't actually get to the very top of Kinder Scout, but it was nevertheless a highly symbolic act. They met up with a contingent who had come over from Sheffield, probably around 400 strong in total, and both groups soon returned their separate ways. In fact, many of the established ramblers' federations didn't support the trespass, amid claims that the organisers, the left-wing British Workers' Sports Federation, were hijacking the campaign for their own political ends. One or two leading ramblers even felt that the wider battle for access would actually be put back by their actions. Despite this, the event made lurid newspaper headlines, not so much because of the trespass itself but due to the harsh reprisals that followed. Following arrests, five ramblers were found guilty on charges of occasioning bodily harm and incitement to cause a riotous assembly, and were sentenced to jail for terms ranging from two to six months. It added to the sense of injustice and galvanised public opinion further. A few weeks later, up to 10,000 ramblers took part in a rally in the Winnats Pass, in the Peak District near Castleton, to call for greater public access.

Although the campaigners might not have seen eye to eye over the Kinder Scout event, with some at the time suggesting that the trespass itself would soon be forgotten, it was in fact one of a series of rallies and protests that were steadily growing in number and intensity as people objected to the denial of basic public access. As far back as 1826, a court case at Flixton, near Manchester, had been fought over the closure of local paths. It led to the formation of the Manchester Association for the Preservation of Ancient Public Footpaths, which later became the Peak & Northern Footpaths Society, whose familiar and reassuring dark-green signposts still guide ramblers across the Pennines to this day. (In fact, there are a number of these signposts on this opening stage of the Pennine Way, perhaps most helpfully a low post at a path junction on Mill Hill indicating the direction of the Pennine Way to the Snake Pass Inn and Bleaklow.) Seventy years later, in 1896 there was a celebrated trespass on Winter Hill, in the West Pennine Moors above Bolton, when local people protested against the landowner's decision to close off a well-used public right of way.

At first glance, this fight for the freedom of the open moors might seem a little disconnected from the Pennine Way, which was opened over three decades after the Kinder Scout Mass Trespass took place; but the genesis of Britain's first long-distance path lies in the struggle for the right to walk in the hills – a struggle that defined the modern access movement and ultimately secured the freedoms that we now enjoy today. It's no coincidence that the Pennine Way begins in Britain's first national park, the Peak District, created by the National Parks and Access to the Countryside Act 1949, which also, of course, paved the way for long-distance paths. A little over 50 years later, the Peak

District was also where the Countryside and Rights of Way Act 2000 was officially rolled out, extending a right of open access to mapped mountain, moor, heath, down and registered common land and opening up further significant areas of the Pennines. Indeed, in the Peak District National Park alone, it more than doubled the amount of accessible open country to over 200 square miles. As I began to learn on my journey northwards, the Pennine Way's story is about far more than a simple path.

I trotted along the straight and seemingly unending line of paving stones across Featherbed Moss with something akin to renewed vigour. Looking back, I could just make out the impressive rocky battlements of Kinder's upper northern face. Once they disappeared from sight into the mist, I plodded on and, after what seemed like ages, finally reached the top of the Snake Pass, where the trail crosses the A57. It's a featureless and rather forlorn place. I took some photos, mainly I think just to record the fact that I had got there.

The Snake Pass has itself played a part in the great Pennine Way adventure, albeit rather a sorry one. There are tales of miserable, limping walkers throwing in the towel when they reach the A57, less than ten miles from the start at Edale, and wearily trudging the two and a half miles down the road to the Snake Pass Inn, or even west to Glossop. Others use the location to jettison unwanted items. A national park ranger told me that they regularly find what they believe is the detritus from Pennine Way walkers dumped by the side of the road. Apparently the most commonly found items are lightweight tents and tins of baked beans.

Over the years, the rangers have quite frequently had to come to the aid of Pennine Way walkers in difficulties. Until he retired in 2002, Gordon Miller was a national park ranger for over three decades and for much of that time covered Kinder Scout and the start of the Pennine Way from his home at Edale. He and three other volunteer rangers walked the entire path in 1966, but after that most of his work was spent assisting fellow walkers, since he also helped out with the local mountain rescue team. After completing my Pennine Way walk, I met up with him in the Old Nags Head at Edale and he remembered a particular episode. 'One day we had a call that a Pennine Way chap had fallen over some rocks and was hurt. We went up to find that his backpack was so huge and so heavy, piled high above his head with all kinds of stuff, that when he stopped to peer over some rocks he literally toppled over as his centre of gravity shifted and he lost control. He fell some way and was quite badly hurt, with broken bones, but we got him down OK. However, it took two of us to carry his pack down the hill because it was so heavy.'

Gordon (who during his 34 years at the national park was affectionately known as 'Gordon the Warden') also recalled some of the other bizarre sights witnessed at the start of the Pennine Way during the early days of the trail. Brenda Smith, former landlady of the Church Hotel (now the Rambler Inn), told him about the Japanese gentleman who set off to walk the Pennine Way in the late 1960s with a donkey – to the understandable bemusement of local people. Although no one knows exactly what happened, apparently he returned three days later, tied up his beast at Edale and set off again to walk the path, but this time on his own.

'In the early 1970s, there was also an enterprising reporter from the *Daily Express* who declared he was going to complete the Pennine Way on horseback,' remembered Gordon. 'He took the Jacob's Ladder route but found it hard work and at the end of the day had only reached Kinder Low. He camped below the summit, but unfortunately his horse bolted during the night and after that he packed it all in.'

Perhaps the strangest sight, from the early 1970s, was a man that Gordon encountered walking down Grindsbrook Clough who said he was finishing his Pennine Way walk from north to south tossing a caber the whole way. 'He was wearing a kilt but had a proper rucksack and boots,' recalled Gordon. 'He seemed entirely normal and rational, except for the fact that every few strides he was heaving a small telegraph pole in front of him and said he had been doing that all the way from Scotland.'

Beyond the Snake Pass is Bleaklow, a huge, lofty morass of wet and inhospitable moorland that is every bit as inviting as its name. Dutchman Gerard de Waal, writing about his Pennine Way walk in the

1980s, describes Bleaklow as an 'indeterminate wilderness of peatbogs' and tells of how he and his companion frequently became submerged up to their waists. For such an unpleasant and presumably hair-raising experience, his description of how they extricated themselves is remarkably composed and matter of fact. 'When it happened – it is always unexpected – we kept calm. We found, by experimenting, that you should not try to withdraw one leg at a time because the full body weight applied on the other leg will make you sink further. Another real danger is that suction will remove your boot, leaving you in a terrible predicament. The practical answer was to bend our bodies forward until they were supported by the ground. And, like members of the Amphibia, we then crawled out of the peat inch by inch, leaving the burbling ooze to settle.'

I shuddered at the thought of immersion, to any depth, in this cold black quagmire, but luckily conditions have improved since then. Still, Bleaklow's upper slopes were wreathed in dark and threatening clouds and the omens were not good that afternoon. The long and winding path made its way over a sandy depression and up into the mist, then it started raining again. There was absolutely nothing to see – no views, no wildlife, no people. Bleaklow Head looked like something out of a 1970s horror film; if a lumbering creature had emerged from behind a rock or jumped out of a swampy hole, I wouldn't have been surprised. The summit was marked by a pile of stones with a long pole crudely sticking out of its top, as though someone had been hastily buried on a battlefield. I think it was more by luck than by judgement that I found my way off the top of the hill. I bumped into a father and his dejected-looking son, who were also trying to escape, and as we exchanged pleasantries it began to really bucket down. When the austere grey shapes of Longdendale emerged from the gloom below, I was relieved. Day 1 on the Pennine Way wasn't meant to be like this, but at least it was almost over.

A couple of hours later, in dry clothes and with a hot cup of tea clasped in my hands, I sat chatting to my B&B hosts at the Old House above Rhodeswood Reservoir. With the closure of Crowden Youth Hostel to individuals a few years ago (group bookings only now), their establishment is one of the few options left for Pennine Way walkers looking for a roof over their head in this sparsely populated valley. For 17 years, Joanne and her husband James have run a mix of guest house, bunkhouse and café rolled into one, with Pennine Way walkers making up 90 per cent of their overnight customers. So, bearing in mind that they're at the end of most people's first day from Edale, what state are most walkers in when they cross their threshold? Do they get many people wanting to give up? 'Yes, there's some that tell us they've had enough,' replied James. 'They say "I can't do another 260 miles of that", but I tell them you've walked 15 miles from Edale today, then it's 12 miles to Standedge tomorrow – take it each day at a time, it gets much easier!' He paused for a moment and lowered his voice. 'Of course it doesn't, really, but you have to encourage them.'

Even for those that have reached Crowden without mishap, the end of day 1 is a time for reappraising your kit list, as James knows only too well. 'The weight of your pack is absolutely vital and people tend to set off carrying far too much. We have literally bin bags full of gear that walkers have left here, including tents, sleeping bags, clothes, camping stoves – you name it. I make them put their names on the bags and say if they don't come back and claim them by the end of the year they're all going to the charity shops in Glossop.'

Then there are those walkers who, to put it mildly, have drastically underestimated the Pennine Way. 'There was the American man who set off from Edale in patent leather shoes. He made it as far as the Snake Pass but chartered a taxi the rest of the way to us,' said James. 'Another Pennine Way walker who was booked in for the night rang me on his mobile and said he was lost. I asked him to describe the view, what he could see, so I could try and work out where he was. He said he couldn't see anything because he was in a wood. I was a bit puzzled, but I supposed he was already down among the trees of Longdendale. It turned out he had got completely disorientated on Bleaklow and had ended up walking in the opposite direction back into the Ashop valley. He still made it to us, mind you, and carried on the next morning.'

Of course, plenty of Pennine Way walkers have no problems on the opening day – Kinder Scout and Bleaklow in favourable conditions offer invigorating walking – and indeed, some particularly fit and determined individuals stride on well beyond Crowden. But, James confided, what really riles him are the walkers who have an unrealistic expectation of the Pennine Way and complain that the trail is not properly maintained. 'They imagine the Pennine Way is a clearly defined, well-walked trail and so they moan when they find there aren't signposts all over Bleaklow showing them where to go. They seem to expect a surfaced path the whole length, so they won't get lost. One party who got lost blamed it on the fact that the trail of orange peel they were following just stopped in the middle of the moor. Lots of people don't seem to be able to read a map properly or use a compass, even though they're often carrying them!'

James looked ruefully out of the window at the late afternoon drizzle and shook his head. 'They read some online diary of a bloke who's yomped it over from Edale in five hours and then are surprised when it takes them over eight and they're utterly exhausted.'

My conversation with James was given added poignancy by the arrival of two other Pennine Way guests that night. They traipsed in wearily and wetly some time after 7pm, having taken the best part of nine hours to cover the 15 miles from Edale. Both in their 60s and evidently ill-equipped for a long-distance walk, the two men had got lost on Bleaklow and had walked half way to Glossop before working out where they were.

Later on, in the pub at Padfield, I gently tried to coax more of their story out of them. How, for instance, had they been navigating? It turned out that one had been using a mapping program on a small hand-held electronic device. Some sort of GPS? No, just a free download from a website; but the rain had got into it and apparently the thing hadn't loaded properly anyway. What about a guidebook? Surely they had a Pennine Way guidebook between them? The second man fished a small, rather soggy hardback volume out of his pocket and passed it to me. It was Wainwright's *Pennine Way Companion*, the once popular if somewhat idiosyncratic guide to the trail written by the famous fellwanderer just three years after the trail was officially opened. Since the 1990s, the book had been revised several times to take account of route changes, new paved sections and so on. I flicked to the front to check which of the recent versions they were using and was astounded to see that it was an original copy, published in 1968. They had been navigating using out-of-date maps and an uncorrected route description that was almost as old as me. I didn't see them at breakfast the next day and learnt later that they had given up that morning.

It is very easy to chuckle at people who set out in the wrong footwear, or to disapprove of those who can't use a compass properly and who get hopelessly lost on the moors, but at some point or other most of us have been out of our comfort zone in the great outdoors. Arguably, the only way to achieve and develop as an individual is to push yourself to the very edge and test the limit of your ability. For me, it's summed up by a slogan that used to adorn the front cover of the Sheffield Clarion Ramblers magazine: 'The man who never was lost, never went very far'.

Of the many Pennine Way guidebooks and articles I dipped into before I embarked on my own walk, one of the most thought-provoking was a short piece by Dr A Smith and Mr M Imrie in the 1985 *Pennine Way Booking Bureau* booklet, published by the Youth Hostels Association (YHA). The two men had successfully completed the Pennine Way in 1984, but both were interested in the effect that it had on their bodies and minds, even though one was already a marathon runner. The back story lay partly in the fact that YHA wardens along the Pennine Way were concerned about the number of walkers who didn't complete the trail because they were fundamentally ill-equipped and ill-prepared. At the time, it was claimed that around a third of walkers attempting the Pennine Way, or at least a third of those staying in youth hostels, gave up, a figure that showed no sign of improving. (A report by the Pennine Way Management Project in 1991 went even further: 'Unsubstantiated opinion suggests a drop-out rate of 70 per cent at the end of the second day, around Standedge to Mankinholes, this massive defeat being the result of exertions on the first two most strenuous and demanding days of the entire expedition.')

In their fascinating and thoughtful article, called 'How to complete the Pennine Way', the two scientists said that amid all the advice on what boots or equipment a prospective Pennine Way walker needed, there was virtually nothing on the main reason for walkers giving up – 'body chemistry'. The article explained how the first few days on the Pennine Way prove an enormous shock to the system for most people. 'The normal store of muscle glycogen and free blood sugar is used up, giving rise to hypoglycaemia (shortage of blood sugar),' they explained. They went on say that despite the consumption of sweets and energy bars the body will start to access its fat store, but unless you are a regular athlete this turning of fat into sucrose will be a slow and inefficient process to start with. 'You will feel hungry, tired and depressed due to a low blood sugar level. The conversion of food into mechanical energy is inefficient, the majority turning into heat. The body then counters heat by sweating. Sweat is a mixture of water and body salts, mainly sodium chloride. Loss of body liquids and salts can result in partial dehydration leaving you weak and shaking. Most of the essential B vitamins are water-soluble and excessive sweating can result in a temporary deficiency. Such deficiencies will result in a reduced efficiency in converting fat into energy as well as producing depression, irritability, diarrhoea, etc.'

The authors suggested a number of ways to counter these problems, including taking vitamin B supplements, using salt on your food and taking a supply of ripe oranges for liquid and sucrose/energy (but not too many as they can act as a laxative!). And there were four additional tips: take a companion; avoid thinking of the days ahead and concentrate on tonight's objective; pack a good pair of trainers so you can switch from your boots on drier ground or if blisters develop; and use Vaseline on sore patches on your feet in conjunction with stretchy plasters.

The article was written over 30 years ago but the message is still relevant: walking 268 miles in less than three weeks across rough ground in all weathers is an extreme and in most cases unique challenge to the human body, so it pays to do more than simply program the GPS and buy a decent pair of boots by way of preparation.

Mike Imrie went on to walk the Pennine Way a dozen times and for a decade was membership secretary of the Pennine Way Association, so it's fair to say he knows a thing or two about the art of completing a long-distance challenge on foot. He wrote an equally interesting follow-up article (called 'Health Revisited'), this time for the Pennine Way Association's newsletter in spring 1995, in which he looked at how to achieve the right balance of vitamins and minerals in a long-distance walker's body (in particular, B vitamin complex and vitamin C). As befits a nuclear scientist, it was typically well researched and extremely comprehensive and is worth tracking down to read in full.

However, for northbound walkers contemplating day 2, he and Dr Smith had some crumbs of comfort. They suggest that if you set off from Edale and make it as far as Malham, then your body will have largely adapted to the new regime and you should have overcome any initial problems. And they offer this concluding observation: 'If you complete the walk despite suffering you will be twice the person you were. If you give up you will be diminished. Good luck!'

CROWDEN – HEBDEN BRIDGE

Repairing the green trail

Longdendale wasn't exactly alluring the following day, murky and uniformly grey with moisture heavy in the air. It was one of those mornings, I told myself, where you simply have to get up and get going without too much thought in between. I crossed a former railway line that now forms part of the east–west Trans Pennine Trail, a coast-to-coast walking and cycling route from Southport, near Liverpool, to Hornsea, beyond Hull. It was as deserted as the lifeless reservoir below, one of five (Bottoms, Valehouse, Rhodeswood, Torside and Woodhead) that occupy almost the entire valley floor. The only activity seemed to be on the far side, where an endless stream of vans and articulated lorries were growling their way along the A628, which links Manchester and the M1 via the high and bleak Woodhead Pass.

Once clear of Longdendale, I slithered up the damp hillside into the cloud above Laddow Rocks. The sodden undergrowth made short work of my dry trousers. I waded through a stream where the slab bridge had partly collapsed and tried to negotiate several patches of spongy ground and bog, before finally embarking on a paved section that marked the long, gradual ascent of Black Hill. My feet were sodden and squelching and all I could see was wet, lifeless moorland. It was not a great start to day 2.

I plodded on for a bit, then decided to call a halt and maybe cheer myself up with a chocolate bar that had been earmarked for a likely afternoon treat to head off flagging energy levels; but much to my surprise I realised I was nearly at the top of Black Hill. I stopped by the trig point and, as I poured a cup of coffee from my flask, the thinning clouds finally parted and a little watery sun shone through. This was better. I celebrated by eating some chocolate anyway; and my spirits were raised further by a short but good-natured chat with a passing walker, a local man, who told me that in his opinion Black Hill was a fine place and unfairly treated by the walking guidebooks.

Mind you, by all accounts, Black Hill's bad press was once well deserved. Writing in 1968 in his *Pennine Way Companion*, Alfred Wainwright described the summit as a 'desolate and hopeless quagmire' where the peat was 'naked and unashamed'. The vegetation had been completely eroded so that the trig point was marooned in a soft bed of glutinous peat and only survived because it was built on a small island called Soldiers' Lump (named after the army engineers who originally surveyed the hill). To physically reach it entailed a dirty and potentially dangerous adventure, as Wainwright himself found out when he became completely stuck in the peat bog. He was rescued by the efforts of his walking friend and a passing national park warden who managed to pull him free.

Half a century later, the summit of Black Hill is almost unrecognisable. The fact that I had reached the top sooner than anticipated, and that I was simply wet rather than covered in bog, is testament to the fact that a slabbed path runs up to and beyond the trig point, which itself now sits on a neat cairn in the middle of a small paved area. More remarkable still is that in all directions there is vegetation: coarse grasses, heather, bilberry, cotton grass and rushes. There are wet patches, of course, as you would expect on any Pennine top, and its sense of bareness and bleakness will never be to everyone's taste, but this is a hill with a new lease of life. It's a far cry from that degraded, boot-sucking sea of exposed peat that once gave Black Hill the darkest of reputations; and it recalls not just the low point in the Pennine Way's fortunes, but the moment when the path's very existence came under threat.

By the mid 1980s, it was clear that sections of the Pennine Way were in serious trouble, principally where the heavily used path crossed fragile, peat-based moorland, and especially in the Peak District and South Pennines. After years of official inaction, the case for some sort of intervention was now irrefutable.

In 1987, the Peak District National Park Authority and the Countryside Commission established a three-year management project to examine ways to repair the worst-eroded sections. They had found that, since a survey in 1971, the width of the path had widened dramatically in certain places as successive walkers tried to avoid the exposed and glutinous peat, which of course only made the erosion worse. What was once a 6ft-wide path on Black Hill had increased to 71ft across, while between Slippery Moss and Redmires to Blackstone Edge the width of bare path had grown by a staggering 900 per cent!

In the first phase of the project, led by Molly Porter, various techniques were trialled, some with more success than others. Since digging out the peat to the bedrock was not a realistic option, most techniques involved floating an artificial path on top of the soft surface. There were wooden duckboards, strips of black plastic matting anchored to the ground, elaborate raft paths that floated on geotextiles, and even sheep's wool. Chestnut fence palings, wood chippings and brash were laid in long lines to try to provide a firm walkway across the peat. Most succumbed to the harsh Pennine weather and actually became eyesores and tripping hazards, so were later removed, but it was valuable experience and lessons were learnt. Some techniques were truly experimental, such as the construction of a short path on Snake summit consisting of expanded polystyrene blocks covered with loose stone. It was based on road construction methods over deep peat sites in southern Norway, which effectively allowed the highway to float. Initially the results were very encouraging, but heavy downpours and poor drainage made the blocks too buoyant and caused them to split, so that the path began to wobble alarmingly, much to the consternation of passing walkers.

In 1991, Mike Rhodes was appointed as project manager. Reflecting on some of the highs and lows in a report ten years later, he described the time when he was walking alone to his car on the Snake summit one winter's afternoon after a site visit. 'It was going dark, it was misty and I was tired from the miles of dodging slurried peat bogs. Suddenly, without warning, I found myself up to my waist in cold liquid peat. I clung to a tussock, hauled myself out and sat there, soaking wet and stinking of rotting vegetation.'

Mike later became Access and Rights of Way Manager for the Peak District National Park Authority. He told me that, 30 years ago, the conditions were so bad that it was make or break for the Pennine Way. 'In the mid 1980s it got to the stage where the impact of the Pennine Way on the Peak District moorland was so severe that it threatened the Pennine Way's actual existence. It was a choice of either making a major intervention and spending a significant amount of money to make the route sustainable – or close it. At one point the National Park Authority was even discouraging people from using the trail.'

A maintenance team of four (later five) was established to carry out large-scale repair and maintenance works. It was long, hard work in sometimes extreme conditions, often involving a walk of several miles across pathless bog just to get to the site. Martyn Sharp, one of the original members of the maintenance team, was appointed in 2003 as the Pennine Way Ranger for the Peak District stretch of the national trail. 'The top of Black Hill was in a sorry state back then,' he admitted. 'You couldn't reach the summit without sinking in up to your knees or above. There was an attempt to redirect walkers away from the very top, around the edge, but in the end we had no choice but to lay stone slabs to the trig point.'

The reaction to the team from passing walkers wasn't always appreciative either, as the project report from the time notes: 'It seems that some of the Pennine Way walkers thought they were there for a working holiday, and some thought they were convicts.'

In 1991, after the failed experimental surfacing techniques, the team began introducing traditional methods of repair using stone paving and, on some of the steeper slopes, stone pitching. It would prove to be the most long-lasting solution, as well as arguably the most appropriate, because from the beginning the choice of remedial action was based on a careful assessment of the location and a desire to respect the essential wild character of the upland landscape.

The flagstones came from the floors of derelict mills in the West Pennines. They were destined to be broken up as waste but instead were lifted, packed in crates and flown by helicopter to the Pennine Way. The large rectangular slabs of Bacup sandstone were placed rough side (underside) upwards in order to give maximum grip to walkers' boots. Laid directly onto the ground, in effect they float on the soft peat as their size spreads the surface area loading. As far as possible, they were laid in gentle curves following the natural undulations and contours and so avoided artificially straight lines. Since the stones were recycled and 150 years old, they were already weathered and didn't have the look of newly quarried material. Some still had the drilled holes that were once used as the footings of looms.

'We were aiming to recreate the traditional techniques of causey paving and stone pitching that have been used for centuries on the packhorse routes across the Pennines, but adapting them for a modern recreational route,' explained Mike Rhodes. 'Look at places like Blackstone Edge on the Pennine Way, or Stanage Edge in the Peak District, for examples of these old surfaced routes. We used natural local stone originally cut from the Pennine hills for use in the mills and factories. And now we were returning that stone to the same hills. The stones are natural products and part of the Pennine landscape.'

It's an interesting reversal of the process described by Ted Hughes in his poem 'Hill-Stone was Content', in which Hughes wrote of the Pennine stone being cut, carted and 'conscripted' into the mills, forgetting 'its wild roots/Its earth-song'.

There's an uncanny but powerful sense of coming full circle. Stones that were originally quarried from the Pennine hills were used to build the mills that fed the Industrial Revolution; the workers looked to escape the weekday drudgery by rambling in the same hills; when they finally achieved decent access and people walked for leisure, some of the moorland paths became eroded and needed repairing; the mills closed down and the redundant stone was returned to the hills to form durable and lasting pathways. How neat is that?

Much of Mike's work on the Pennine Way and for the national park has been about balancing the conservation and protection of the moors with enjoyable recreation. 'One of the fundamental principles of footpath repair is that you make it a good path that people will walk on. And when I see people coming out to walk the Pennine Way without leaving an impact then I consider that my job will be done. I really do think we're beginning to get there now.'

However, paving the Pennine Way was only part of the story. The next phase saw the revegetation of the surrounding ground, which had begun in earnest with the management project in the 1990s. In 2003, an initiative was launched called Moors for the Future, an ambitious partnership of public and private bodies that before long ran one of the biggest moorland conservation projects in Europe. Such was its success that in 2015 the partnership received the largest ever award made by the European Union to a UK-based nature conservation project – the small matter of €16 million (over £12 million) for its MoorLIFE 2020 project. It began by installing new hilltop fencing to control sheep numbers and prevent overgrazing, then launching fire awareness campaigns, since over 400 fires have been recorded on the national park's moors since 1982, many with devastating consequences for the moorland vegetation. Around 10,000 tiny dams were constructed to prevent damaging surface run-off (a technique known as gully blocking), and systematic fertilisation and reseeding began. In addition, over 750,000 plugs of native moorland plants were planted (by hand!) and sphagnum moss was reintroduced to begin the long process of restoring the blanket bog and stabilising the peat.

Funding also came from the water utility companies, for whom discoloured water washed off the eroded peat costs millions of pounds to treat each year. There were separate initiatives to replant clough woodlands on the edges of the moors and a community science project to help people better understand moorland ecology, since research into moorland conservation techniques was integral to the Moors for the Future programme.

If you're wondering how relevant all this is to a walk along the Pennine Way, then read Wainwright's description of Black Hill in the 1960s in *Pennine Way Companion*; or look at photos of walkers floundering on Kinder Scout in the 1970s and 80s. There are still visible scars on Featherbed Moss where successive Pennine Way walkers tried to dodge the worst of the bog (the average 'trample width' here was measured at over 170ft); and even the first mile out of Edale across the grassy expanse of Grindsbrook Meadows on the original route was once eroded into so many parallel paths, thanks to the tread of walking boots, that Gordon Miller described it to me as the Pennine Way motorway – three lanes north, three lanes south.

The transformation has been startling, and walking the Pennine Way through the Peak District is now a much more pleasant experience. However, Martyn Sharp is at pains to point out why the work was carried out in the first place. 'People have to understand that we didn't put the slabs down to make the Pennine Way easier to walk but to protect the rare habitats,' he said. 'We took some criticism over the slabs to start with, but the older paving stones have blended in and the vegetation has grown back around them really well.' In fact, it's done so well that Martyn now has to strim vegetation encroaching the path at one point.

Black Hill seems like a place reborn. It's still a big, stern lump, but these days it's more green than black. 'I have a special affinity for Black Hill,' admitted Martyn. 'It's not as busy as Kinder Scout but to me it's every bit as special. There are mountain hares and short-eared owls up here now, it's a place that's alive once again.' And he says the views can be just as commanding as elsewhere on the trail. 'If you stand on the northern side of Black Hill, a little beyond the trig point, you can see Pendle Hill and even Pen-y-ghent on a clear day. It's an exhilarating place.'

And as for that famous trig point, once the only piece of dry and recognisable land amid the summit bog, it also seems to have an admirer. 'Every year a local man walks up the hill along the Pennine Way to repaint the trig point,' says Martyn. 'I try and get up to see him and I've even offered to supply the paint, but he politely refuses.'

From the summit of Black Hill, the Pennine Way originally struck north-westward across Dean Head Moss to reach the A635 Saddleworth–Holmfirth road, then continued across White Moss opposite. However, the ground here was notoriously wet and marshy and there were regular horror stories from Pennine Way walkers. In his 1975 guide to the long-distance footpaths of northern England, Geoffrey Berry observed: 'The peat here is softer, stickier and deeper than any we have experienced, and that alone, on its part, is no mean achievement.' Wooden fence palings were laid across the worst bits in the 1980s, but these soon deteriorated and were eventually removed, so in 1990 an alternative route across Wessenden Head Moor and then along the Wessenden valley, a little to the east of the original, became the recommended route and is now the permanent path. I followed it to the A635, a high and open moorland road with good views, not particularly busy at that moment, so I dropped my pack, leant against the wall and rested.

For over 30 years, this isolated lay-by has been the location of the legendary Snoopy's snack van, a mainly weekend phenomenon that appears to be celebrated largely on the strength of the generous size of its bacon butties and the huge, steaming mugs of tea served up to Pennine Way walkers, who are no doubt grateful for a hot drink and a chat. Whether they open the serving hatch or conduct business from the door at the end depends on the strength of the wind, I was told.

Looking back, Black Hill was now more or less clear of cloud, although a little to the east my eye was irresistibly drawn to the 750ft pencil-thin mast of the Holme Moss transmitter, which was erected in 1951. Although pinned down with five sets of steel stays, the 140-ton mast looked incredibly fragile. Beyond the mast a low, grey blanket still enveloped Bleaklow. I sighed deeply. I had got over the first hurdle, seen off the opening test on the Pennine Way. But was this the right way to look at it?

Long before I took that first step at Edale, I decided I had to try to get to the bottom of the popular notion of the Pennine Way as simply a hard, uncompromising slog. The physical and mental challenge, the arduous miles of bog and bare moorland, the blisters and pain. Surely there was more to the Pennine Way than that? But the Pennine Way has always seemed to carry its reputation before it. In his book *The Wild Rover*, Mike Parker set the Pennine Way alongside the many hundreds of other domestic walking trails and described it as the 'undoubted alpha male of the pack, the toughest, hardest bastard there is'. It seems to be the only British long-distance path that everyone has heard of, even those for whom walking for fun is as alien a concept as deep-sea diving or eating snails. In the preceding months, whenever I mentioned that I was going to walk the Pennine Way people tended to respond with terms like 'long', 'hilly', 'tough', 'rain' and 'bogs'. Others offered a shake of the head or a roll of the eyes and in their minds they probably added 'nutter'.

In their 1980 guidebook to backpacking, *Britain at Your Feet*, David Wickers and Art Pedersen were pretty blunt about the Pennine Way, calling it 'a 250-mile wet slog up the middle of England'. They described how 'the going is rough and can be a real body wrecker ... there are exhausting hours to be spent bog hopping across the peaty plateaux, just like wading through a giant squelchy grow bag. And the weather can be truly violent, with low flying rain clouds, sleet that comes hard and horizontal, and pea souper mists that can brew up within minutes, even on the gentlest of summer days ... there are certainly moments when you have to convince yourself it is doing you good, and when the very idea of the Pennine Way being a public "footpath" seems an utter euphemism.' You get the impression they didn't like the Pennine Way very much.

Of course, walking along the top of the Pennines is always likely to have its challenging moments, whatever route you take and however you choose to walk it, and that's what distinguishes it from the Cotswold Way or Thames Path. The Pennines are a high, often remote chain of hills, the western facing slopes in particular prone to rain, and where there's peat underfoot the ground is always likely to cut up. Long-distance walks are about experiencing the elements, moving slowly through different natural landscapes and being outdoors. And they're about testing your mettle. But how far does testing your mettle mean that a walking trail should be so exacting as to make endurance rather than enjoyment the watchword?

More than almost any other UK walking trail, the Pennine Way seems synonymous with sheer physical challenge. The South West Coast Path may be much longer (630 miles compared to the Pennine Way's 268 miles) and the overall height gain much greater (115,000ft against the Pennine Way's 37,000ft, give or take a bit), but you rarely go half a day without dropping down to a village, café or beach. When you set off for a day on the Pennine Way, on the other hand, in most cases you don't see a shop, pub or café until nightfall; and if you camp you might not see one at all.

As I walked north to Scotland, I pondered the question of toughness and challenge and talked to others about it. Where precisely do you strike the balance between maintaining the trail's sheer physical (and mental) test and making it sufficiently accessible so that enough people feel both inspired and capable of attempting it? Reading accounts of early trail completions in the 1960s and 70s, I was struck by the fact that most people seemed to accept the boggy and sometimes treacherous conditions underfoot as simply part of walking along the top of the Pennines. It might not have been altogether pleasant at times, but coping with it was part of the adventure.

So was it right to tolerate the sort of erosion that I'd already heard about in the Peak District or could (and should) the path be better maintained but still remain a walking challenge? After all, a walking route that is so long, high, exposed and remote is surely challenging enough, regardless of the surface beneath your boots?

The Pennine Way's creator had a clear view on this. In an article in *The Great Outdoors* magazine in April 1993, journalist Roly Smith quoted from a conversation that he had had with Tom Stephenson in 1976. Did the scars on the landscape caused mainly by the feet of Pennine Way walkers upset the route's architect? 'No, it doesn't offend me in the slightest,' Tom replied. 'The way I see it is that this route has given so much pleasure to so many thousands of people who perhaps otherwise might have not ventured on to the hills. That is what I wanted in the first place, and when I see young people enjoying themselves on the Pennine Way, it makes it seem worthwhile.'

Others have pointed out that the relatively small cost of repairing a stretch of worn footpath, when compared to the cost of building just a few yards of new road, for instance, is a price worth paying, especially when you factor in all the physical and mental benefits associated with taking exercise in the outdoors. A well-used and eroded path is evidence that people are walking it and want to walk it, so the argument goes.

However, 50 years on and attitudes have shifted. It might still be just as important to encourage young people onto the hills, but it's no longer acceptable to sit by and allow such obvious environmental damage to take place. I suspect, too, that many outdoor users are increasingly aware of their individual impact and uncomfortable with the notion that their own feet are damaging the very same wild and beautiful landscapes that they come to enjoy. And such damage, too. A full condition survey of the Pennine Way in 1989 showed that for the trail south of the M62 (including all of the Peak District), the average worn or trampled width was found to be 40ft; but on the summit plateau of Kinder Scout the trample damage spread up to half a mile wide!

As I left the Peak District, on the newly laid causey paths amid recovering moorland, I really couldn't see that there was any other option but to repair and renew, even up here where by rights it should be wild and untouched. Indeed, I even felt a faint sense of hope that amid so much wider ecological destruction that we have been wreaking on the planet for the last couple of centuries, we still have it in our gift to step back and, through purpose, ingenuity and hard work, rectify the damage. Either way, the Pennine Way had been pulled back from the brink.

I turned my back on Black Hill and that soggy first day and headed off down the increasingly sunlit Wessenden valley, now on a firm and inviting track past a string of small reservoirs. At the top, by the roadside, was a National Trust interpretation board that explained how this part of Marsden Moor was once known as the Black Moor because it was covered by soot from the surrounding mills and factories. It also featured an old photo of the long-vanished Isle of Skye Hotel, which once stood near this spot, describing how day trippers used to walk up to this lonely moorland pub for ham and egg teas.

The building has long since gone, compulsorily purchased and demolished in the 1950s by a water company for fear that their nearby reservoir water would be polluted; but the pub lives on in the local name for the A635 (the Isle of Skye road), as well as in the name of the annual Four Inns race, for which it is the starting point. This long-running team competition is held around Easter and involves a 45-mile non-stop walking/running route over the rough moors of the Dark Peak, linking four pubs: the Isle of Skye (site of), the Snake Pass Inn, the Old Nags Head at Edale, and the Cat and Fiddle on the moors to the far west. Of course, two of these pubs are on the Pennine Way, and the Snake Pass Inn just off it. The winning teams often take as little as six or seven hours, while others walk through the night and stumble in after 20-plus hours.

At Standedge, more a location than an actual settlement, the route crosses the A62 Huddersfield–Oldham road. In the early years of the Pennine Way, Peter's Transport Café was a fixture of the hilltop car park, a refreshment stop for lorry drivers and commercial traffic in a pre-M62 era when the trans-Pennine road was much busier. Judging by the accounts of Pennine Way walkers at the time, the café was also a welcome sight for walkers at this remote location; but alas, it burnt down in 1970 and, like the Isle of Skye Hotel, has been consigned to the stuff of memories.

The route was now obvious, direct and mostly firm underfoot, with sections once notorious for their bog tamed by paths of aggregate and slabs. After the cloud and rain of the Peak District, it was now blue skies and sunshine in the South Pennines, bright and incredibly clear. Below me the high-rise buildings of Rochdale looked almost within touching distance, which was both fascinating and slightly unnerving at the same time. Between Crowden and Hebden Bridge, the Pennine hills seem to take a sharp intake of breath: the bare upland spine separating Oldham, Littleborough and Greater Manchester from Huddersfield, Halifax and West Yorkshire to the east is just a few miles wide. It seemed as if the ribbon of undeveloped upland trodden by the Pennine Way was the only thing stopping northern England from turning into one giant retail park or housing estate.

This sense of walking through an almost semi-urban, man-made environment was compounded by a string of small reservoirs. Further afield and off the main Pennine chain, there were a growing number of wind turbines visible. In particular, even as I watched, a large wind farm seemed to be taking shape north of Rochdale, with cranes hoisting gigantic shafts and propellers skywards. But it wasn't just a visual assault on the senses. The growl of the M62 was first audible at least half an hour away, until eventually the trail dropped down to a cutting below Windy Hill in order to cross the motorway via a high and slender footbridge.

Originally it seems that the plan was for the Pennine Way to cross the M62 slightly east of its present line, following the A672 as it passed underneath the motorway at junction 22; but – the story goes – Transport Minister Ernest Marples (a keen rambler, it was said) insisted that the Pennine Way should have its own footbridge. And not just any off-the-shelf urban design either, but a reinforced concrete three-hinged arch with a span of 220ft, complete with counter-curve and side cantilevers. In other words, the Pennine Way got the sort of elegant and bespoke bridge that the country's foremost long-distance footpath deserved, which I find very satisfying.

The M62 bridge was completed early in 1971 and Pennine Way walkers were crossing it before the motorway tarmac had even been laid. The *Manchester Guardian* carried a splendid photo by Robert

Smithies of almost 100 ramblers from the Peak & Northern Footpaths Society, who were the first to cross the new bridge on Easter Sunday. The photo was reproduced on the front cover of the Society's annual report for 1971–72 and shows a line of waving figures stretching right across the new structure, with just bare earth and a couple of diggers below. (Incidentally, when Smithies died in 2006, his obituary in *The Guardian* described how he enjoyed recounting the background to one of his other Pennine Way pictures – a walker struggling through winter blizzards – which had his editor in raptures. 'I just drove up the Snake Pass, between Sheffield and Manchester, parked up where the footpath crosses and turned the car heater on,' he recalled. 'Then I waited for the first silly sod to materialise out of the snow.')

Perhaps not surprisingly, this section of the M62 is the highest point of any motorway in England, peaking at 1221ft. And with Scammonden Bridge (the longest single-span concrete arch bridge in the UK) and the well-known Stott Hall Farm (where the motorway carriages were built either side of the building, so marooning it in the middle) just to the east, the Pennine Way footbridge is in noteworthy company.

I stood mid bridge and took a photo of the endless stream of traffic 65ft below. A lorry hooted and I waved. I looked down as vehicle after vehicle sped underneath at what seemed to be breakneck speeds. A few drivers glanced up at me, perhaps fearful of what I was about to hurl down on them, or maybe wondering why a fully grown man was spending a July morning taking photos of motorway traffic.

The M62 is just one of numerous trans-Pennine roads that the Pennine Way hops across. Beginning with the Snake Pass and A628 Longdendale highway, there are five other major A roads that cross the Pennines within a few short miles; and at Standedge the railway and canal also go deep beneath the surface. On occasions, walking the Pennine Way seemed like an exercise in geometry, at least at its southern end.

At Blackstone Edge, the modern A58 linking Littleborough and Ripponden is also eclipsed by more historic thoroughfares. For a short distance, the Pennine Way drops downhill on a line of neat dark setts, the smooth grey stones standing out vividly against the grassy Pennine hillside. It was originally a packhorse track that was widened to become a turnpike, although some have claimed that its origins go all the way back to the Romans. It's certainly a location that has been well documented by travel writers over the centuries, many of whom seemed to find it particularly daunting. As far back as 1696, Celia Fiennes reported that the 1500ft-high hilltop was 'noted all over England for a dismal high precipice'. Daniel Defoe crossed the Pennines in 1724, referring to them as 'the Andes of England', which is perhaps stretching it a bit. He described a tortuous journey in a blizzard over the moors from Rochdale to Halifax, where the wind blew so strong he could hardly open his eyes and snow obliterated the track. Perhaps most oddly of all, it was in mid August.

Already the Pennines were changing and the walk taking on a subtly different character. The trail remained doggedly high but as Greater Manchester finally disappeared from sight and the hilltop obelisk of Stoodley Pike loomed ever closer, the path swung round and the deep green gash of the Calder valley was revealed. I gazed down at Todmorden and at the narrow valley snaking its way eastwards across the Pennines towards Hebden Bridge. A train clattered somewhere deep below and all along the bottom there were mill chimneys and densely packed houses clinging to the lower hillsides, since this was once a highly industrialised place. But they were broken up by extensive clumps of woodland and a lush green patchwork of fields that spread steeply up the hillsides. High pasture could be glimpsed above and there was a distinct feeling that the Pennines were about to raise their game.

A path peeled off to Mankinholes, where the youth hostel, occupying a former 16th-century manor house, has long been a popular stop-over for Pennine Way walkers. Incidentally, if you want to see how a stone-slabbed track beds down over time to become part of the landscape, then look closely at this historic causey path. Also known as the Long Drag, it leads down to the hostel from the moorland top. It was built to provide paid work for men whose families were starving as a result of the so-called Cotton Famine (the severe depression in the Lancashire cotton textile industry in the early 1860s, caused in part by the American Civil War, which halted the regular supply of imported raw cotton bales).

Closer to hand, though, there is a monument that dominates the view: as hilltop edifices go, Stoodley Pike is an impressive sight. Work started on a permanent memorial on this spot in 1814 to mark the defeat of Napoleon. It was promptly stopped when he escaped from the island of Elba and was completed when he was finally finished off after the Battle of Waterloo in 1815. Unfortunately, in 1854, the whole thing collapsed, supposedly after being weakened by an earlier lightning strike, and a more lasting, solid version was built. Someone also had a sensible afterthought and a lightning conductor was added a few years later. I'd read that it also came under threat of demolition in World War II, when there were concerns that it might be used to guide German bombers. However, it still stands today, a 120ft-high needle-shaped point partly coated in black soot. There's an outside balcony 40ft up, which offers even better views, but to access it you have to run the gauntlet of an internal spiral staircase covered in broken glass in the near darkness. I fished out my head torch to help me find my way and soon I was leading a merry gang of ramblers and sightseers into the gloom.

If the Peak District grouse moor owners and their gamekeepers were staunchly against allowing ramblers greater access to the Pennine tops, then the water companies who owned large tracts of moorland in the South Pennines were equally resistant. Although the last two reservoirs I had passed, White Holme and Warland, were in fact built primarily to feed the Rochdale Canal, most of the reservoirs in this area were constructed to satisfy the thirst of the industrial communities either side of the Pennines. The water companies claimed that allowing public access to their upland catchment area would lead to contamination and spread disease, and they had acquired and demolished cottages, farmhouses and even, as I'd seen, a pub through compulsory purchase for this reason. There was little hard evidence to back up their claim – after all, livestock often grazed the moors – but in an era before treatment works were widespread, it was a strong and evidently persuasive argument. However, occasionally there was a glimpse of an ulterior motive. In his book *Forbidden Land*, chronicling the struggle for access to mountain and moorland, Tom Stephenson quoted the British Waterworks Association's opposition to the Access to Mountains Bill 1939: 'Among their general objections they included "the tendency of such areas (ie mountains and moorlands) to become a resort for undesirable characters among whom immorality and licentiousness is rife".'

In the period between the two World Wars, frustrated ramblers and access campaigners looked for ways to overcome these seemingly implacable obstacles. There had been the rallies and trespasses, of course, most publicly on Kinder Scout, where the mass trespass had made national headlines and highlighted the woeful lack of access to the Peak District's moorlands. But for one journalist, walker and activist, there was another ploy.

Tom Stephenson was the 'open-air correspondent' for the popular *Daily Herald* national newspaper. He wrote a now famous, double-page feature entitled 'Wanted – A Long Green Trail', which appeared in the newspaper on 22 June 1935. This was the first time that an idea for a walking route the length of the Pennines had been properly aired. Reading the article today, it seems likely that Tom and probably others had been considering such a route for a while. As my own walk progressed, I would learn much more about the self-effacing and remarkable Tom Stephenson, creator of the Pennine Way and tireless access campaigner.

The spur for Tom's article was a letter that the paper had received from two American girls asking for advice about a 'tramping holiday' in England. Tom explained to readers that the Appalachian Trail and John Muir Trail stretched thousands of miles through the girls' homeland but that England had nothing to compare. Instead, despite the popularity of walking in England, our own hills were ringed with what he called 'wooden liars' – notices declaring that the land was strictly private and that trespassers would be prosecuted. He invited the reader to consider how, little more than a century before, people were walking unhindered along old Roman roads, pilgrimage routes, shepherds' trods and drove roads, criss-crossing the hills for a variety of purposes, but now many of these routes had been lost and access closed off. Ramblers might pour into the likes of the Peak District every Sunday to enjoy good open-air recreation, but their freedom to roam the hills and moors was severely curbed. The answer, Tom artfully suggested, was 'something akin to the Appalachian Trail – a Pennine Way from the Peak to the Cheviots'.

Walking a long distance for recreation and fun, as opposed to doing it for work, a religious pilgrimage or because you had no other transport, was something that had actually begun in continental Europe some years before. As Colin Speakman explains in his 2011 book *Walk!*, the Westweg (West Way) had been developed in the Black Forest of Germany in 1900 by the Black Forest Society, and before long other popular trails emerged and similar networks grew in places like the Vosges. Young Germans (who called themselves *Wandervögel* or 'wandering birds') poured out of the cities to explore the countryside. They began to enjoy a growing and ever more intricate system of marked paths linking one walkers' hostel to another, the paths often depicted by no more than simple splashes of paint on a tree trunk or rock.

This idea of purposefully creating a waymarked long-distance walking route soon spread to Sweden, then crossed the Atlantic to America, where the 265-mile Long Trail was established in Vermont, stretching from Massachusetts to the Canadian border. However, the Appalachian Way (or Trail), completed in 1937, was the first long-distance path that really captured the national imagination and whose scope (2100 miles from Georgia to Maine) matched the ambition and grandeur of the United States.

While recognising the achievement, Tom Stephenson was keen to ensure a sense of proportion for any such route along the Pennines. In his *Daily Herald* article, he painted a picture of how the Pennine Way might look: 'This need be no Euclidean line, but a meandering way deviating as needs be to include the best of that long range of moor and fell; no concrete or asphalt track, but just a faint line on the Ordnance Maps which the feet of grateful pilgrims would, with the passing years, engrave on the face of the land.'

He outlined a likely course, which with the exception of Boulsworth Hill and Pendle Hill was uncannily like the final agreed route, and in a nod to the prevailing royal jubilee he suggested it could be called the Jubilee Way or Georgian Path. The name was clearly of less importance than the overriding desire to secure a public foothold in these forbidden lands. The idea of the Pennine Way had arrived.

3

HEBDEN BRIDGE – MALHAM

Tom Stephenson's big idea

The next morning I sat in the kitchen of a terraced house in Hebden Bridge. It belonged to a small woman in what I judged to be her late 60s or early 70s, who I had never met until the previous evening, nor was I ever likely to again once I had left. As I sat quietly, she busied herself preparing breakfast, humming gently as she stirred the scrambled egg and checked the toast. I looked round the neat but homely room, at the postcards on the fridge door and a vase of fresh flowers by the window. There was a small pile of ironing on a chair by the door and a few cookery books on a shelf. Outside, some children walked past noisily on their way to school. And as I sat there at the kitchen table, surrounded by all the trappings of everyday life, but an everyday life that belonged to a complete and utter stranger, it struck me that bed and breakfast is a most peculiar arrangement.

Mind you, if bed and breakfast is by definition peculiar, that's nothing compared to the phenomenon that is the Pennine Way B&B landlady. After I had arrived the previous afternoon, weary and slightly footsore, I went through the customary greetings and then made the grievous mistake of imagining I could simply walk down the tiled corridor towards my room still clad in boots and rucksack. After all, my boots were clean after walking through the town and my pack was completely dry. Short and slight but with a commanding voice that could probably be heard the other side of the valley, Miss B announced that boots (whatever their condition) were to be removed before entering the premises. That's perfectly fine, I thought, as I sat outside the back door on a bench evidently provided for that purpose. A wide, shallow tray lined with newspaper was produced, on which I was invited to place my boots. I then stood up and shouldered my pack, but was promptly informed that rucksacks were not allowed to be worn when inside the house but instead had to be carried in the arms in a forward position. I stood, slightly stupefied, wondering what on earth I had let myself in for tonight. I had visions of being stood over in the bath by this officious lady instructing me how to scrub my back. Sensing my bewilderment, Miss B relented and explained that she had had too many pictures knocked off the walls of her narrow landing by young men wearing 'enormous' rucksacks. I finally made it to my room, clutching my rucksack before me, and opened the door in trepidation, fearing what other house rules I might inadvertently break.

In the end, I must say I warmed to Miss B. I learnt that she had been providing bed and breakfast for Pennine Way walkers on and off for over 30 years ('but I only open in the summer months – you shouldn't be walking it at other times'); and despite her stern manner, delivered in the style of a short-tempered maths teacher, I think she may have developed a soft spot for walkers. We chatted over breakfast and she told me she had had a serious operation at the beginning of the year and wasn't going to do B&B this season. 'But then Pennine Way walkers began ringing up to book for the summer and I just couldn't turn them down.'

Half an hour later I said goodbye and, armed with her hand-drawn map showing me the best way to regain the trail above the town, I left the home of a complete stranger to walk 16 miles to that of another.

Miss B is just one of many Pennine Way accommodation providers who have developed a special bond with the walkers who periodically stagger through their doors. The Pennine Way Association's indispensable accommodation guide first appeared in 1971 and ran for over four decades, edited by the late John Needham. In an article he wrote for the spring 1989 issue of the association's newsletter, he recalled that in the first edition there were 75 establishments listed and the average price of an overnight B&B stay on the Pennine Way was £1.25 (by 1989 it had hit the heady heights of £8!). John also observed how accommodation provision had shifted to meet demand over the years, so that in 1972 there was only one listing for the Hebden Bridge area but by 1989 there were seven. Pennine Way walkers also made it clear what they thought of the generous hospitality they were shown. 'It is pleasant to report that we get few complaints; most of the writers have nothing but praise for the ladies who took them in, fed them, and dried them out.'

Some B&Bs were in there more or less from the beginning and became legends among regular trailwalkers. Chris Sainty, former chairman of the Pennine Way Association, is one of many who remembers Ethel Burnop, of Woodhead Farm in Lothersdale, with particular fondness. 'She was one of the early B&B providers and I remember Tom Stephenson used to drop in if he was in the area,' he said. 'It was a working farm in those days and very basic, but you always got a fantastic greeting and a cup of tea with lashings of cake. Her breakfasts were enough to keep you going all day and she never turned anyone away. She loved what she called her "Pennine Highwaymen". They were her family.'

Teacher and guidebook writer Alan Binns also recalled how the Burnops were always kind and welcoming to his groups of schoolboys on their Pennine Way walks in the 1960s and 70s, never once refusing anyone shelter. The record, he believes, was probably set in July 1968, when on just one night there were 26 walkers inside the farm and 46 tents in the field outside.

David Blowers was another who used the pages of the Pennine Way Association's newsletter to praise the Burnops' unfailing hospitality. He recounted the highlights from his walk along the Pennine Way in July 1979 with two fellow sixth-formers:

Woodhead Farm was such a welcome sight and we had been told that a meal from 'the Burnops of Woodhead Farm' was something not to be missed, so our first approach to Mr Burnop was tactful: we asked if the pub in the village served meals and to our delight he answered by saying that his wife may cook us a meal. Feeling in a better mood we went to put the tent up.

A paragraph dedicated to Mr and Mrs Burnop:

These are the most amazing people that I have ever come across. They allowed us, and the two French ladies [also walking the Pennine Way], who were having bed and breakfast and evening meal, to use their washing and toilet facilities. Not only that but they were friendly and the meal, well just take a look at this: Soup, roll and butter, roast steak, roast potatoes, boiled potatoes, sprouts, carrots, runner beans, cabbage, cauliflower, biscuits and cheese, strawberries and ice cream, tea … wonderful.

We spent most of the evening in their house, both before and after the meal, talking just as if we were at home. Mrs Burnop even asked us what we would like to watch on the television … such luxury.

The Pennine Way deliberately bypasses Hebden Bridge, because when the route was originally plotted there was little to attract walkers. Early in the last century, it was a prosperous mill town, famous as the centre of the trade in fustian (thickly woven cotton cloth with a short nap or pile, like corduroy and moleskin); but bust followed boom and by the 1960s it seemed to be in terminal decline. Some industry limped on, but shops were empty, houses were being pulled down and the valley was littered with redundant and dirty mill buildings. In his 1967 book *A Guide to the Pennine Way*, Christopher John Wright describes the scene: 'This very narrow gorge of the River Calder has cotton manufactures, clothing mills and dye works crowded into the valley, and the smoke and smell of industrial effluent fills the lungs.'

Then, during the 1970s and 80s, Hebden Bridge began to reinvent itself as an influx of artistic and creative people moved into the valley; and after that a new wave of wealthier, trendy incomers brought in further vitality. There are still the steep cobbled streets and tightly packed rows of traditional 'double-decker' housing, but the once grimy old mill town now boasts dozens of small independent shops, as well as cafés, bars and places to stay.

I walked into the town centre to soak up the atmosphere of what *The Times* described in 2013 as 'the coolest place to live in Britain'. It's likely that if the route of the Pennine Way was being plotted today, it would pass through Hebden Bridge, not least because it was also the first official 'Walkers are Welcome' town in the UK. This initiative was launched in 2007 and now includes over a hundred towns and villages nationwide where visiting walkers are assured of the best possible service.

The latest development is the Hebden Bridge Loop, a new walking route connecting the Pennine Way with the town centre to encourage walkers to stop and visit. The idea came from Dave Brooks, co-director of Hebden Bridge Hostel. When he walked the Pennine Way in 2012, it occurred to him that trailwalkers were missing out by not entering Hebden Bridge or nearby Heptonstall. Dave and the local walkers' action group worked together to create a waymarked route from Callis Wood to the town centre, then up to Heptonstall to rejoin the Pennine Way near Hebble Hole. And what, I asked him, about those purists who say it's not the official route? 'Well, what about the Bowes Loop?' replied Dave. 'If Bowes can have a Loop, then so can Hebden Bridge.'

The Bowes Loop, much further along the path, is an alternative section of the trail via the County Durham village of Bowes. It was introduced early on, to offer more accommodation choices, but ironically there are few places to stay in Bowes these days so the Loop has lost much of its original purpose.

I do like what the enterprising folk of Hebden Bridge have done and I like the idea that the Pennine Way can evolve and improve, offering future walkers more choice and a better experience. I also like the fact that Dave proudly displays a large map and photos of his own Pennine Way walk in the entrance of the hostel. This comfortable and welcoming independent hostel adjoins the Birchcliffe Centre, a former Baptist Chapel that is now the base for a lively arts and heritage charity called Pennine Heritage (which Dave is also involved in). The charity is devoted to preserving and promoting the landscapes of the South Pennines, and its local oral history recordings and photographic collections include, most fittingly, archive material from the Pennine Way Council (which later became the Pennine Way Association).

Some short but lung-busting climbs were needed to finally exit the Calder valley and leave the colourful denizens of Hebden Bridge behind. The noise and bustle far below fell silent as I steadily made my way up across sloping pasture and deserted lanes towards the expanse of Heptonstall Moor.

Before I climbed the last field, I took a breather and veered off to visit Highgate Farm, just off the route. This is the site of a small but legendary shop known as May's Aladdin's Cave. It all began 35 years ago when farmer's wife May Stocks was asked by some passing Pennine Way walkers if she could spare any fresh milk or eggs for their breakfast.

This kept happening, so she asked what else they needed and, as her daughter-in-law told me across the counter, it just grew and grew. The converted stable building is crammed full of everything Pennine Way walkers could possibly want – hence the Aladdin's Cave tag – from toiletries and newspapers to tinned food and cold pies, fresh fruit and home-made cakes to ice creams, bottled beer, and spare hats and socks. There's a deli counter, fresh sandwiches and jars of sweets.

'We stock what walkers ask for,' I was told. 'Plasters, talc and gas canisters seem to be popular.' She went on to explain that it has become a community shop for the residents of Higher Colden, and as I stood there agonising between a giant square of flapjack and a tempting sticky bun, there was a regular stream of local people popping in for this and that, or simply to chat. Although Pennine Way walkers are no longer the shop's mainstay, they remain important to May, a sprightly 76-year-old who still has a regular newspaper delivery round. You can camp for free in the field by the farm, and over the years she has dried boots, sown broken rucksack straps and offered moral encouragement to those wearying of Calderdale's steep slopes. In the end I bought the enormous square of chocolate-covered flapjack, thick and rich and very filling. It kept me going till teatime.

I finally reached the top of the slope and stepped out onto the high open ground. Ahead of me, the hills broadened out and there was quite a lot of nothing. By this I mean that there were some small, far-off reservoirs, a few farms and clumps of trees, but above all a lot of open pasture and moorland. It felt like a landscape emptying out – but in a nice way – as if the Pennine landscape was pushing back its shoulders after all that built-up stuff and reasserting its more natural self (not that reservoirs and grouse moors are all that natural). I was struck, in particular, by the incredibly open vistas, how the yawning moorland rolled away, one gentle ridge after another. It wasn't a dramatic landscape in the conventional sense of the word and there were, for instance, no plunging gorges or soaring peaks that grabbed your attention, but the general wash of this bare Pennine canvas was oddly mesmerising. I went back to the words of Tom Stephenson, a man so attuned to the hills of northern England, to see whether he could explain the effect of these moors on the senses. In an interview with Marion Shoard in 1977 (reproduced in *The Rambler* magazine of February/March 1989), he said: 'You get the idea of a flat skyline, but you're up and down all the time. It's that attraction of them: the long lines, the level lines in the landscape characteristic of a sort of table with a sharp nose … you get the effect of plains receding as far as you can see, as one range of moorland succeeds another. That gives you a great sense of distance you wouldn't get in the Lake District because you have a mountain interrupting your view in one direction or other.'

What was especially noticeable was the lack of people. A solitary runner, a post van and a couple of tractors were the sum total of life for the best part of two hours that morning, as I made my way by path and lane via Graining Water and the trio of Walshaw Dean Reservoirs. I paused on the far side of the middle one to read some large and evidently VERY IMPORTANT public notices. Huge boards, in vivid colours, shouted warnings at me that cold water kills, bathing was prohibited and there was a danger of falling along the bywater channel. I didn't even know what a bywater channel was, but walking along it sounded risky. In fact, I found out that it was simply an artificial trench running alongside the main reservoir to carry away excess water, and I found this out because the Pennine Way now ran beside it.

Beyond the reservoirs, the path took to slabs as it gradually made its way up to the top of the hill. However, unlike some of the newer paved routes that I'd been treading over the last couple of days, this one was laid as long ago as 1989 by Calderdale Countryside Service and it was interesting to see how well it had bedded down, with vegetation fringing the stones all the way along. New moorland vistas now opened up ahead, with Haworth and Keighley over to the right. But the main attraction was much closer to home. The trail descended to a ruined building, variously called Top Withins, Top Withens or simply Withins. The main part of what was evidently once a small, simple dwelling was roofless and sat in isolation next to a couple of trees towards the top of the moors. In any other situation this would be just another neglected and unremarkable old building, slowly decaying year by year; except here small knots of people all over the hillside were making a beeline for it, following waymarked paths from Haworth that even included signposts in Japanese.

A prominent plaque fixed to one of the walls explained that the building was associated with the Earnshaw home described by Emily Brontë in *Wuthering Heights*. Erected by the Brontë Society in 1964, the plaque and its carefully chosen wording interested me as much as the dilapidated building. It was a masterclass in non-committal. 'The buildings, even when complete, bore no resemblance to the house she described. But the situation may have been in her mind when she wrote of the moorland setting of the Heights.' The notice finishes with the slightly irritable comment: 'This plaque has been placed here in response to many inquiries'. You can almost hear the author of the notice sighing.

There wasn't too much to see and I felt slightly out of place among couples in white trainers and sunglasses. I wondered what they expected to find there, and whether they felt their three-mile trek across the moors from Haworth was worth it. I did consider making the reverse trip, perhaps nosing round the Parsonage Museum for an hour; but the sun was shining and I thought I'd really rather be up on the moors on my own than jostling with holiday crowds in a busy tourist village.

The last 20 miles or so had reminded me how the South Pennines have a surprisingly rich literary association. Near the path back at Standedge there had been a memorial to Ammon Wrigley, a local poet from Saddleworth, little known today but in the early 1900s he had a large and enthusiastic following. The Calder valley, and in particular Mytholmroyd and Heptonstall, was the stomping ground of the young Ted Hughes, whose poetry captures the sparse Pennine landscape in much the same way that the Brontë sisters evoked the mood of the windswept moors a century earlier. As I'd noted a few miles back on Heptonstall Moor, from a purely scenic point of view these rather bare and bleak uplands are no match for the preceding Peak District or for the Yorkshire Dales that follow; but for many artistic types, and evidently some Pennine Way walkers, this very emptiness gives the South Pennines a special character. It's as if the sheer desolation fires the imagination and the wide and rather featureless horizons unlock some creative spark. As Ted Hughes observed in his poem 'Pennines in April': 'Now, measuring the miles of silence/Your eye takes the strain'.

There's certainly something about these stark and deserted moors that touches you. Already I felt it, even if I wasn't entirely sure what it was, let alone had the eloquence of Emily Brontë or Ted Hughes to express it. For 50 years, the Pennine Way has shone a light on our relationship with high and open country, on our basic need to have access to natural and uncluttered spaces where we can be challenged like this. It doesn't matter whether we walk the Pennine Way for a fortnight, a day or even just an hour or so. Even up here, sandwiched rather ingloriously between Burnley and Bradford and where the endless slopes of heather and acidic grasses can sometimes verge on the drab, this path is our portal to another world. It's an interface between people and landscape, and a reminder that there are other things in life besides email, shopping and celebrities.

I wasn't finished with the Brontës quite yet. Dropping down sharply to Ponden Reservoir, I paused to admire Ponden Hall, a 17th-century farmhouse that's reputed to be the Thrushcross Grange of *Wuthering Heights*. After climbing back up even more steeply, I strode out across Ickornshaw Moor and realised I really was on my own. There was absolutely no one around. A skylark trilled somewhere above me; in the far distance, a faint whine could have been a chainsaw; but otherwise there was just me and an awful lot of silent and rather featureless moorland. I stopped to have a break, resting my back against a stone wall and staring out in an unfocused way across the open slopes. Just an hour before, the moorland had been positively teeming with life above Haworth, and yet here, in the middle of July, the Pennines seemed utterly empty. The same had been true this morning around Walshaw Dean Reservoirs. It might not be the pristine wilderness experience but in these pockets of the unfashionable lower Pennines there were snatches of solitude that I hadn't really expected.

Again, returning to Marion Shoard's article in *The Rambler* magazine, I found that Tom Stephenson had summed it up well: 'There's a silence that you can almost hear. The wind in the different kinds of vegetation: you hear that in different tones – a whisper or a rustle on the ground, the heather and so on. There's the sound of a curlew, the plovers, the little plaintive peep peep, and the snipe drumming in season. They're all part of the attraction. Then there's the different shades in the vegetation: grey-green, grey in winter with the heather sooty black. It's surprising what different tones you get in the landscape. I like the moors at all times of year. The Pennine moors are even more colourful in winter than in summer.'

I spent the night at Cowling, an untouristy Pennine village just off the trail on the A6068. There seemed to be an unending stream of traffic heading from Burnley to Keighley, or Keighley to Burnley, including huge wagons that made the pavements shudder. My B&B was tucked away just off the main street, a short terraced row where Susan and Sandy couldn't have done any more to make a footsore Pennine Way traveller more welcome. As soon as I arrived, I was ushered through the kitchen and sat down in the tiny back conservatory amid the geraniums and wellies, a cup of tea and slice of home-made lemon drizzle cake thrust into my hands whether I liked it or not. Where had I walked from? How did I feel? What was the weather like? Susan, in particular, was a keen rambler herself and empathy flowed in waves. Cowling might not have been the prettiest place I stayed in, but the welcome at Woodland House was certainly among the warmest.

A couple of hours after I arrived, another Pennine Way walker plodded wearily through the door. I'd already encountered Barry several times on the trail since Edale, including amid the murk of Kinder Scout on day 1; but although our walking schedules were overlapping, we hadn't had much chance to talk and swap stories. Middle-aged and single, average height with thinning dark hair and a rounded face that easily burst into a smile, Barry was a paramedic from south London and was looking, he said, to get away from it all for a while. He was affable and interesting, but he was also exhausted and wanted an early night. Judging by his limp, he was also suffering with from sore feet, so we agreed to set out together the next day.

The following morning, as I prepared to go down to breakfast, there was a distinctive smell in the house, an almost medicinal odour that seemed faintly familiar. I presumed Susan had been cleaning the kitchen or unblocking the drains. Barry was already seated at the breakfast table, a sheepish grin on his face. As the odd smell intensified, he pushed back his chair, unclipped his sandals and raised his bare feet. Ugly great blisters covered almost all of his toes and one of his heels in great weals, the like of which I'd only seen in photos in first-aid books. Barry had evidently been treating the blisters with an antiseptic powder, and presumably before that they had been liberally sprayed with some sort of industrial-strength solution – hence the all-pervading smell throughout the house. It awakened dim and not altogether comforting memories of bathrooms and communal changing rooms from my youth. Susan came in with plates of bacon and eggs and promptly went back out. I told him to put his revolting feet away and we tucked into breakfast.

So how on earth had he managed to get this far with such debilitating injuries? Didn't they hurt? He explained, with a wink, that he had a 'well-stocked' first-aid kit, by which I think he meant that there were perks to being a paramedic. He mentioned the strong painkillers that he'd been taking since day 1, plus the various foot ointments, lotions and second-skin dressings that now adorned his beleaguered digits. I got the impression that his first-aid kit not only accounted for a significant proportion of his rucksack weight but also probably contained items that were kept under lock and key in most dispensaries. When we finished breakfast, I asked to look again at his bare feet, oddly fascinated that blisters could appear in such dramatic shapes and sizes, one of them spanning several toes, and wondering at what point the patient should be hospitalised. My feet, in comparison, were blister-free and in decent shape. I took a couple of close-up photos, which made Barry hoot with laughter and Susan, who had come in to clear the table, scuttle back to the kitchen once more. Looking back at those photos afterwards, I marvelled at how he carried on. The pain might have been dulled by pills and the toes cushioned with artificial-skin dressings, but it clearly still hurt. Evidently grit and determination count for much on the Pennine Way.

However, the emergency treatment seemed to be working, at least for now, because when we set off together Barry kept up a reasonable pace with only the trace of a limp. As we made our way slowly through the fields and along the lanes, I gently began to coax his story out of him and understand more about his motivation for walking the Pennine Way. It transpired that he'd fairly recently broken up with his long-time partner, and acrimoniously too, so I immediately assumed that plunging off head first into something as different and extreme as the Pennine Way would provide a welcome distraction and perhaps a chance to recover some self-esteem. But Barry didn't labour the point and I sensed there was more to it than that. In conversation over the next few miles with this sociable, gentle man, one or two more pieces of the jigsaw emerged and slotted into place. As we stood above Lothersdale and gazed down at the village tucked away in the fold of the hills, and to the moors peeping over the horizon, he spoke about how all he could see from the window of his town centre flat was the side of another house. He told me how, as a paramedic for the last few years, he was regularly called out to people our own age who, through drink, drugs, smoking or obesity, were killing themselves before his eyes. Then when one of his own close friends, an ostensibly healthy 40-something, suddenly dropped down dead, it really shook him. 'I told myself, you have to live life, make the most of this one chance you've got. But when I told my daughter I was going off to walk the Pennine Way she said I must be mad, at my age!' He chuckled, but with a look of resolve.

At Lothersdale, Barry decided he would take a breather. Since I was keen to press on, we said our goodbyes and I climbed up to the bumpy open top of Pinhaw Beacon. Suddenly new vistas were revealed as the ground fell sharply away to the lush green fields of the so-called Aire Gap, the first of three distinct geological breaks in the Pennine chain. To the west, the distinctive outline of Pendle Hill filled the view, while ahead the Yorkshire Dales were beckoning and the Pennine Way was about to go through one of its most exciting transitions.

It's useful to have some basic understanding of the rocks that underpin the Pennines, in order to grasp how it's translated on the surface and what that means for the walker in terms of visible scenery and likely conditions underfoot. Until now, I had been walking largely on gritstone and shale, over rounded moorland covered by thin, harsh, acidic soils, water-retaining peat and blanket bog, an environment that supports only a few plant species. Soon I would switch to limestone, a light and permeable rock created by the deposits in a shallow sea

300 million years before. In a limestone environment, most of the surface water disappears underground and the thin, turf-covered soil is punctured by cliffs and rocky scars. A few prominent peaks, such as Pen-y-ghent and Ingleborough, stand proud due to their harder caps of millstone grit. Further north, a volcanic injection of dolerite into the rock strata created the distinctive Whin Sill, today visible as a highly resistant dark rock that forms the crags of High Cup Nick, the waterfalls of Upper Teesdale and the high points of Hadrian's Wall. In the far north are the older Cheviot Hills, with their hard and resistant granite core, which also owe their height and shape to volcanic activity.

All that was to come. For now, the Pennine Way dropped steadily towards the leafy fields around Thornton-in-Craven and, for the next few miles, traversed a landscape of very small grassy hills known as drumlins, formed out of glacial deposits. A waymarked path peeled off to the left heading for Earby, a mile and a half off the route and an unwarranted diversion for Pennine Way walkers if it wasn't for the presence of a small youth hostel.

One of the enduring charms of Pennine Way youth hostels is their sheer variety. In contrast to the busy modern hostels at Edale, Malham and Hadrian's Wall, you also get the likes of Earby, located in the back streets of a former mill town between Burnley and Skipton. The 22-bed, self-catering hostel is a modest and unremarkable terraced cottage and the sole reason it's a hostel is that it's the former home of Katharine Bruce Glasier. She was a Quaker and early campaigner for women's rights, co-founder of the Independent Labour Party, together with Keir Hardie and Ramsay MacDonald, and altogether a remarkable all-round social reformer. After her death, the house was bought with donations to a memorial fund and presented to the YHA in 1958. When the hostel was threatened with closure, Pendle Borough Council stepped in to save the property, then leased it back to the YHA. It's typical, quirky Pennine Way.

This short westward extension to Earby might have had a precedent, back in the days when the Pennine Way was simply a provisional line on a map. The original plan was for the Pennine Way to reach Malham by a slightly more westerly route, via Widdop Cross and Wycoller. The grouse moors around here were, like those of the Peak District, among the most fiercely guarded in the Pennines in the 1930s; and in fact it wasn't until the Open Access legislation of 2000 that you could legally access much of Boulsworth Hill for the first time. This was undoubtedly in the mind of Tom Stephenson when the idea for a continuous walking trail the length of the Pennines was first aired in his 'long green trail' article. What could be done to unlock these private moors so that the public could walk them in freedom?

Tom was born in Chorley in 1893 and spent his early years at Whalley, just a few miles away from where I was standing, on the far side of Pendle Hill. He stayed in full-time education until the age of 13, which was quite rare for a working-class Lancashire lad in those days, then began work in textile printing. Despite the (illegal) 66-hour week, he managed to escape the calico factory and, on the first Saturday after starting work, climbed Pendle Hill. It was a transformative experience and one that inspired his lifelong love of walking and the countryside. In his memoirs, *Forbidden Land*, he wrote: 'Across the valley were the Bowland Fells; and away to the north Ingleborough, Pen-y-ghent and the other Pennine heights, all snow-covered, stood out sharp and clear in the frosty air. That vision started me rambling, and in the next sixty years took me time and again up and down the Pennines and farther afield.'

In a later conversation with Gerard de Waal, he went further: 'That's where the Pennine Way was born. I was just 13 years old when I climbed Pendle Hill. I can remember standing on the top and thinking how I wanted to climb each and every one of the hills I could see.'

Despite the long working hours, Tom regularly walked four miles to Clitheroe library to continue his reading; then, after scraping together 30 shillings, he bought an old bike so he could complete a 16-mile round cycle ride to Burnley for night classes. Eventually, after much hard studying, he won one of only two scholarship places to study geology at the Royal College of Science (now Imperial College) in London. What seemed a promising future was scuppered by the intervention of World War I. Tom, already an activist in the growing Labour movement, declared himself a pacifist and was initially given an exemption; but later he was arrested, court-martialled and sentenced to 12 months' hard labour at Wormwood Scrubs, followed by a further term at Northallerton jail.

Upon release, he continued his political activity, any chance of resuming his studies now gone. Initially he returned to printing, but before long began to develop a successful career in journalism, writing about walking and the countryside and repeatedly pressing the case for greater access to the Pennine hills. By the early 1930s, he was reaching a national audience, first as editor of the TUC-controlled *Hiker and Camper* magazine, then via his regular contributions to the widely read *Daily Herald* newspaper. The editor gave him more or less free rein to press the ramblers' cause, and this was the platform that allowed him to conjure up the idea of a long green trail.

Many years later, when the Pennine Way was officially opened, Tom was quoted as saying that, when he wrote the famous 1935 article, he never imagined the Pennine Way would ever be realised and that he was taken aback at the public's enthusiastic response. Perhaps he was being typically modest, but immediately following publication of the article, he and fellow access campaigner Edwin Royce were persuaded to persevere with the idea by T (Thomas) Arthur Leonard, another of the great campaigners of the time, who among other things co-founded the Co-operative Holidays Association.

So, three years after the article appeared, in February 1938, a Pennine Way Conference was held at Hope, in the Peak District, in a guest house run by the Workers Travel Association. The aims were to consider the proposal in more detail with like-minded people and to decide what to do next. Among the invitees were ramblers' federations, YHA groups and footpath preservation societies. Both the invitation and the full minutes are reproduced in Chris Sainty's 2014 guidebook *The Pennine Way* and are available to view in the Ramblers' Association records held at the London Metropolitan Archives. They make fascinating reading.

Tom was clear that a new walking trail would act as the catalyst for a drive for greater access. He told the meeting: 'A Pennine Way would introduce more people to the hills and not all of them would be content to follow a defined path.' And resistance from landowners to creating a linear trail would ultimately play into their hands: 'If we can create a public opinion believing it is indefensible to withhold a few miles of footpath from the people we shall have made some advance.'

The letter of invitation from Tom and his co-signatories made it plain that the Pennine Way was not in lieu of any wider campaign for access, but instead was bound up in it. 'It is not suggested that the Pennine Way should be regarded as an alternative to complete "Access to Mountains", nor that it should lessen the demand for that full measure of freedom. Among the keenest supporters of the Pennine Way are some of the staunchest advocates of Access to Mountains, and they believe that the attainment of the lesser scheme may well prove a useful step towards the realisation of the greater measure.'

The Conference heard that the planned route was approximately 250 miles long, with roughly 68 miles over ground not presently covered by any track or right of way. Of those 68 miles, around 50 miles were over land where ramblers currently had no right of access, with about 30 miles in the hotly contested Peak District and South Pennines. Conflict with landowners was already rife – the Kinder Scout Mass Trespass had taken place just a few years before; and despite the Access to Mountains Bill currently under discussion on the national stage, little headway had been made towards securing greater access to moorland. Indeed, some attendees wondered whether the goal of securing a Pennine Way through the Peak District might be hastened by agreeing to 'deviations' away from disputed ground, even to the extent of moving the beginning of the Pennine Way a little further north. In response, GHB Ward from Sheffield & District Ramblers Federation was adamant that 'we should not give way before we had begun' and that the wider ideal that the Pennine Way stood for was something not to be relinquished.

The Conference concluded by endorsing the idea of a Pennine walking trail and agreeing to press ahead with a full survey of the proposed route. The final resolution was clear about the benefits that a new trail would bring, declaring that 'it is in the national interest, on the grounds of the physical and spiritual well-being of the Youth of Britain'. The statement went on: 'Further, this Conference agrees that the wider health-giving moorlands and high places of solitude, the features of natural beauty and the places of historical interest along the Pennine Way, give this route a special character and attractiveness which should be available for all time as a national heritage of the youth of this country and of all who feel the call of the hills and lonely places.'

It's worth dwelling on these weighty words, which appear to embody what the founding fathers of the Pennine Way had in mind: 'in the national interest ... well-being of the youth ... health-giving moorlands ... call of the hills'. It wasn't just a nice walk across the moors, but something to physically and spiritually enrich young people, in particular.

So the Conference ended with a blueprint for the Pennine Way. A committee was established (the Pennine Way Association) and a number of organisations were identified to carry out the survey work and negotiate to develop individual stages of the proposed route. The same local ramblers' federations and youth hostel groups that supported the Conference would be in the vanguard, researching the new route on the ground. In an era of limited leisure time and scarce resources, the scale of their task was daunting. Simply reaching what were often remote locations was difficult enough, but then the detailed survey work started in earnest. They had to compile a list of available accommodation up to a mile either side of the proposed route; inspect any records for common land holdings and inclosure awards; mark up a map showing all existing paths, stiles, gates and footbridges; make detailed observations about the nature of the ground (whether pasture, heather, bog, etc); draw up a register of all landowners on the pathless sections; and, where possible, try to give an indication of attitudes towards the Pennine Way from local landowners.

Following the Conference, the idea for a 250-mile walking trail along the Pennines was widely reported in the national media and, with Tom's guiding hand, more articles and commentary were generated. The *Yorkshire Post* reported how, at the Conference, 'twenty feet of Ordnance Survey maps were spread out ... and a thin green and red mark [was] carefully studied by men and women representing the national and local organisations interested in rambling.' The *Evening Chronicle* (Newcastle) welcomed the promise of 'a sky line trail from Wooler to Derbyshire'; while the headline of the *Daily Despatch* (Manchester) simply said the trail 'will be heritage for youth'. In *The Observer*, Ivor Brown told his readers how the 'organised pedestrians of the North have been discussing a plan to prepare and, where necessary, open up a walkers' track, which will run right up the spine of England.'

A year later, in November 1939, Tom Stephenson reported on progress in a follow-up article for the *Daily Herald*. He said that the Rev HH Symonds, secretary of Friends of the Lake District and one of the founders of the YHA, 'considers the scheme for a footpath way from Peak to Cheviot is a valuable anticipation of National Parks', while he quoted Edwin Royce as saying: 'The Great North Trail should be the first of a series of new footpaths to compensate the walker for the paths he has lost in the last hundred years.'

Unfortunately, circumstances then took a difficult turn. Despite promising much, the Access to Mountains Act 1939 ended up actually strengthening landowners' hands, rather than allowing greater public freedoms; then World War II broke out and not unnaturally the public focus shifted elsewhere. It would be a lengthy wait before Tom's long green trail would ultimately be realised.

From Pinhaw Beacon to Malham, the trail threaded its way through the gentle, lush pastures of Craven. Quiet country lanes, a canal towpath, riverside meadows – it's as if the Pennine Way was taking a breather in readiness for the next upland instalment. A short burst beside the Leeds and Liverpool Canal, at 127 miles the longest in northern England, took me beneath the so-called double-decker bridge near East Marton, where an extra upper arch was added later to raise the level to that of the A59 trunk road.

All too soon, I left the towpath for more field-hopping to reach the large village of Gargrave and a welcome café stop in a trail favourite. As I tucked into a particularly tasty Welsh rarebit, the café owner explained that they have had plenty of experience of satisfying hungry Pennine Way walkers. Linda took over the Dalesman Café, Tearooms & Sweet Emporium (to give it its full title) in January 1999, but it's been a café since the mid to late 1960s and generations of Pennine Way walkers have stopped here for refreshment. It's small and homely, and a little old-fashioned, and I'd imagine half a dozen dripping backpackers could cause minor havoc among the tables and chairs, but Linda said she didn't mind in the slightest. 'I find Pennine Way walkers very

Tom Stephenson, whose 1935 newspaper article sparked the idea for the Pennine Way. (photo: Ramblers' Association archive)

The eroded start of the Pennine Way across Grindsbrook Meadows, Edale, in the 1970s. (photo: Peak District National Park Authority)

Above A plaque at Winnats Pass, near Edale, commemorates the place where ramblers staged mass rallies in the 1930s calling for greater access to the Peak District's moors.

Below The Old Nags Head pub, Edale, at the southern end of the Pennine Way.

Above A Pennine Way walker stranded amid the peat hags of Kinder Scout in 1978. (photo: Chris Sainty)

Below In the 1960s, Burnley teacher Alan Binns led parties of schoolboys along the length of the Pennine Way – here is one group at Kinder Downfall on the first day of their adventure. (photo: Alan Binns)

Tom Stephenson inspecting experimental matting on the Pennine Way at Snake Pass, 1976. (photo: Mike Williams)

Right inset Walkers following the Pennine Way across Featherbed Moss in 1987 on chestnut paling, laid down in an unsuccessful attempt to counter the mounting erosion. (photo: Chris Sainty)

Below inset The eroded top of Bleaklow, with the Pennine Way running across the middle. (photo: Moors for the Future Partnership)

By 2011 the revegetated summit of Black Hill had been transformed. (photo: Moors for the Future Partnership)

Above A Peak & Northern Footpaths Society signpost indicating the Pennine Way near Blackstone Edge, with a new wind farm in the far distance.

Below The Pennine Way footbridge across the M62 under construction in 1971. (photo: Tom Stephenson/ Ramblers' Association)

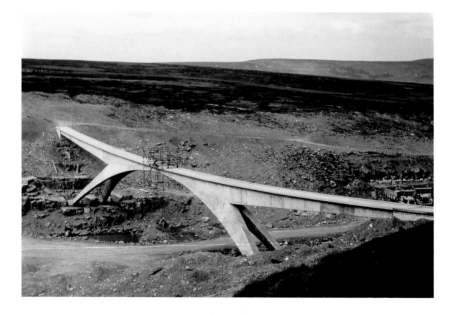

friendly and engaging,' she said. 'Yes, they tend to unpack their whole rucksack or come out of the toilets having changed all their clothes, but it's not a problem. They eat and drink plenty and are prepared to spend their money, not like some of the day ramblers.'

The café has a visitors' book, which Pennine Way walkers have traditionally signed, plus a specially made and rather fetching Dalesman Café Pennine Way mug; and outside the entrance stands a much-photographed Pennine Way signpost (it says Edale 70 miles, Kirk Yetholm 186 miles, but it's probably best not to take that too literally). If all that wasn't enough, the café boasts that it is the only dedicated sweet emporium on the whole of the trail. Jars of traditional sweets offer the weary traveller an instant sugar hit, but which is the Pennine Way walker's sweet of choice? 'I'd say mint cake and midget gems are probably the most popular,' Linda replied after some thought. 'Jelly babies always go down well, plus dolly mixture and sherbet lemons. I think most walkers are probably after a little boost at this point, maybe something to keep them going and lift their spirits.'

4

MALHAM – HORTON-IN-RIBBLESDALE

'We have waited long enough'

Malham was busy, very busy indeed. I had not only entered the Yorkshire Dales National Park but had arrived at one of its honeypot sites; and it was a weekend in mid July. The little village seemed awash with walkers; but luckily, and rather surprisingly, few of them seemed bound for Malham Cove at precisely the same time as me, so I approached the rock face largely on my own, stood at its foot and gazed up in awe. Massive vertical cliffs 260ft high towered above me in a natural amphitheatre. Several hundred years ago a mighty waterfall cascaded from the top, but the water had long ago found its way through the cracks and instead bubbles up just south of Malham village. (Later in 2015, however, following persistent heavy rainfall, water briefly flowed over the top of the Cove for the first time, it was claimed, since the 1700s.) Since 1993, a pair of nesting peregrines has added to the Cove's appeal, with telescopes provided to watch the birds close up, but I was told that the young birds had already flown the nest by the time of my visit.

I made my way up the steep path to the left and reached the top of the cliffs for part two of the spectacle. The view back across to Malham and the hills to the far south was impressive enough, allowing me to trace the course of the young River Aire, which had provided such a gentle and peaceful end to the previous day; but what was underneath my feet was equally arresting. Now that I'd swapped millstone grit for carboniferous limestone, I'd entered a whole new landscape of scars and sink holes, cliffs and pavements. The natural 'pavement' that was spread out at my feet above the Cove was made up of bare limestone, weathered over time by water into distinct blocks (clints) and divided by deep cracks (grikes). Damp-loving ferns and other plants, such as herb Robert, bloody cranesbill and maidenhair spleenwort, poked out of these shady crevices.

It's a truly unique and fascinating landscape, but for the Pennine Way walker with a heavy rucksack and weary legs it's also one to be careful on – with so many tripping hazards, and also slippery when wet, it's a potential ankle-breaker. Still, Malham is a great introduction to this bright new karst landscape, which also includes nearby Gordale Scar, a deep and spectacular chasm in the cliffs. It's a startling change after days of rather sombre moorland.'

The area also has a special significance for the Pennine Way, for it was at a ceremony at Malham Moor (sometimes called Malham Lings) on Saturday 24 April 1965 that the Pennine Way was officially opened.

Following the 1938 Pennine Way Conference, there was enthusiasm in the air as ramblers' groups and other organisations prepared to go off and survey the proposed line of the new trail. World War II then intervened and life became dislocated; but, despite the difficulties, the Pennine Way Association persevered with its work.

In 1942, the association presented a memorandum to the Scott Committee on Land Utilisation in Rural Areas, a move by the government to develop more coordinated rural planning policy and preserve rural amenities. The submission outlined the background to the proposed Pennine Way, its likely route and the need to create new public access. It painted a picture of an unobtrusive walking trail that fitted into the landscape, pointing out that the pre-war development of motor traffic had made the roads and even the country lanes unsafe and unsuitable for pedestrians. The memorandum concluded with a statement that encapsulated the Pennine Way vision: 'There are good reasons for believing that after the war rambling will be still more popular, and it will be very regrettable if young people seeking harmless exercise find themselves barred from the wild and lonely places. The discontent and resentment likely to arise from such a state of affairs could, we believe, be avoided by the adoption of the Pennine Way and other schemes of similar character. The Pennine Way would meet a very real need and be a boon to thousands of young people, and an encouragement to them to learn in the best possible way something of the geography and history and varied beauty of their native land. It would provide an escape to lonely heights and refreshing solitudes for many condemned to spend their working lives in mean cities and ugly towns.'

Ironically, the hardships that brought the country to its knees and the subsequent post-war desire for change and a new start almost certainly made it easier for the Pennine Way to become a reality. After considering all the evidence, the Scott Report recommended setting up national parks and recognised the need for long-distance paths. It was followed by an influential report by John Dower in 1945, which provided the real blueprint. John was the secretary of the Standing Committee on National Parks, formed in 1936, and one of the few real allies of Tom Stephenson in official circles, at a time when there were still plenty of sceptical voices about greater access to the countryside and the notion of a Pennine Way. (Incidentally, John Dower lived at Kirkby Malham, on the Pennine Way just a few miles back down the valley, and this highly talented architect and visionary planner also designed Malham Youth Hostel, which has served Pennine Way walkers for many decades. Sadly, he died of tuberculosis in 1947, aged just 46.)

The Dower Report, as it's often called, was taken up by others, culminating two years later in a recommendation by Sir Arthur Hobhouse's committee that the government should press ahead and establish not just national parks but also a network of long-distance footpaths. The legislation that finally achieved this long-cherished goal was the National Parks and Access to the Countryside Act 1949. Most visibly, it established Britain's first ten national parks, as well as national nature reserves and a requirement for local authorities to produce a definitive map recording local public rights of way; and, for the first time, it allowed for the creation of official long-distance footpaths. In addition to the Pennine Way, the Hobhouse Committee suggested creating the Offa's Dyke Path, the Ridgeway (from the Chilterns to the south Devon coast), the Pilgrim's Way from Winchester to Canterbury (part of which was included in the North Downs Way), the South Downs Way and a Thames towpath route from Teddington to Crickland (now part of the Thames Path). There were also coastal trails around each of the proposed new national parks, including Pembrokeshire, the North York Moors (Cleveland Way) and parts of Exmoor (later to be the South West Coast Path).

The 1949 Act was certainly ground-breaking and a giant step forward, but it was not without its flaws, as it failed to deliver unhindered access to uncultivated uplands – the right to roam – that the Ramblers' Association and others had hoped for. However, even getting the Act onto the statute books required considerable groundwork and lobbying behind the scenes, in which, rather inevitably, Tom Stephenson played a significant role.

By now, Tom had left the *Daily Herald* and was a press officer for the new Ministry of Town and Country Planning. He used this position, and all his guile and political know-how, to lobby for the creation of the Pennine Way, but he was under no illusions about what he was up against. Writing in his memoirs, *Forbidden Land*, he described how, in 1945, a small exhibition about the proposed Pennine Way in the entrance hall of the Ministry attracted a great deal of interest. 'This led one assistant secretary to complain that all the publicity about a Pennine Way might lead to a demand for something actually to be done about it.'

One of Tom's boldest and most effective stunts was to organise a three-day walk along the projected route of the Pennine Way for a group of prominent MPs, taking in the splendours of Teesdale, High Cup Nick, Cross Fell (on top of which they just happened to meet a rambling club from Darlington calling for greater access to mountains) and Hadrian's Wall. The party included Hugh Dalton, until recently Chancellor of the Exchequer, and Fred Willey, who was soon to be a government minister. The others were Arthur Blenkinsop, Julian Snow, George Chetwynd and Geoffrey de Freitas, plus rising star of the left Barbara Castle, who later became a prominent Cabinet figure.

They were all Labour MPs, of course, since this was the immediate post-war period when social reform and a new beginning were in the air. Although the young, comparatively affluent and increasingly mobile middle class were part of the great surge in rambling and outdoor recreation, it was also abundantly clear that the campaign to create the Pennine Way was wrapped up in the wider struggle by working-class people to reclaim the land and secure legitimate access to the hills. Young communists had been in the vanguard of the Kinder Scout Mass Trespass in 1932, while Tom Stephenson's own left-wing leanings were well known. It must have seemed to some that the Pennine Way was simply another manifestation of the class-based assault on the landowning tradition. Certainly it was no surprise to learn that plenty of Labour MPs were drawn to Tom's cause. Hugh Dalton had just been made the new president of the Ramblers' Association, while Geoffrey de Freitas was already president of Nottinghamshire Ramblers. During the walk, Dalton told the *Daily Mirror*: 'Some selfish landlords would like to keep us off the Pennines. They are not going to get away with it.' He also made news on the second day of the walk by raising the red flag on the top of Cross Fell. 'Dalton takes "red flag" to the Pennines' ran the *News Chronicle* headline, although its reporter then admitted that in fact Mr Dalton simply tied his red handkerchief to a stick on top of a cairn.

It is almost inconceivable to imagine a group of politicians, including some senior figures, undertaking a three-day hillwalk in that manner today, but it clearly worked, and the walk in May 1948 received considerable press attention. However, according to Barbara Castle (writing in *The Spectator* a month after the walk), the MPs also quite liked the tables being turned. 'Whether the reporters and photographers enjoyed themselves equally is a different matter. The one who asked on the evening before the start: "Let's get this straight. Are you really walking this route?" soon woke up to reality. The physical endurance of the Press was, in fact, the best news story of all, if only there had been someone to report the reporters. The Parliamentarians threatened to turn their own cameras on the photographers as they charged backwards and forwards at the double with their load of gear, seeking perilous vantage-points from which to surprise the plodding cavalcade.' Mrs Castle was clearly impressed that some, at least, were up to the rigours of the high Pennines. 'One newspaperman walked for two and a half days in lounge suit, town mac and lightweight shoes, and still looked the complete Lobby Correspondent at the end of it.'

Meanwhile, Mrs Castle's own performance was admired by the reporter from the *Daily Mirror*: 'At the end of the first day's walk, Captain Julian Snow, MP, 6ft 6in and 16st, and Mr Geoffrey de Freitas, 6ft 4in, complained about their feet. Said perky Barbara Castle, 5ft 2in, and burdened by a hefty rucksack: "What you need is more exercise". They chased her down the village street.'

Journalists and politicians gently sparred from the beginning. In fact, before the walk had begun, the *Evening Gazette* had led with an article entitled 'MPs will find this a hard walk'; and the *News Chronicle* seemed to revel in warning of the dangers of the Helm Wind and rainstorms on Cross Fell ('apart from that they'll merely be exposed to anti-tank fire on the War Office practice range at Bowes Moor'). While out on the walk, the politicians had to be careful of their own behaviour, as Barbara Castle noted at High Force. 'Here Hugh Dalton turned to squire me over the man-sized rocks, only to be rewarded by the publication next day of a photograph captioned: "Mr Dalton in difficulties".'

Even the group's lunch breaks were newsworthy. The *Daily Mirror* reported how the MPs stopped at the remote farmstead of Birkdale, in Upper Teesdale. 'There, Miss Mary Airey, 58, had been planning the lunch for a fortnight – tongue salad, peach trifle, cakes and tea. "Two shillings each, if you don't think that's too much," said Miss Airey. "Nonsense," boomed Mr Dalton. "I have no economic ties now." And Miss Airey got much more than 14s for her work.'

The MPs' high-profile walk kept the issue of outdoor access and countryside legislation firmly on the table, so that afterwards Hugh Dalton publicly called for the creation of national parks and a strengthened rights of way network. And he added: 'We stand also for completion of the Pennine Way, remembering that this splendid project was first outlined by our good friend Tom Stephenson in 1935. That was thirteen years ago. We have waited long enough.'

There must have been a sense that, finally, the time had come, as the 1949 Act received all-party support and passed into law. Certainly some politicians seemed determined that there would be no further delay. Two years after the Act was passed, the Minister for Local Government and Planning – the same Hugh Dalton – formally approved the Pennine Way on 6 July 1951, just 15 days after being presented with the proposals. It remains one of the speediest confirmations ever executed by a government minister. In doing so, he announced that the route would run through nine counties south of the Scottish border, and perhaps rather surprisingly explained that it was intended for both walkers and riders on horseback. 'Much of this walking or riding will be through rough country and pretty strenuous. The Pennine Way is not for motorists. Here and there it goes, over short distances, along made up roads, but it is not part of our plan to make up any more of it. The intention is that it should nowhere else be more formal than a rough, moorland track, and adventurous cyclists will be able to tackle a good deal of it, but not, I think, some of the roughest parts.' He also confirmed that it would be necessary to create another 70 miles of rights of way to complete the continuous trail; and that the relevant local authorities should waste no time in doing so. 'If they can secure these by voluntary agreement, well and good. If not, I shall not hesitate to authorise compulsory powers.' (Hugh Dalton's long statement was reproduced in full in the Pennine Way Association's newsletter in autumn 2000.)

However, if approving it was one thing, then realising it on the ground was quite another. From 1949 to 1953, Tom was a member of the new National Parks Commission (later the Countryside Commission) but although he was chosen to chair the long-distance routes sub-committee, he was unable to bring the Pennine Way to fruition during his tenure. In fact, it took at least another decade – fully 30 years after his 'long green trail' article originally appeared – before the Pennine Way was finally declared open.

The reasons for the delays were perhaps inevitable, given the historic resistance of many of the owners of the Pennine moors. Even though the 1949 Act gave local authorities the powers to create new public rights of way in order to realise long-distance paths, the process was slow and cumbersome. Some landowners remained dogged and defiant until the end, most notably the water authorities.

Huddersfield Corporation objected to the designation of a 'bad weather' alternative Pennine Way route from Black Hill to Wessenden Head, claiming that it might pollute nearby Digley Reservoir, even though it was newly built and incorporated all the latest treatment facilities. A public enquiry was held in 1954 and the Inspector decided that the risk of harm was so remote that the objection couldn't be sustained.

Next up was Manchester Corporation, who wanted to stop the section of the Pennine Way from Longdendale north to Black Hill, even though well-used roads and a railway already ran virtually alongside their existing reservoirs. The *Manchester Guardian* covered the subsequent public enquiry, reporting (on 31 July 1954) that a medical witness was called by the Ramblers' Association to give an expert's opinion. Dr Wilfred Fine said that the numbers of typhoid carriers had declined to 2.9 per million of the British population. In those under 44 years old (the group most likely to walk the Pennine Way), he estimated that it came out as three carriers in 4 million. The population nationally for that age group was about 30 million, so taking an annual Pennine Way usage by 10,000 members of this age group it would take 300 years for 3 million people to pass. 'As there were only three carriers in 4 million people of this age group,' said Dr Fine, 'in 300 years, in round figures, two carriers could be expected to pass along that part of the Pennine Way.' (For a fuller account of the enquiry, see Chapter 4 of Tom Stephenson's *Forbidden Land*.)

Despite the weight of evidence and expert opinion, the Inspector sided with Manchester Corporation and it took over a decade, when a new filtration plant in Longdendale was completed, for the Pennine Way to be restored to its original route via Laddow Rocks to Black Hill. Until then, walkers had to follow an indistinct path from Hey Edge over Westend Moss and Tooleyshaw Moss.

The proposed route of the Pennine Way was based on maps prepared by the Pennine Way Association, but negotiations between the Peak Park Joint Planning Board and landowners dragged on, and for some time walkers were still prevented from following the route from Mill Hill over Featherbed Moss to the top of the Snake Pass. By March 1954, there were still 51 miles left to obtain; but despite this, Tom Stephenson, writing around this time in a YHA pamphlet (*The Pennine Way*, published by YHA Manchester & District and North Midlands), exhorted ramblers to explore the new trail regardless: 'On the rest of the route, *even* where no legal right of way exists, one is unlikely to encounter serious opposition. Admission that no right of way is claimed will usually be sufficient to obtain permission to proceed. If, however, such permission is not forthcoming, it should be remembered that you cannot be compelled to retrace your steps but only directed to the nearest right of way.'

And there was a helpful note of advice on navigation for anyone planning to explore the new route: 'Those unacquainted with the Pennines should note that a 1 inch map and a compass are essential. In places the route is across trackless moors as yet unmarked by cairns. Recently a mile-eating foot-slogger set out from Rowlandcote

[Edale Youth Hostel] to walk the 250 miles of the Pennine Way to Kirk Yetholm in five days. He carried neither maps nor compass. It was not surprising, therefore, to read that instead of walking the Pennines he traversed industrial South Lancashire and found himself at Preston, some 40 miles off the route.'

The last disputed section of the Pennine Way, in Northumberland, wasn't eventually resolved until a public enquiry in Bellingham in 1964, after the Hon CGW James had first objected to the proposed route crossing his land in Upper Redesdale, then the Ramblers' Association protested that the alternative suggested by the National Parks Commission through the forest involved too much road-walking. Hugh Dalton's original approval of the path seemed a long, long time ago.

From the top of Malham Cove, I followed a dry and narrowing valley past bare cliffs, screes and angled drystone walls. Soon I emerged onto a wide, grassy plateau, reaching a car park that was steadily filling up with chattering groups of ramblers adjusting gaiters and rucksacks and attempting to fold maps in the gusty wind. A farm vehicle approached slowly down the lane, pulling a small mobile snack bar, and then carefully mounted the open verge ready to do business.

Marked on the map, in almost every direction, were shake holes and swallow holes, small depressions in the ground where surface water literally disappears down through the cracked and porous bedrock. Strange, then, that up ahead was Malham Tarn, a broad lake made even more incongruous in this mostly treeless landscape by its conspicuous leafy fringe. For an explanation, you have to go back to the last ice age when a glacier scoured out a large shallow basin, which was then dammed by moraine and made impervious by an underlay of marl on top of Silurian slate.

The broad path swept around the edge of the water and I stopped several times to take photos of the waves, whipped into white horses by the keen wind. Amid the shelter of the woods on the far side, the route passed Malham Tarn House, an imposing country mansion that was originally a shooting lodge but was extended in the 1850s by millionaire William Morrison. A keen supporter of the arts, he hosted guests such as John Ruskin, Charles Darwin and John Stuart

Mill, as well as Charles Kingsley, who was so captivated by the place that it inspired his book *The Water Babies*. Since 1947, the house has been managed by the Field Studies Council, who use it for educational courses; and it played its own small role in Pennine Way history in 1965 when VIP guests at the trail's opening had lunch at the house. To celebrate the 50th anniversary, staff at the centre held an evening of special Pennine Way events; and the Field Studies Council has also produced fetching fold-out colour charts featuring some of the common birds, mammals and plants that walkers on the Pennine Way might encounter.

It might have taken 14 years from confirmation to official opening, but eager ramblers didn't wait for the tape to be cut. The Pennine Way was already being walked long before a few thousand people gathered on Malham Moor, near the Tarn, on a chilly April morning in 1965 to mark its formal unveiling. HF (Holiday Fellowship) and the YHA had been organising led walks along the likely route since the late 1940s; and the first guidebook appeared in 1960.

According to a list compiled by Chris Sainty, there are now more than 50 separate publications about the Pennine Way (one for every year of its life), including not just full-length guides but several featuring circular day walks from the path: the Pennine Way National Trail website (www.nationaltrail.co.uk/pennine-way) even has its own selection, dubbed 'the Pennine Way in a day'. The notion that you're only a true Pennine Way walker if you complete it in one go might still resonate with a few purists, but in fact it never stood up in the first place. A surprising and, I suspect, little-known fact is that neither Tom Stephenson nor Alfred Wainwright actually walked the full length of the Pennine Way in one continuous outing, although both must have known the route like the back of their hands.

Among the many guidebooks to the Pennine Way, one published in 2015 takes yet another interesting and novel approach. It focuses not on the entire route but only on the 165-mile middle section between Hebden Bridge and Hadrian's Wall, through the Yorkshire Dales and North Pennines. Writing in the *Yorkshire Dales Review* in summer 2015, Colin Speakman praised Tony and Chris Grogan's *Heart of the*

Pennine Way, saying that Tom Stephenson would have been delighted as it would encourage more people to enjoy the Pennine Way.

Back in April 1965, mind you, ordinary ramblers were simply pleased that the path was at last officially opened. Among those present was a young Colin Speakman. I tracked him down on my way through Malham and asked him what he remembered about the day.

'I was 23 and a teacher at Bingley Grammar School,' he said. 'I'd been getting involved with West Riding Ramblers and on that day a coach had been laid on for our group to walk to Malham and back, so we could attend the opening of the Pennine Way. It was a cool, grey April day and there was a large marquee for the VIPs which people tried to crowd into. But I had little interest in listening to the platitudes of the gathered government ministers and officials, since I only wanted to hear from Tom Stephenson, one of my heroes.' Colin described how the 72-year-old Tom, dressed for the hills, spoke to the eager and appreciative audience, his warm and rolling Lancashire accent clearly full of passion. He told them that he hoped the National Parks Commission would safeguard the Pennine Way from tarmacadam, pylons, afforestation and reservoirs, and that the accommodation gaps would be addressed, especially in the Cheviots.

Before Tom spoke, Lord Strang, chairman of the National Parks Commission, opened the proceedings by admitting that it had taken an 'unconscionable long time' to get to this stage. The Rt Hon Fred Willey, Minister of Land and Natural Resources, then said that he hoped the 1949 legislation could be amended to ensure that such a delay wouldn't happen again. Earlier that morning (and apparently dressed in lounge suit and shiny black shoes), the minister had accompanied Tom in scaling Pen-y-ghent, reportedly meeting other walkers on the summit, who were heading southwards for the opening celebrations.

Reporting on the opening in *The Dalesman* magazine three months later, WR (Bill) Mitchell described how 'the moor became dotted with celebrities, but most eyes were on the erect, bespectacled, tanned, grey-thatched figure of Tom Stephenson. His hand was clasped several hundred times. He was patted on the back. When he rose to speak in the largest of the tents, there were shouts of "Good old Tom". During the day, Tom conducted a number of newspaper interviews, including one with a cub reporter from the *Manchester Guardian*, Bernard Ingham, who later went on to become the press secretary for Prime Minister Margaret Thatcher.

So what was it like running the launch event? Responsibility for organising it beforehand and managing it on the day fell to the head warden of the West Riding section of the Yorkshire Dales National Park. Wilf Proctor, who when he joined the National Park Authority two years earlier was its first ever paid warden, recalled the event in an article he wrote for the volunteers' newsletter *Waymarker* in 2005. He remembered how the remote moorland site just south of Malham Tarn proved a logistical challenge, involving closing the roads so that a lorry could safely deliver the marquee, and trying to find a caterer capable of producing high tea for 200 assorted VIPs in the middle of nowhere. Eventually, the canteen manager for toothpaste firm Elida Gibbs, who had an establishment in Leeds, rose to the challenge: 'He organised chairs and tables, cutlery and crockery, cheerful Yorkshire waitresses, water for tea (in milk churns from Tarn House) and all the food. Two hundred guests sat down to ham salad, cream cakes and cups of tea ad infinitum.'

Wilf's team of 40 voluntary rangers excelled themselves on the day, plying traffic-control policemen with sandwiches (a one-way system was in operation around local lanes) and responding to unexpected situations with typical resourcefulness ('A lady fainted in the crowded marquee during the speeches … and the only way to get [her] into fresh air was to push her under the tent side'). One warden even cut short his holiday in the Grand Canyon to make sure he got back for the opening, much to his companion's surprise ('My friend said I was daft, but it meant a lot to me').

Wilf shared some of his other memories from the day: 'of Miss Chesterman, my contact at the [National Parks] Commission, introducing me to Mr Willey; of the firm handshake from Tom Stephenson, whom I had previously met on several occasions; of Lord Strang who so kindly sought me out to say "Thank you, Proctor"; of Mrs Pauline Dower, widow of the man who conceived the Commission; of the three sixth formers from Bradford Boy's Grammar School who, in response to a challenge I had issued when lecturing at the school, had walked the Pennine Way from Kirk Yetholm, timing themselves to arrive at the ceremony just before the crowd dispersed, but just in time for tea and cakes! And of some senior civil servants wearing rather puzzled expressions … a gradely "do" like this was outside their ken.'

Wilf died in 2007 but I spoke to his widow, Joan, who had attended the opening with her husband. She told me that her own abiding memory was the sheer spectacle of people arriving on foot from every direction. 'It was quite amazing – whole families, people of all ages, walking down the lanes and along the paths to be at the event. There were mothers with pushchairs and even toddlers on tricycles. It meant so much to them, they all wanted to be there. The opening of the Pennine Way was such an important and symbolic moment for us all.' The annual report of the National Parks Commission published later that year stated that there were 3000 people at the event, although other accounts quote a figure of 2000.

Not unnaturally, the opening of the country's first official long-distance footpath created press headlines far and wide. Previewing the event in *The Guardian* (17 April 1965), Geoffrey Moorhouse wrote: 'The Americans have their Appalachian Trail, the New Zealanders their Milford Track; next weekend we shall have our Pennine Way which is neither as grand or as formidable as the other two but which is good enough for this claustrophobic country.' Eric Newby, then the travel editor of *The Observer*, walked 120 miles of it, and in his article on 11 April 1965 introduced it to readers as 'the longest and toughest continuous walk in Britain' and 'no *autostrada* for pedestrians'. In the *Daily Worker* (17 April 1965), Tom Spence explained to readers that the Pennine Way had been opened 'despite the money-merchants who view land only as green pastures for making more money.' Meanwhile, in an article in *The Lady* magazine (July 1965), Elizabeth Coxhead predicted that the Pennine Way 'will never be tamed, or likely to be crowded, but at least, if you slip and twist an ankle, somebody may be along in the course of a day'.

As far as anniversaries were concerned, it was no coincidence that the Pennine Way was officially opened on 24 April. Thirty-three years earlier – to the day – the Kinder Scout Mass Trespass had taken place. It confirmed not just the Pennine Way's pivotal role in the wider struggle for public access to the hills, but its own unique place in the history of outdoor recreation in Britain.

Malham Tarn began to recede as I plodded up the long and unending side of Fountains Fell. There were quite a few other walkers about, little knots of people wandering the paths and open slopes. Towards the top, I stopped and looked back eastwards over the Yorkshire Dales spread at my feet. The weather was fresh and bright, with patches of dazzling blue sky, and although there were still some menacing dark clouds about, they were zipping over quickly in the keen wind. When the sun periodically emerged, it was like a light switch had been turned on. The grassy hillsides were plunged into almost iridescent shades of green and light brown, while the bare limestone rock and screes shone a vivid off-white. It was a view to savour. However, it was also apparent that, possibly for the first time since leaving Edale, there were no pylons or wind turbines in sight, no hilltop monuments, transmitters, chimneys or reservoirs. There were no villages nor even any farms, since Tennant Gill Farm far below was hidden in a fold of the slope and the single track lane linking Malham to Arncliffe was more or less anonymous. The urban Pennines had become the wild Pennines, and it was uplifting.

I finally crossed over the top of Fountains Fell, named after the famous abbey that once owned huge tracts of land in these parts, and the wind really hit me. Starting to get cold, I descended the hillside in haste, trying not to lose my footing as I gazed at the irresistible prospect of Pen-y-ghent now ahead. I overtook what I assumed was a Duke of Edinburgh Award group of four young people, plodding slowly but purposefully with large packs, wrapped up against the keen wind. I'd seen a couple of other groups already that day, and having just passed the Field Studies Council centre at Malham Tarn, with a small squadron of minibuses parked up outside, it set me thinking about the role of the Pennine Way in terms of outdoor education.

The Pennine Way Conference in 1938 was adamant that establishing a walking trail along the Pennines was a matter of national interest 'on the grounds of the physical and spiritual well-being of the Youth of Britain'. Tom Stephenson had been quite clear that he wanted to see 'young people enjoying themselves on the Pennine Way'. In our modern digital age when there are so many leisure choices for young people, including lying on your bed for hours on end with a smartphone or laptop, it's worth reminding ourselves that there was once a time when a walking expedition through the hills was, for some at least, the epitome of an adventure. Reading accounts of early walks along the Pennine Way by groups of young people, I'd been struck by the sense of excitement and daring, despite the hardships and occasional pitfalls.

I'd already learnt that the Pennine Way was being walked well before its formal opening, and throughout the 1960s and into the 70s parties of schoolboys marched from Derbyshire to Scotland on teacher-led expeditions that are almost inconceivable now. Numerous people told me how, during those years, every boy supposedly wanted to walk the Pennine Way. Not long after the path was officially opened, Sir John Hunt, who led the first successful Everest expedition, was part of a group that walked the new trail; John Noakes and his dog Shep tackled it as part of his *Go with Noakes* TV programme (in an episode entitled 'The walk will do you good'); and legendary football manager Brian Clough even walked it for a few days to raise money for a good cause. For boys (and now men) of a certain generation, this was hero time.

So why is this sort of group walk for young people so unlikely now? Is it just because it's less fashionable? Or is it logistically more difficult to walk a long-distance path like the Pennine Way? Are there too many other attractive alternatives, or are health and safety regulations more stringent? But as I read some of these hair-raising early accounts, another thought kept occurring to me, a thought expressed by many others before me, that perhaps we're simply getting a bit soft these days.

Alan Binns wrote an early guidebook to the Pennine Way, published by Frederick Warne in 1966. A tough Burnley schoolteacher, he had some sage advice for would-be trailwalkers: 'I am as good a walker as the next man, a rugby union forward, a teacher of physical education, and yet I remember vividly the blackness of exhaustion coming over me when, driven from the Cheviots by wind and rain, I slumped to the floor in the tiny post office at Hownam on a bitter day in early June.'

In 2014, Alan published his memoirs, in which he devoted a small section to walking the Pennine Way, describing how, during the 1960s, he led parties of schoolboys along the newly formed trail. Some of their experiences make you gasp. 'In the southern Pennines we had to cross many areas of bog and soft peat. One of the boys boasted that you didn't have to walk round the muddy areas and if you ran fast enough across the boggy pool you didn't sink in. This worked on the small pools but he tried it once too often on a bigger pool and far out from the edge he slowed up and sank quickly to the depth of his legs. I believe that he had reached the floor of the mud pool and was on a more solid foundation but he could easily have vanished from sight. He was stuck and we cut sods of tussocky grass to make a series of footholds to reach him with a section of rope and we hauled him out. The force needed to extricate him from the clinging mud almost pulled his hips out of joint. He never again tried this foolish theory.'

Despite this, Alan told me, the overall experience for most of the boys was unquestionably life-enhancing: 'To walk 250 miles over such severe terrain and sometimes in such severe weather conditions was a great test of character. Boys who succeeded were very proud of themselves and they would remember their achievement for the rest of their lives.'

Preceding Alan Binns was Kenneth Oldham, author of the very first guidebook to the Pennine Way, published by Dalesman in 1960. He, too, was a teacher who had led parties of schoolboys along the route as far back as the early 1950s; he is believed to be the very first to have done so. After his appointment as headmaster at Whitehough Camp School in Barley, Lancashire, he was responsible for over 30 successful completions of the Way by parties of 'young folk'. Indeed, on his retirement in 1983, he was credited for introducing two generations of Lancashire schoolchildren to outdoor education. In his guidebook *The Pennine Way*, he includes some notes entitled 'Planning an Expedition' which offer no-nonsense instruction, including what sort of trousers to wear: 'Light clothing is always an advantage on a strenuous trail such as the Pennine Way and during most of the year, shorts are preferable to long trousers ... I know countless cases where those in long trousers have slipped into bog and continued the remainder of the route with the unpleasant reminder every time it rained or they walked through wet vegetation. Legs are easily washed and are dry almost as soon as the rain stops or you pass from wet grasses to shallow turf.' There is plenty of other sensible advice, such as the absolute necessity for a brew of tea on arrival at a camp or youth hostel (to ensure morale among the party, as well as to boost energy levels); and peppered throughout the book are almost throw-away references to how he and his party of boys had to wade through swollen rivers or navigate down a steep hillside in a force 10 gale.

In his long and highly distinguished career, Kenneth Oldham advised the government on outdoor education, led mountaineering expeditions and even, according to one account, used his specialist knowledge of the Pennines to help the police locate the scene of the Moors Murders from a small photographic snapshot. However, when he died in 2004, an obituary in a national newspaper quoted him as saying that his proudest achievement was passing on his love of the outdoors to schoolchildren, particularly those who had once been wayward pupils like himself.

I thought back to the warning signs around the reservoirs on the moors near Haworth, as well as to the newly paved paths and some walkers' expectations of signposts and waymarks across Bleaklow, such a contrast to the approach of the intrepid teachers and eager young lads in shorts and woollen jumpers jumping through the bogs 40 and 50 years ago. At what point did we become so safety-conscious and preoccupied with assessing risk that the raw thrill and trailblazing spirit of the Pennine Way got lost? Physical and mental challenge is inherent to the Pennine Way and part of its original design, but I worry that society's attitudes to risk-taking and calculating danger are shifting so much that we might end up with a new generation who actually find escape and adventure an alien concept and are fearful of the great outdoors.

In his book *The Adventure Alternative*, Colin Mortlock described what he called the four stages of the 'outdoor journey'. It begins with play, then goes on to adventure and frontier adventure, and ends with misadventure. By its design and nature, the Pennine Way represents (for most of us, at least) frontier adventure, that crucial stage where a person is likely to be taken out of his or her comfort zone and is no longer in full control of the situation, but where with effort, skill, good judgement and a bit of luck he or she can still succeed and in so doing derive great satisfaction and pride at that success. Whether you call it personal development or character-building, the Pennine Way above all other domestic walking trails offers that sense of frontier adventure. If it's true that you can only truly achieve when you really push yourself to the edge, then this high, exposed and rugged upland trail still provides that opportunity.

Fifty years ago, the done thing was to walk the Pennine Way in shorts, stay in draughty old youth hostels and navigate the bare moors by compass. Nowadays there's a wide choice of expensive breathable fabrics, centrally heated B&Bs and navigation by GPS. And if you really fancy it, you can have your luggage transferred by a van while you walk. Put in these terms, concepts of challenge and adventure might seem rather tame, but gone are the days when Alan Binns led parties of intrepid schoolboys along the trail, relying on caches of food that he had buried in holes in the ground in advance. We need the Pennine Way as much in the future as we did in the past, to offer successive generations fresh air and exercise, open and wild spaces, and the opportunity to push personal boundaries and explore our capacity to learn and develop.

There are few English hills so distinctive in shape and recognisable as Pen-y-ghent. It may not be the highest but it's certainly one of the highlights on the Pennine Way; and because it's relatively accessible, it can also be quite popular. There was a steady stream of people clambering up its steep southern flank that afternoon, an ascent involving a short burst of scrambling, but in truth nothing quite as arduous as the hill's severe outline at first suggests. Rather oddly, the name Pen-y-ghent is believed to come from the Welsh for 'hill of the winds', which in the blustery conditions was highly appropriate.

Soon I reached the top, where an elegant curved stone seat formed part of the wall across the summit ridge. It was built to mark the 50th anniversary of the Yorkshire Dales National Park in 2004. Of the three national parks that the Pennine Way visits, the first to be created, in 1951, was the Peak District (one of the initial group of four established by the 1949 legislation, the others being the Lake District,

Snowdonia and Dartmoor); the Yorkshire Dales followed in 1954 and Northumberland in 1956. Ironically, the Pennine Way then had to wait almost another decade before its own official launch.

I didn't make use of the seat because it was being sat on. In fact, I had to momentarily wait to reach the summit cairn because there were so many people milling about. Walkers of all shapes, sizes and ages kept appearing from various directions, but what really caught my attention was a small group of staggeringly underdressed youngsters who were laughing and jumping about for each other's photos, obviously celebrating their mountain conquest. Good on them, I thought, as I stood there watching, me dressed in fleece jacket, Goretex coat, warm hat and long trousers, they in little more than shorts, T-shirts and trainers. Maybe it's an age thing? Or perhaps it's me that's becoming risk averse?

5

HORTON-IN-RIBBLESDALE – HAWES

Racing and relaxation in the open hills

It was the end of the day from Malham and I was sitting in the pub at Horton-in-Ribblesdale, sorting out maps and writing my diary, a pint of beer half drunk before me. All of a sudden, the door burst open and in poured a group of about a dozen young men, smiling and laughing. They were loud and a little boisterous in a good-natured way, all except one who lay down on a bench in the corner and closed his eyes, moaning gently to himself. It transpired they had just completed the Three Peaks Walk, the popular one-day challenge walk taking in Pen-y-ghent and the neighbouring hills of Whernside and Ingleborough. (It's sometimes called the Yorkshire Three Peaks Walk in order to distinguish it from the equally hare-brained challenge of climbing Ben Nevis, Scafell Pike and Snowdon all in one go – the so-called National Three Peaks Walk.) The 24½-mile route must be completed within 12 hours and it's incredibly popular, not just for individuals and small groups but often attracting hundreds of competitors in mass fundraising events organised by national charities and companies on team-building exercises. It's a fairly serious undertaking, involving over 5000ft of ascent and requiring good navigation skills if the weather is rough.

By their age, apparel and conversation, the lads before me were probably college undergraduates, reasonably fit but certainly not hillwalkers. (The one prostrate in the corner was almost certainly neither fit nor a hillwalker.) After a noisy 45 minutes in which a vast quantity of Guinness was consumed and the premises emptied of crisps, a cry went up that the minibus had arrived and they all trooped out. A comforting hush descended throughout the pub, as the landlady began collecting glasses and rearranging the stools and tables. I asked her about the Three Peaks Walk. I knew that for many years there had been problems with footpath erosion because of the sheer number of people walking the route, but surely it was good for trade in Horton?

'Well yes, some of them come in and have a beer at the end, occasionally a meal, but usually all they want to do is change and go off. And they try and come in here to do that.'

I said I'd seen the sign in the gents saying this is a pub toilet not a changing room.

'Don't get me wrong, some of them are very nice,' she said. 'This lot tonight were fine, very friendly. But others empty their rucksacks and leave loads of litter for us to clear up and some are quite rude when you confront them about it. And it's the sheer numbers we have to deal with. Literally hundreds and hundreds sometimes turn up at weekends and invade what is really just a small village. Some local people breathe a sigh of relief when the weekend's over.'

She began loading the glasses into the dishwasher with a frown. I gave her a few moments and tentatively asked another question.

'So what about Pennine Way walkers? What are they like?'

'Oh, you lot are fine,' she replied with a laugh. 'You have a drink, eat a meal, then you fall asleep in the corner.'

The Three Peaks Walk traditionally starts at Horton-in-Ribblesdale, where for many years the Pen-y-ghent Café on the main street has clocked walkers in and out to record their times (if you do it within 12 hours you are then eligible to join the Three Peaks of Yorkshire Club). However, calling in the following morning for a quick coffee, I was far more interested in the relationship of the long-standing walkers' café with the Pennine Way.

The café has been run by the Bayes family since 1965, the same year that the Pennine Way was opened, which I'm fairly certain makes it the only family-run business on the trail still catering for Pennine Way walkers 50 years on. For most of that time, Peter Bayes and his wife have been in charge, but latterly son Matthew and daughter Melanie have taken over its day-to-day running. From the beginning, they have kept a record book for Pennine Way walkers to sign, huge black-covered tomes sitting on their own dedicated shelf behind the far end of the counter. There are already five complete volumes and now I proudly added my name to the sixth and asked whether I could glance through some of the older ones. They were brought over for me to inspect. As

I carefully turned the pages, it felt like I was handling some valuable literary manuscript, which in many ways it was. I wondered whether I should be wearing white gloves, perhaps dimming the lights? The books contained thousands of names, dates and short comments from men and women who for five decades have been walking this famous trail. I was literally touching a little bit of Pennine Way history – and in my own small way was making it, too.

The Pen-y-ghent Café is the sort of place every long-distance footpath needs. You can get a filling and inexpensive meal, whether it's the staple full breakfast or beans on toast and rhubarb crumble, or you can push the boat out just a little bit for a spicy banana toastie. Maybe you fancy an ice cream, need a spare pair of socks or insect repellent, want to order a take-away packed lunch or just sit in the corner with a brew and spend a rainy hour leafing through old walking magazines? When they ask you how you like your tea, they mean it; and if a walker has a problem that needs solving or a question to be answered, the queue at the counter will not necessarily hurry along until one of the many members of staff have solved it.

Melanie told me how, over 50 years, the Pennine Way had changed in their eyes. She remembered how, when she was small, her mum would help sick walkers to bed upstairs to wait for a doctor, but now they'll have already called for help on their mobile long before they reach the café. 'But you learn to spot a Pennine Way walker,' she said, 'through what they're wearing and carrying. Especially those who have been camping or bivvying, there's a fresh air-ness and clarity in their eyes.'

It was also clear that the Bayes family have enormous respect for Pennine Way walkers, which is evident in the attitude and reception you get from all the staff behind the counter. You can trace this back to the 1970s, when Peter Bayes decided to produce a badge for Pennine Way walkers as a mark of recognition. He wrote to everyone who had signed the café's Pennine Way book and asked them to submit log sheets of their own walks in return for a badge. It became an annual competition and the best entry won a modest cash prize – funded, of course, by Peter.

Pennine Way walkers still come in and sign the book on a regular basis and Melanie said it's become a unique record. 'We get lots of people who visit and say that they walked the Pennine Way years and years ago, so we go through the volumes and find their individual entry from that time. They are really ecstatic, genuinely thrilled at seeing their own entry again!'

As I climbed gently out of Horton that morning, the Three Peaks route came in from the right. You could tell this not just from the signpost but also because the track widened and the hard surface improved. The challenge walk is so popular that the Yorkshire Dales National Park Authority employs an extra ranger to maintain the walking route between the three summits and it's paid for by a special project. In 2013, a major route diversion took the path away from the sensitive and increasingly eroded track over Black Dubb Moss and Horton Moor north-west of Pen-y-ghent. The route now follows the Pennine Way off the mountain westwards, then via a newly engineered path over Whitber Hill it joins up with the trail again at the point where I was now standing.

If a brand new path seems a little drastic, it's because we're talking exceptional numbers. My guidebook warned me to expect hundreds of fellow walkers over the next quarter of a mile, especially at weekends. Every year, 100,000 people walk the Three Peaks, according to the National Park Authority, which by my crude reckoning is probably something in the region of 50 times more than annually complete the Pennine Way full distance. No wonder the pub landlady of the night before was concerned about the impact that all these walkers have on such a small rural community. By contrast, it was hard to see how a long-distance path like the Pennine Way, even in its heyday, could have anything like the same social impact, with lower numbers and a more transient type of user. It was just the surface that occasionally got hammered.

However, as if to show that that there is in fact some Three Peaks downtime, on this mild, sunlit Monday there wasn't a soul about and I had the route entirely to myself. I assumed that July would be a popular month for Thee Peakers and that such competitions or challenges are mostly seasonal. After all, who would want to tackle some of northern England's toughest hills and most remote moorland in winter when the daylight is short and the weather is often inhospitable? The answer, of course, is that there are plenty – and it gets more extreme still. Welcome to the Spine Race.

Billed as 'Britain's most brutal race', the Spine Race takes place along the Pennine Way each winter. On the official website (www. thespinerace.com), the organisers describe what would-be competitors are likely to be up against: 'Expect to race through extreme weather, deep snow, ice, mud, bogs, strong winds and rain in a gruelling non-stop seven-day race from Edale to Kirk Yetholm.' Yes, that's right, seven days or less, non-stop along the Pennine Way in early January! If that sounds a bit much, you could always opt for the shorter Spine Challenger competition instead, which is a non-stop 108-mile race along the Pennine Way between Edale and Hawes with a time limit of 60 hours.

Whether you choose the Spine Race or the Challenger, the organisers pull no punches: 'It's not just the conditions that are against you – your own body could become your worst enemy with tiredness, fatigue, sleep deprivation, exposure and the general pains of wear and tear playing havoc with your performance. To finish you must be prepared and willing to push yourself harder than ever before.' The winner of the 2016 Spine Race, 'ultra-runner' Eoin Keith from Cork, smashed the existing record by completing the 268-mile route in 95 hours and 43 minutes (24 competitors finished out of a field of 60 starters).

Although for most of us, myself included, just completing the Pennine Way in two or three weeks is a test in itself, there are some for whom covering as much distance as possible in the shortest time is evidently the ultimate goal. According to the Pennine Way National Trail website (www.nationaltrail.co.uk/pennine-way), most end-to-end walkers take 16–19 days to complete the trail; and a Countryside Commission survey in 1990 gave the average as 17 days. At the time of writing, the same website also states that the record for the fastest completion is held by Mike Hartley, who in July 1989 ran the whole route in 2 days, 17 hours, 20 minutes and 15 seconds. It took him two years to prepare for his run and at the height of his training he covered 170 miles a week along the trail. Apparently, he stopped only twice during his epic completion, for 18 minutes each time, including once for fish and chips in Alston: surely this must have taken a toll on his digestion? It certainly did on his feet, as he ran the last 40 miles using a borrowed size 10 shoe on his (ordinarily) size 8 right foot.

Running the Pennine Way in the fastest time has proved an irresistible challenge since the early days. Chris Brasher was one of a relay team that in 1971 ran the route in 33 hours, then three years later Joss Naylor, the remarkable Lake District sheep farmer and fellrunner, completed the Pennine Way on his own in 3 days, 4 hours and 35 minutes.

Covering well over 250 miles on foot along the Pennines in three days or less is clearly exceptional, and probably a little mad, but there are a surprising number of other walkers, obviously fit and incredibly motivated, who manage to walk the route in an unfeasibly short time. One such is John Needham who, with a small group in the 1970s, completed the whole path in seven days.

In the Pennine Way Council's spring 1978 newsletter, he explained how they went about the task. Heading north to south and with most of their supplies carried by a support vehicle, each day involved around 30–40 miles of walking. The weather seemed typically varied, from sunshine between Greenhead and Dufton (one day's walk) to snow the next day at High Cup Nick. John appeared to walk quite a lot on his own and finished that day from Dufton at the Tan Hill Inn at 10.30pm; then the next 39-mile day at about the same time.

However, the last day, from Ponden to Edale, covered 54½ miles and just reading about it is exhausting. Although they made reasonably good progress throughout the day, by the time John and his companion reached the trig point on Black Hill, darkness had fallen. They eventually made it down to Longdendale around midnight and had something to eat in the back-up car at Torside. John explained what happened next: 'Snow began to fall as we sat in the car. Jack said he couldn't go any further without sleep – I said if I stopped now I'd never start again, so about 12.45 I started alone to cross Bleaklow, with a sleeping bag wrapped around my shoulders, two torches and food. As I climbed up Torside, snow was falling and I could see nothing, but plodded on up to the top. I sat down and ate – then off again. I lost the stakes, wallowed in peat streams and groughs, found the stakes again.'

Luckily, he spotted the torches of two others in the support team, one of whom said he would walk with John to Edale. 'It was nearly dawn when we set off across Featherbed Moss for Mill Hill. After the short, sharp climb on to the Kinder Edge, life seemed to go out of me and from a reasonable pace I went into a shuffle. I'm sure I couldn't have found my own way across to Grindsbrook, but eventually I stumbled over the log bridge into Edale and we were all soon on our way to Sheffield by car.'

All this talk of physical endurance and against-the-clock racing left me breathless, even though I knew that a key ingredient of my own Pennine Way walk was not necessarily speed but seeing if I had the strength, stamina and resolve to rise to the challenge of a long expedition on foot. Could I still do this sort of thing at 50? Was I strong enough, both physically and mentally? For all the enjoyment of soaking up the natural wonders of the Pennines, the freedom and solitude, meeting like-minded people and sampling local real ale, it was also about testing my capabilities. Whether you term it a midlife awakening, opportunity, transition or crisis, there is definitely something about getting to that point in your life when you assess – either by force of circumstances or a gradual realisation – that you have a finite time left on this planet and it's time to recognise it, celebrate it and of course make the most of it.

By way of response, the Spine Race may seem a little excessive, but since the early years of the 21st century there has been a growing phenomenon of middle-aged men (and it is nearly always men) taking up extreme sports and physical tests, opting for 100-mile cycle rides, sponsored mountain climbs and running ultra-marathons. 'Triathlon is the new golf!' was one startling headline I saw shortly before I began my walk. I guess, on the face of it, it's simply middle-aged men wanting to prove their vitality to themselves (and others), staving off thoughts of retirement and turning to extreme physical sport instead of more clichéd behaviour like buying a high-powered motorbike or dyeing their greying hair. In a *Mail Online* article ('The new mid-life crisis: Today's men seek their thrills on boys' own adventures', 2 November 2011), Rachel Porter interviewed several bewildered wives trying to make sense of their husbands' new-found love of adrenaline-pumping outdoor action. Mary from Oxfordshire, whose previously sedate partner Brian was now training to walk to the North Pole, said: 'I do understand the need for something to fill the gap when life gets a bit easier and you're not ready for retirement, but I thought he'd join the Rotary Club.'

I'd also read an online article entitled 'Mid-Life Transition', challenging the common perception that physical decline is an inevitable consequence of ageing and that as we get older we tend to slow down and do less. In it, Dr Andrew Weil argued, with some cogency, that regular exercise helps you take charge of your own health and remain active and independent; and that much of the physical frailty attributed to ageing in fact results from inactivity, disease or poor nutrition. In an article in *The Telegraph* online ('Midlife crisis "replaced with graceful midlife transition"', 22 January 2010), Matthew Moore suggested that the best way to avoid a 'midlife crisis' was to appreciate how many years you have left and make imaginative plans for using them. 'An increasingly confident and resilient generation are embarking on productive "second lives" as they reach 50, aware that they still have 30 good years ahead of them,' he said.

This trend seems to be reflected in the age profile of those walking the length of the Pennine Way, which over the years has been gradually rising. In the Countryside Commission's Pennine Way Survey of 1971, the vast majority of 'whole way' walkers were aged 15–44 (93 per cent) with the 45–64 age group accounting for just 7 per cent. The next full survey, almost two decades later in 1990, showed that long-distance Pennine Way walkers were getting older, since although there were still 71 per cent in the 16–44 age range (classed as 'young adult'), those over 45 years old walking the full distance had risen to 21 per cent. By the time of the National Trails survey in 2007, the most populous age group walking the Pennine Way – for whatever distance, since it didn't differentiate this time – had switched to 45–64-year-olds (48 per cent), with the 18–44 age range accounting for just 33 per cent.

On the face of it, this suggests that the average Pennine Way walker, at least among those going long distance, was now more likely to be middle-aged or older, depending on what point you judge midlife to start. It also confirms that gone are the days when bold and occasionally reckless groups of young lads embarked on a boy's own adventure by tackling the Pennine Way. Instead, it's likely that summit-bagging and adventure-based sports appeal more to the younger generation, who perhaps might go on to walk the Pennine Way when they get older, slower and more reflective. Still, with full-distance walkers far outnumbered by those enjoying shorter outings ('thru hikers' and 'section hikers', as they're known in American trailwalking parlance), it was necessary to keep all this in perspective; but the profile, appeal and pattern of use of the Pennine Way has clearly changed.

I plodded slowly but contentedly up the track towards distant Hawes, enjoying the peace and quiet in the gentle sunshine. With a straightforward stage ahead of me and the weather set fair till later, it would be true to say that I almost dawdled. The Three Peaks encounter, in particular, reminded me that long-distance walking is certainly not the same thing as challenge walking; and that if time is all that matters, you'll almost certainly miss out on something fundamental that the Pennine Way offers – the sense of place and moving slowly through a changing landscape with self-awareness and understanding. I was already finding that a journey on foot along the Pennine Way, day after day, was allowing me to immerse myself in space and calmness and to enjoy the opportunity for reflection that a mad 24-hour dash can never do. I was still walking some long distances every day, and it was hard work at times, but already I was falling into the steady rhythm of the long-distance walk – something familiar to most seasoned trailwalkers.

Today, in fact, the Pennine Way seemed to be telling me to slow down, look around and enjoy. There were good views of Ingleborough and Whernside over to the west and intermittently of Ribblehead Viaduct. I stopped once or twice to inspect things that interested me, most notably several holes in the ground next to the path. Descending to Horton the day before, I had diverted to look at Hull Pot, perhaps one of the largest and most spectacular potholes in the Dales, but this morning I passed a series of seemingly impenetrable rocky openings and depressions in the limestone that gave way to extensive caving systems. Sell Gill Holes has a pitch 150ft high leading to a huge underground chamber, and similarly Jackdaw Hole and Long Churn are further portals to amazing subterranean networks. I have to say

I prefer my recreation on the surface rather than under it, especially when coming across such treasures as Ling Gill Nature Reserve. This small gorge falls away steeply by the side of the path, richly clothed in ash, wych elm, rowan and birch, and is a reminder that once upon a time the hillside was covered in deciduous woodland.

Beyond the shallow stream, the Pennine Way continued across the increasingly barren hillside, steadily gaining ground, with conifer plantations away to the right. There were occasional waymarks, including most appropriately for the new Pennine Bridleway, officially opened in 2012, since this was once a well-used packhorse route: a couple of centuries back, Ling Gill bridge would have echoed to the sounds of hooves as trains of tough little ponies were led over the Pennine hills carrying food, textiles and coal. Yesterday I'd walked past the site where the Pennine Way was officially opened half a century before, and here – with the Pennine Bridleway – was a sign of just how far we've come since then in developing recreational routes across the northern hills.

For many years, national trails (called long-distance paths before the inevitable rebranding) had their own dedicated trail officers, centrally funded by government, but budget cuts have meant that Natural England (once known as the Countryside Commission and then the Countryside Agency) has changed its approach. The premier tier of recreational routes in England and Wales is now managed via locally run trail partnerships, but with funding and support from Natural England. There's still an officer in charge of day-to-day coordination, and for the Pennine Way that person is Heather Procter, who works out of the Yorkshire Dales National Park Authority.

After completing my Pennine Way walk, I met Heather to learn more about looking after the Pennine Way, both now and in the future. Heather's official title is Pennine National Trails Partnership Manager, since she has dual responsibility for both the Pennine Way and the Pennine Bridleway, and she explained that a key part of her work is coordination. 'Managing all 268 miles of the Pennine Way only really works through a successful partnership,' she said. 'That includes all the local authorities up and down the trail, the three national parks and North Pennines Area of Outstanding Natural Beauty, Natural England and a regeneration partnership called Pennine Prospects that covers the South Pennines. My role is to work with all these different organisations, for instance helping them look for funding to cover maintenance work on the trail.'

Day-to-day repair work is probably the most obvious task that the partners carry out, mending stiles and bridges and improving eroded surfaces, and for that Heather has the support of two Pennine Way lengthsmen (rangers to you and me) covering the Peak District and Yorkshire Dales. Having these two professionals whose sole task is to maintain and, where possible, improve the Pennine Way on the ground is probably one of the trail's greatest strengths from a management point of view. This day-to-day attention – whether unblocking drains and culverts or replacing broken signs – helps to prevent overall deterioration and ensure a positive trailwalking experience, whether you're out for an hour, a day or a fortnight.

However, footpath maintenance and repair is just one aspect of a trail officer's work. 'Getting a decent and consistent standard of path is obviously important,' Heather explained, 'and there are still a few badly eroded locations which we will probably have to deal with, but there are plenty of other aspects to my work on the Pennine Way as well. For instance, how do we promote the trail and are we sure about the "offer"? The image of the Pennine Way as a tough and adventurous walk is certainly correct, but we need to work out how to convince people to enjoy this unique outdoor challenge in their own country when it seems to be just as easy and affordable to go abroad for that once-in-a-lifetime physical challenge.'

Heather also talked about the need to look at plugging the accommodation gaps on the trail, of promoting local buses and trains to make it easier to explore the Pennine Way using public transport, engaging more volunteers to help care for the route and seeing what can be done to involve local communities a little more closely. However, one of her regular tasks is to complete an annual 'condition survey' of the path. 'I walk a section of the route and check the condition of the surface and all the path furniture,' she explained. 'I carry a hand-held tablet with a program that shows every signpost, gate and stile, each precisely located and with its own code. I record whether it's in a good condition or not, or if it requires any maintenance and what priority should be given to it, then via a mobile app this data is electronically submitted, a paperless report is generated and sent to the relevant highway authority to consider action. The precise surface of the path is also documented all the way along, broken down into different types, so that I can monitor any deterioration or note problems with drainage or encroaching vegetation.'

I walked past another sign for the Pennine Bridleway, impressed again by the ambition of this 205-mile route the length of the Pennines. The idea of long-distance recreational routes is now so well established that we've moved on to developing continuous coastal paths, of course, but there must still be something of the pioneering Pennine Way spirit about creating a new route from scratch. It's envisaged that around 30 miles of new rights of way are required to complete the Pennine Bridleway; and there was more than double that for the Pennine Way half a century earlier. Not only did the National Parks and Access to the Countryside Act 1949 empower local authorities to impose new access links in the proposed long-distance path, but Section 54(2) also gave the local authorities specific powers to provide other facilities where they were found to be lacking. Its scope was surprisingly wide: 'Arrangements for securing, at places in their area convenient for persons using the part of the route in question, the provision, whether by the authority or other persons, of accommodation, meals and refreshments (including intoxicating liquor).'

The 1949 legislation goes on to say that a local planning authority may erect buildings to carry out such a function and even acquire land compulsorily for these purposes. Another section of the same Act also gave local authorities the power to provide and operate ferries for the purposes of achieving long-distance routes. This may not have much relevance for the landlocked Pennine Way, but again it gives some idea of both the vision and the purpose of the legislators, as well as a recognition that there were likely to be gaps in the provision of certain services for walkers. However, whether the national trail office has ever provided weary walkers with intoxicating liquor seems rather unlikely.

On the high, western slopes of Cam Fell, the Pennine Way joins a wide track known as Cam High Road. It's another historic route, used since the Romans and in particular by cattle drovers who led huge herds across the wild tops of the Pennines, as well as by wool traders and other merchants. The route climbs steadily across the bare and open hillside, feeling ever more remote, with moorland and valleys radiating out in all directions. From this watershed, the Wharfe flows eastwards through Yorkshire, becoming an important tributary of the River Ouse and reaching the North Sea via the Humber Estuary, while the Ribble heads south through Lancashire to issue out into the Irish sea near Preston.

Once, this wide, well-used route was quite natural and unsurfaced, described by Tom Stephenson in his 1969 guidebook *The Pennine Way* as a 'grass grown track running along a ledge of the fell'; but in the early years of the 21st century it was damaged through intensive use by recreational motor vehicles and trail bikes; then, after they were banned, logging wagons began thundering in and out as the plantations on the east of Cam Fell began to be cleared. The surface has evidently been upgraded into a hard and rather unforgiving track, presumably to cater for these huge trucks, one of which rumbled past me now in a cloud of dust, not slowing down for a moment. I carried on along the single-track route to find, most bizarrely in this remote and otherwise traffic-free location, that a minor traffic jam had occurred. The logging truck had met a small oil tanker, presumably returning from supplying the remote farmhouse at Cam Houses ahead, and one of the two was going to have to give ground and reverse some distance. I tiptoed round the sparring vehicles and continued briskly up the track towards Cold Keld Gate, the sense of height and remoteness growing with every step.

In addition to rubbing shoulders with the Pennine Bridleway, for a while the Pennine Way also falls into step with another historic long-distance footpath. The Dales Way was co-devised by Colin Speakman, who I met at Malham recounting his memories of the opening ceremony of the Pennine Way. The 80-mile Dales Way from Ilkley to Bowness-on-Windermere is an altogether gentler affair ('more of a beginner's trail' confided Colin to me). Now with links to Leeds, Bradford and Harrogate, it stretches the length of Wharfedale and over the years has proved enormously popular. In fact, as Colin explains in the 11th edition of his official guide to the route (*Dales Way: The Complete Guide*), the first organised walk along a section of the proposed Dales Way happened as long ago as 1969, at a time when the Countryside Commission was considering a possible walking link between the newly opened Pennine Way and the Lake District. In the end, the Dales Way was developed in its own right, largely thanks to the efforts of the local Ramblers' Association and then the Dales Way Association. Nevertheless, it provides an excellent complement to the Pennine Way and is perhaps another example of how the recreational trail network began to flourish once the Pennine Way caught people's imagination.

The very top of the track felt like a proper pass, almost 1900ft high and above the heads of several valleys, and from here the Pennine Bridleway headed off westwards towards Dentdale while the Pennine Way made directly for Hawes. The sense of light and open space was palpable. It was remarkably peaceful and I could pick out very specific sounds: a curlew trilled its watery call from the bleak moorland away to the east; a hairy cow further down the hillside snorted noisily. I stood for a couple of minutes, simply absorbing this bare but magnificent landscape, the huge sky and the endless hillsides stretching out in all directions. Eventually I decided to move on, since the light mist of the afternoon was gradually turning to drizzle as the weather deteriorated. I picked up the pace and began the long descent to Hawes, the busy market town of upper Wensleydale, eventually entering round the back of the famous Creamery. I was looking forward to replenishing supplies and re-entering civilisation for a while.

So it was that around 4pm I found myself standing outside the Spar supermarket on the busy main street, contemplating fresh fruit and just possibly an ice cream. I noticed a young man bent over a large rucksack nearby, so I went over and asked if he was walking the Pennine Way. He said he was and stood up, grinning from ear to ear. Edward was a tall, gangly-looking 20-year-old with long floppy hair and a pleasantly dishevelled air. Was he walking solo like me?

'No,' he replied, 'well yes.'

'Pardon?'

'I set off with a mate, but he got poisoned and has just gone to hospital. So I'm carrying on alone.'

'Poisoned?' I asked with some disbelief, but just a little concern as well. I could do without a serial poisoner on the trail.

Edward explained how they had been wild camping, including a night on the top of Pen-y-ghent in the lee of a wall, which given the recent wind must have been some experience. But they had also been drinking from streams along the way, which might just have accounted for his friend's predicament.

As he was explaining all this, Edward had returned to his rucksack and resumed packing the groceries he'd just bought from the shop. I noticed that in one of the side pockets he had emptied a bag of loose, dried pasta. Now he was decanting a jar of tomato pasta sauce into a small and rather flimsy-looking plastic bag, talking away all the time as he did so. He lobbed the empty glass jar into a nearby bin and then, after pinching the clip along the top of the bag, proceeded to squash the bulging bag into another rucksack pocket. I watched with growing consternation as the bag appeared ready to burst, all the while still trying to follow his tale of two lads bivvying in field barns and falling down hillsides.

Edward had spent a couple of days in Hawes sorting himself out and asking chemists about different types of poison. Now, on a drizzly late Monday afternoon, he had decided to set off once more, which I guessed was par for the course for his approach to the Pennine Way. I said I'd walk with him to the edge of town, where my B&B was located.

'So why are you walking the Pennine Way?' I asked, curious to discover what motivates two young men to backpack the Pennines when they could be hanging out in some warm, southern European capital instead.

'Well, I've never really walked anything like this before, but a few months ago I went to see that film *Wild*. You know, the one where Reese Witherspoon walks along a trail through the North American mountains.'

I said I hadn't seen it but I'd read the book, about a young woman who sets off to walk the 1100-mile Pacific Crest Trail from Mexico to Canada.

'It looked really cool. So afterwards I told my dad that I was going to walk the Pacific Crest Trail over the summer before I went back to uni in September.'

'And what did he say?'

'He said go and walk the Pennine Way first and see how you get on.'

I told Edward his dad was probably right.

That evening, I went to watch an artistic performance described as 'walking and dancing the Pennine Way'. I didn't know anything about it until I got to Hawes, but in one of those serendipitous moments I'd picked up a flyer from a café in the town about a show called *50 Steps*, one of a series of events celebrating the 50th anniversary of the trail. It was to take place at the Dales Countryside Museum in Hawes, which had previously staged an exhibition about the Pennine Way. Tonight, for one night only, there was to be a live performance featuring three dancers, a musician and a video artist, who were going to translate the Pennine Way into movement and music. I got there slightly early in case it was busy (it wasn't) and took my seat. I mentioned at the front desk that I was actually walking the Pennine Way at the moment, not because I was seeking adulation but just to see whether I could get in for free (I couldn't). However, word quickly spread and I was soon singled out by the cast and some of the audience, which was faintly embarrassing. It also meant that I had to stay awake the whole evening, which proved a bit of a challenge as it wore on and fatigue set in.

The show featured three women dancing in front of a screen showing footage of the Pennine Way near Hawes, filmed earlier in the day. Accompanied by some moody guitar strumming, the women (who had all been out on the path) then translated their experiences through the medium of dance. There was a lot of waving of arms, bending and jumping around, which struck me as a bit energetic for most Pennine Way walkers, but when one limped slowly across the floor and slumped down panting I thought she was probably nearer the mark.

This was the third of five performances at different locations on the route (including Edale and Garrigill), so afterwards I asked them about their impressions of the Pennine Way. One described how, when she was striding out rhythmically, the ground seemed to almost move her along, as if it had a great power. Another spoke expressively about the space and openness and about how humans seem so insignificant in such an awesome landscape. I knew exactly what they meant. We talked all too briefly about being close to nature, the weather and attitudes to the hills; but they were already packing up because, as they told me rather apologetically, they wanted to get to the chip shop before it closed since none of the cast had eaten yet. I guess it's hungry work dancing the Pennine Way.

6

HAWES – KELD

A tale of two trails

The next morning, feeling fresh and ready for the trail once more, I wandered into the centre of Hawes to pick up some snacks. I'd already been tipped off by some other Pennine Way walkers that the pies at the family-run baker's and butcher's JW Cockett & Son (est. 1854) were second to none, but Tuesday was also market day so, after stocking up with some goodies, I continued up the main street to the fruit and veg stall. It all looked very fresh and appealing, but I had a rather awkward question to ask. Could I buy a single banana, please? Not a bunch, just one on its own. The young man next to the cash desk nodded, although not terribly enthusiastically. I selected a bunch and tore off what I judged was the largest fruit, just to reassure him that I wasn't *that* mean, and asked how much it cost. Without weighing it he said '45p', which gave me the impression that he had just made it up, but I wasn't going to argue.

Clutching my large yellow fruit, I moved off to the edge of the stall, took off my rucksack and crouched down next to it in order to locate my banana case. Now, I'm not particularly interested in gadgets and gizmos, and my walking kit is by and large fairly unshowy and rudimentary, but I do rather like my bright yellow plastic banana case. It's quite large and, as you might expect, shaped like a banana, and it does a wonderful job of keeping bananas (or any other delicate foodstuffs, for that matter) intact and uncrushed, even after a full day stuffed down a rucksack. I now unclipped the case and carefully slotted the banana inside, straightening it out ever so slightly as the degree of banana bend was just a little too acute for the uniform curve of the case. I tend to take this part of the process quite slowly, as I don't want to face the disappointment of unclipping the case a few hours later to find that the skin has split or started to go brown. When the banana was satisfactorily housed in its casement, I snapped the lid shut, making sure that the banana was snug inside and wasn't either squashed too tight or couldn't move around too freely. It was only then that I looked up to meet a sea of faces staring down at me, a little knot of shoppers with expressions that varied from the curious to the mildly amused. I smiled rather apologetically. I really wanted to explain why I had a banana case and how it worked so well, but I sensed the good folk of Hawes might not be on my wavelength. And judging by the look of the stallholder, buying bananas individually was not something he wanted to encourage among his customers. I packed up and, replete with fruit, headed for the hills.

Unfortunately the hills were not very welcoming. The goal was Great Shunner Fell, the third highest point in Yorkshire, but so far that morning it had been obscured by cloud and squally showers. I dallied for a while at Hardraw Force, the highest single-drop waterfall above ground in England, which whooshes a spectacular 98ft over the rocks. Even more remarkable is that a 19th-century tightrope walker once crossed the small gorge and even stopped midway to cook an omelette. It seemed only marginally more daft than walking up a huge wet hill that morning.

It was a very long four and half miles to the top of 'Shunner', not exceptionally steep or difficult, just a tiring plod through the wind and rain. A notice explained that the moors were important for the rare black grouse, but the birds had more sense than to be out on a day like this. Inevitably, the only form of life either brave or foolhardy enough to battle with the conditions were Pennine Way walkers. Towards the top I caught up with three men who I had first met on the approach to Pen-y-ghent a couple of days before, chatted with over a pint at Horton later that evening and then not met again until now. (Such are encounters with other trailwalkers on a path the size and scale of the Pennine Way, that unless you are locked into their daily stages you end up on an unpredictable cycle, encountering them one day, passing them on another, then not seeing them for several days.) Probably in their late 50s or 60s, a more friendly and easy-going trio you could hardly wish to find. Derek, Steve and Tim were evidently firm walking buddies. Their daily 'penninewayers' blog (https://penninewayers.wordpress. com) is an amusing and illustrated diary of their walk, supplemented by a 'beer blog' describing in some detail what pubs they visited (most, by the sound of it), what real ale they came across and what it was like.

As we huddled at the summit shelter and ate our lunch, the three men explained that, for them, the Pennine Way was unfinished business. They had tried to walk it in June 2012, but the weather was so bad that they were forced to abandon after managing to get as far as Dufton. 'It rained hard every single day,' said Derek. 'Remember the Hebden Bridge floods? We waded through them!' He went on to describe how every moor and hilltop was shrouded in cloud and there were hardly any views. 'We stood at the top edge of High Cup in thick mist and could sense a huge void below us,' said Steve, 'but we just couldn't see a thing. The rain was relentless and I even took a day out to catch a train to Carlisle to buy new waterproofs. But in the end we decided to quit.'

In comparison, their summer 2015 attempt had so far gone well and the weather was much kinder, so that they were finally enjoying the views denied to them last time. Great Shunner Fell had so far proved the exception; but even now, the rain had stopped and the clouds were beginning to thin. There were fleeting views of far-off slopes, but nothing substantial yet. On a clear day, you can see Cross Fell, Buckden Pike, Pen-y-ghent and even the distant Lake District hills. But – as the chaps had found in 2012 – those days were sometimes at a premium and you had to rely on the guidebook to describe the views.

At 2349ft, Great Shunner Fell was in fact the highest point I had reached so far on the Pennine Way, and once more I had the sense that it was gently testing me. Despite the wind and rain, the route up from Hawes had been fairly obvious, with slabs across the particularly boggy sections towards the top. In the distant past, though, it appeared to be the convention to bypass Shunner altogether if the weather was really rough, with Pennine Way walkers taking to the metalled lane over the Buttertubs Pass to the east in order to reach Swaledale. Some years were drier than others, of course, as this item from the Pennine Way Council's newsletter dated August 1976 showed: 'Pennine Wayfarers must be thirsty people, at any rate after traversing Great Shunner Fell. Even in winter the people of Keld and Thwaite have been so inconvenienced by pleas from dehydrated walkers that the Parish

Council last February asked the National Park Committee to provide standpipes and taps. The Committee agreed to do this not only in the two villages but also in Hawes station yard. So walkers need no longer seek to hire camel humps before leaving the existing standpipe by the Malham Information Centre.'

I wondered what it must have been like to walk the Pennine Way without slabs, with few signs or waymarks, and without sufficient drinking water; and, in particular, what it was like venturing onto the Pennine Way (or what you believed was the likely route) before it was even officially opened, with some sections not yet finalised. I found it hard to imagine attempting the route without a proper guidebook or detailed maps, but the more I read the accounts of early completions, the more it conjured up images of pioneers and trailblazers, almost making up parts of the route as they went along.

I decided to seek out someone who had set foot on the trail in those early years and could tell me what it was really like; so before I set off on my own walk, I met Peter Stott. He first walked the Pennine Way in the summer of 1963, then again in stages in the late 1990s, before completing it all in one go once more in 2013, exactly 50 years after his first completion. So how did it feel to be walking the Pennine Way two years before it was officially opened?

'I remember being incredibly excited,' he said. 'I was just 16, but doing it with two older lads. We walked long distances, up to 30 miles a day, as we had to fit it into what was in effect a fortnight's youth hostelling. There were some remarkable places and people, like the helpful warden's wife at Mankinholes who dried our wet leather boots and socks in the oven. It was a terrific adventure, just a real thrill being up there in the hills.'

And what was it like to walk on the ground?

'There were no paths to speak of. Waymarks and direction signs were almost non-existent. We had to interpret our maps, on which we had pencilled what we took to be the line of the Pennine Way based on the Ramblers' Association's sixpenny leaflet, and work with a compass. My mate's mum had managed to get some pre-war maps from West Riding County Council library, but none of them covered

Cross Fell and the ones of Redesdale didn't show any forests! Luckily for us, approaching Bellingham there were occasional "PW" signs and untitled white arrows painted freehand on trees and fence posts. In one or two places the actual route was still being argued about when we were walking it.'

Back in 1963, Peter's kit was also a bit different. 'I had leather boots and two pairs of seaboot stockings, khaki shorts, a cotton shirt and cotton anorak. We carried one change of clothing, a sweater, cycle cape, washing kit and towel, packed lunch and glass water bottle, all in a cotton rucksack.'

Peter admitted that they were a cocky trio of lads when they set off, thinking that they knew it all after hillwalking in the Lakes and the Yorkshire Dales, but the opening day's labours really hit them. 'A 30-mile day was something we expected to take in our athletic stride. But we struggled on the first day from Edale and that night at Holmfirth Youth Hostel we were utterly exhausted. The Pennine Way had shown what it could do to the overconfident, and although our lesson was a hard one to swallow it did help us complete the walk.'

Peter talked about the ankle-snaring heather on the trackless moors and plunging knee-deep into bog. He also vividly remembered getting to Hawes, tired and extremely wet, and looking for somewhere to bide their time before the youth hostel opened at 5pm. 'We went into a café, stripped to the waist to an accompaniment of giggles from the female clientele, put on spare dry shirts – those old cotton rucksacks somehow kept out the weather before polythene bags became commonplace – and we ordered tea. After the tea, it was still too wet and too early to leave, so we ordered fish and chips. When we finished, we lit up cigarettes and ordered more tea. Still the rain hammered down. After a while, the staff began to drop hints that we might be thinking of leaving. Our response was to order fish and chips again, then we asked for more tea. When the rain eased, we paid 30 shillings (£1.50) for the eight helpings of fish and chips and 33 cups of tea. Finally we changed back into wet shirts and anoraks and shuffled out to the damp market place.'

In the absence of a youth hostel at Middleton-in-Teesdale, the trio booked into a B&B and were able to at last have a proper wash. 'That night we had our first bath since leaving home. Few youth hostels had showers in the early 1960s, and no self-respecting man would have been seen dead with a deodorant. I wonder if they ever did get that bath clean afterwards?'

So what had changed 50 years later, walking the Pennine Way in 2013?

'Signage and slabs, which have made it easier, of course, and a defined walking line on the ground. In 1963, for instance, the route from Malham village to the Cove was just a faint line in the grass, not the wide semi-surfaced track it is now.'

So is the Pennine Way a noticeably easier walk today?

'Much of the trickier navigation has been taken out of it, but it's still a long and exacting distance. If you want to know what it used to be like then, go ten yards either side of the walked route and see how you get on. I wouldn't dream of walking it without the slabs, now.'

And how did he feel completing the walk again, five decades on?

'Just as enjoyable as 1963. The feeling of satisfaction when you finish the walk is immense, like you've achieved something private, deep and personal, just for you. No one else can fully appreciate it.'

Peter's online description of his two full-distance walks, 50 years apart, are well worth reading (www.stottiewalks.walkingplaces.co.uk). He's also confident that the Pennine Way will endure. 'It blazed a trail for all the others and is part of our walking heritage. Its fame will help preserve it.'

In 1963, Peter Stott and his mates bypassed Great Shunner Fell because of the bad weather; but it had now relented for me, so I heaved on my rucksack and slowly made my way down the soggy hillside, buoyed by ever-improving views into Swaledale. Coming up towards me was a bearded middle-aged man, well kitted out with waterproofs and walking poles, picking his way quickly over the bumpy terrain. For some reason, I fancied he might be a north–south Pennine Way walker, but when I stopped him to ask, it turned out he only lived a short distance away and was out for a 'quick round' before tea. With a laugh he pointed out his house, waving his arm in the general direction of Thwaite, a village a couple of miles below us. But since the path literally went past his doorstep, had he ever been tempted to walk further along the trail, perhaps the whole of the Pennine Way? 'I'm up here most days,' he admitted. 'I love the wide open spaces of these moors. As a born and bred northerner, this is a special place, grand walking. But the Pennine Way? Maybe one day.' He paused, and with an elaborate wink, added: 'But that would mean leaving Yorkshire, wouldn't it?'

Half an hour later, I trotted into Thwaite and stopped for a drink at the Kearton Country Hotel. It wasn't so much because I was desperate for a cuppa but because there are relatively few opportunities for this kind of pit stop on the Pennine Way. I sat inside at a table near the door, perspiring gently and conscious that my damp rucksack and mud-splattered gaiters didn't exactly fit in with the plush surroundings. Shelves of rather expensive-looking Yorkshire Dales-themed souvenirs and knick-knacks surrounded me, while at the far end of the long room several couples quietly chatted as they tucked into their tea and cake, their comfortable warm cars parked just a few yards away outside the entrance door. When I got up to pay, I joked with the impassive young woman behind the counter that I was about to resume battle with the great outdoors. She looked at me as if I was speaking another language, which to her I guess I was.

My destination for the night was the small village of Keld, just three miles away, but it took an energetic and at times rough path round the upper slopes of Kisdon Hill to reach it. Not that I minded too much. The weather had perked up, there was time in hand, and below me lay beautiful Upper Swaledale. This path stayed high above the deep valley, its steep sides partly cloaked in woodland. Far below, the infant River Swale curved round to the village of Muker and on towards Reeth and Richmond, the valley broadening out into a patchwork of walled fields and numerous tiny barns. Here and there, especially on the upper slopes, there was evidence of past lead mining; while approaching Keld the water skipped over rocky outcrops in a series of waterfalls. As an end to a day's walk on the Pennine Way, it was hard to beat.

Not unnaturally, as the first official Long Distance Route (the term used by the National Parks and Access to the Countryside Act 1949), the Pennine Way remained the best-known and the most popular trail for some considerable time. After opening in 1965, it was followed by the Cleveland Way (1969), Pembrokeshire Coast Path (1970), Offa's Dyke Path (1971), Ridgeway (1972), South Downs Way (1972) and North Downs Way (1978); but none could match the status, reputation and sheer pulling-power of the Pennine Way. It was, after all, the original, and had been a small matter of 30 years in the making.

Precisely how many walked the Pennine Way in the early years is difficult to say, since reliable statistics are hard to come by. The National Parks Commission conducted a small survey in 1965, but it wasn't until the Countryside Commission's Pennine Way Survey in 1971 that a fuller picture of the trail emerged. Although the two studies are not directly comparable because different locations were surveyed, it suggested that numbers of people walking the trail had increased significantly in just the six years since it had opened, possibly by as much as threefold. Both surveys were conducted over a four-day summer period at points along the path, but while the 1965 study recorded 550 walkers (of all types), the 1971 survey registered 1900 walkers expressly using the Pennine Way. There was no attempt to identify seasonal variations, other than the self-evident observation that more would be likely to walk the trail at Easter, Whitsun and in the summer holidays, nor was a total figure suggested, but numbers were evidently high and rising.

The heyday of the Pennine Way was probably in the 1970s and early 80s, but the next full study wasn't until 1990, when the Countryside Commission's April–October survey of that year suggested that the path was used by an estimated 10,000 long-distance walkers and 153,000 day walkers during the seven-month period. Of those 10,000 long-distance walkers, 46 per cent were walking part of the way, 40 per cent were found to be walking the whole way, and the remaining 14 per cent were walking the whole way but over a period of time on selected days or at weekends.

Other findings from the 1990 survey showed that three-quarters of long-distance walkers were male and a quarter walked on their own, or if they were in a group the average number was three. Among day walkers, there were more women (four out of ten) and perhaps unsurprisingly there were more younger and older participants.

That the Pennine Way was popular was clear for all to see. In a walking anthology published in 1981 (*The Winding Trail*), Bob Hankinson describes a winter walk along the Pennine Way in December three years previously, explaining that his unusual choice of when to walk the path was partly to avoid the crowds at other times of the year. 'In summer you can anticipate following dozens of other walkers along a broad black squishy highway … you will see the route as the backs of walkers; a line of diminishing specks on a line leading over the horizon. You will not be alone, certainly not at weekends. You will be one of hundreds who sign their names in the book kept in many of the cafés on the Way; there were six pages of entries for August 1978 at Gargrave.' As I learnt a few days ago at Gargrave, the café's visitor books from those times have long since disappeared, so there was no way I could check this claim, but it seemed to bear out all the other evidence.

Whatever the precise numbers, I assumed that Tom Stephenson would be pleased that the trail was inspiring so many people to venture out onto the Pennines; but then I came across a quote from him in conversation with Marion Shoard in 1977 about the attraction of moorland (reproduced in *The Rambler* magazine of February/March 1989). 'Above all, though, I like the feel of walking on a completely trackless piece of moorland,' he said. 'It's a crude taste I suppose. I would rather walk on the open moor than on a well-made footpath. The Pennine Way is now a great highway. Much of it has lost its attraction for me, because you no longer have the loneliness, though you can still get a mile off the Pennine Way and not see anyone. I have been alone for most of my life. I like to walk alone and feel I'm alone in the world. And I can get that on the moors more than anywhere else in the country.'

From green trail to great highway – the Pennine Way might have taken three decades to get from idea to reality, but after that it seemed to be just a few years before its originator was apparently bemoaning the loss of solitude. And there were more obvious problems beginning to pile up for the country's best-known footpath.

As more and more pairs of boots pounded away, the problem of erosion steadily mounted, especially on the fragile peat surfaces at either end of the route, as I had already learnt in some detail in the Peak

District. This, in turn, perpetuated the trail's reputation as a tough old slog and now the coverage started to become negative. Barry Pilton's 1986 book, *One Man and his Bog*, and a collection of cartoons called *Laughs along the Pennine Way* by 'Pete Bogg' published the following year might have been tongue in cheek, but the images they conjured up were downbeat and off-putting and simply reinforced popular perceptions of the route.

In the specialist outdoors press, things were no better. 'Pennine Problems' was the headline of one article in *The Great Outdoors* magazine (April 1993), part of a series called 'Trails in Trouble'. Prior to that, in December 1988, a letter to the editor of the Long Distance Walkers Association (LDWA) magazine implored event organisers to avoid the Pennine Way. 'In fact, should not the LDWA cease to promote the Pennine Way and omit this grossly over-used route from the Long Distance Walkers' Handbook?' the reader asked.

In an article in *The Great Outdoors* (quoted in the Pennine Way Association's autumn 1989 newsletter), Peter Evans came up with a more radical solution, suggesting that the path had 'taken enough of a pounding' and it was time to give it a good rest. 'Has the hour arrived when the Countryside Commission could perhaps consider "de-designating" the Way? It's happened to Munros … why not a National Trail? The route would still be there but wouldn't have the same kudos … we could have a sort of anti-information campaign … removing its "official" badge. And maybe, just maybe … Tom Stephenson's long green trail could become green again, given an environmentally conscious decade or two.'

About the same time as all this was happening, and almost certainly as one of the consequences, the Pennine Way's supremacy came under challenge from the growing number of other walking trails that had been springing up all around the country. As recreational walking grew in popularity, the other official long-distance paths were joined by an increasing number of regional routes, local trails and unofficial 'ways'. Some were waymarked and promoted by county councils, such as the Shropshire Way, Isle of Wight Coastal Path and Calderdale Way; others were local routes devised by local rambling clubs and even enterprising individuals. If you had the time, inclination and ability to read a map and do some fieldwork, there were any number of long-distance walking routes just waiting to be devised. In 1986, the LDWA's handbook listed 231 unofficial routes, but by 2015 that database had grown to around 1400 paths, trails and defined routes of all descriptions across the UK, covering more than 81,000 miles. Two enterprising walkers, Denis Brook and Phil Hinchliffe, even devised an alternative to the Pennine Way (*The Alternative Pennine Way*), a 267-mile route from Ashbourne to Jedburgh via Ilkley, Kirkby Stephen and Haltwhistle, shadowing the original route. Domestic trailwalking had clearly come a long way in the 50 years since the Pennine Way was established.

With so many more routes, and most of them considerably shorter and more accessible than an arduous high-level trail across the Pennines that was suffering from mounting erosion, the popularity of the Pennine Way waned and the numbers walking it steadily dropped off. By the trail's 40th anniversary, in 2005, the Countryside Agency quoted the then national trail officer who reckoned that around 3500 people walked the full distance of the Pennine Way every year and around 150,000 annually for 'day trips and longer walks'.

It's easy to band these sorts of figures about and trail officers always urge caution regarding their accuracy and interpretation, but for some years there have been automatic electronic devices ('people counters') at hidden locations on the Pennine Way, including at Byrness and Greenrigg in Northumberland and at Crowden and the Snake Pass at the southern end. Given a small margin of error, they show little obvious increase or decrease in the numbers of Pennine Way walkers since 2005. Of course, numbers fluctuate from year to year and there are occasional variations, almost certainly due to the weather, but the view of the present path officer (in 2016 at the time of writing) is that there are now probably around 1500–2000 full-distance Pennine Way walkers a year, while the counters show that the total number of visits on foot to locations on the Pennine Way, for whatever purpose, is between 210,000 and 220,000.

Despite this apparent levelling out, there's still a vague sense of uncertainty and an awareness of ongoing change. In April 2015, a feature in the *Northern Echo* caught my eye, entitled 'Path ahead uncertain as Pennine Way celebrates 50th anniversary'. The article ran: 'The UK's first long-distance trail is facing a midlife crisis, according to those charged with conserving it.' It then quoted the Yorkshire Dales National Park's head ranger, Alan Hulme, who said: 'The Pennine Way is an absolute treasure, but we have to look at how we can promote it as a lot of people are scared of its distance. What people wanted 50 years ago is not what people want now, three weeks' walking is a big ask in this modern era.' He went on to explain how the new partnership managing the trail, led by the National Park Authority, would 'aim to promote the route in different ways, such as promoting single-day walks'.

I remembered my stay at the B&B back at Crowden, where my landlord had explained that they now offer two-day breaks on the Pennine Way, with accommodation and pick-up/drop-off so you can walk just the opening couple of days. It was designed for 'guests who wish to sample the experience of the Pennine Way as a preparation for completing the whole walk at a later time; and for those who only have a limited amount of time available and must complete only one or two sections at a time'.

So is it simply that the Pennine Way is too long and too hard for most of us these days? No doubt Alan Hulme was also alluding to the changing nature and wider choice of leisure pursuits available to us; how walking abroad, for instance, is now so much more accessible than it was 50 years ago; and how all the demands of a modern working life can make a three-week holiday unrealistic. But Edale, Malham and Horton seemed bursting with walkers to me; and surely 1400 logged paths and trails point to a continued enthusiasm with long-distance walking?

As the 20th century drew to a close, trailwalking in Britain certainly seemed to be as popular as ever, judging by the paths I walked, but the Pennine Way was definitely not the league leader any more. Although it might make a catchy phrase in a newspaper, I'm not sure that any walking trail can really have a 'midlife crisis', but the meaning is obvious. Other national trails like the South Downs Way and the South West Coast Path continued to be well used, while new ones like the Thames Path, Cotswold Way and Hadrian's Wall Path emerged; but more than anything the Pennine Way suffered at the hands of the Coast to Coast Walk.

The Coast to Coast Walk begins at St Bees on the Irish Sea coast in West Cumbria, and crosses northern England via the Lake District, Yorkshire Dales and the North York Moors to end at Robin Hood's Bay on the shores of the North Sea. For such a popular trail, it's something of an oddity. It's not an official route in the sense that it isn't a national trail and isn't promoted by a local authority; instead, its success has been largely organic and is purely due to the inspiration drawn from the writings and ideas of its creator, Alfred Wainwright. When compared to the Pennine Way, there are a number of factors weighing in its favour, not least that at 190 miles it can be comfortably completed in two weeks' holiday, rather than in the two and a half to three weeks usually needed for the Pennine Way. It's certainly a long walk, but not too long. Many find the start and finish points on each coast more satisfying and logical than the slightly arbitrary beginning and end of the Pennine Way. Others side with Wainwright for including a crossing of the Lake District fells; and no doubt some simply find it easier to manage because the hilly bits are punctuated with less demanding and lower-level sections. Put simply, it's not as tough as the Pennine Way.

Although Wainwright wrote about both routes, inevitably he favoured his own creation, comparing the two in some 'personal notes' at the end of his Coast to Coast guidebook: 'The Pennine Way is far longer and a greater challenge to stamina, but most of it lies over dreary moorlands. The Coast to Coast Walk is, in my opinion, immeasurably superior in scenic qualities, although it has no Hadrian's Wall to stimulate the imagination. You enjoy the Pennine Way, if at all, because it satisfies an ambition and is a personal achievement; certainly not for its ravishing scenery.' Then, in typical Wainwright fashion, he chooses a gender for each path and throws in a large dollop of sexism to boot. 'The Pennine Way is masculine; the Coast to Coast Walk has feminine characteristics. If there happens to be something in your temperament that makes you like the ladies the odds are that you will prefer the C to C. You may not meet any but you will be reminded of them. On the PW you never give them a thought … well, hardly ever.' And he ends with a flourish: 'I finished the Pennine Way with relief, the Coast to Coast Walk with regret.'

Wainwright's *A Coast to Coast Walk* was published in 1973, five years after his *Pennine Way Companion* came out. As Hunter Davies points out in his biography of Wainwright, by then the author's personal circumstances were much happier, with a painful divorce behind him and happily wedded to Betty, his second wife. It also appears that research for the Coast to Coast Walk was a much drier and more pleasurable experience, since rain seemed to dog Wainwright's Pennine Way experience at almost every turn.

Despite a lack of official promotion, the Coast to Coast route steadily became more and more popular. Latterly it has topped readers' polls in walking magazines and was no doubt boosted by other high-profile publicity, most notably Julia Bradbury's TV series in 2009. For an unofficial path, there are inevitably no proper statistics on user numbers, but pulling together anecdotal information, personal experience, media exposure and the sheer number of walking holiday companies that now cover the route, it's probably safe to say that, as far as long-distance footpaths go, it has comfortably outstripped its competition – including the Pennine Way.

But what goes around comes around, it seems. In the last few years, there have been the first few grumbles about the Coast to Coast Walk becoming just a little *too* popular, the odd complaint about lines of walkers queuing for stiles and accommodation booked up long in advance, especially by walking holiday companies. There have had to be a number of minor diversions and alternative routes created to deal with erosion on the vulnerable moorland sections ... does that sound familiar? One of these is at Nine Standards Rigg near Kirkby Stephen, only a few miles west of my present location on the Pennine Way. When I walked the Coast to Coast, 25 years ago, it already seemed well used; so if that trend has continued, no wonder it's getting a little crowded. Maybe, just maybe, the pendulum could even swing back towards the Pennine Way for those seeking an away-from-it-all northern hillwalk?

That evening I stayed in a B&B at Keld, a lovely hamlet at the very top of Swaledale. There's not much there apart from a few farms and cottages, a chapel and a scattering of accommodation, including a camping field and a former youth hostel that's now a comfortable walkers' lodge; and long-distance walkers were there by the rucksack load. Keld is where the Pennine Way and Coast to Coast Walk bisect; and if my B&B was anything to go by, the overwhelming majority of them were walking the Coast to Coast.

Before dinner, I sat in the residents' lounge with a drink, a map and some very gregarious Americans. They had just finished day 7 of the Coast to Coast Walk and were having a great time, but seemed surprised to come across someone walking another trail. They had clearly never heard of the Pennine Way, and possibly (judging by a few of their looks after my introduction) not the Pennines either. No matter, I began to explain a little about my own walk. One of them cut in and said it just sounded like a long ramble across the moors. I replied that it was a bit more challenging than that. In fact, the Pennine Way was longer, rougher and harder than the Coast to Coast Walk. They seemed a bit crestfallen at this, I think possibly because the walking holiday company they were using had billed the Coast to Coast as England's premier hill trail.

At this point, I'm afraid I may have got a bit carried away. Perhaps it was some misplaced loyalty to the Pennine Way or simply a pint of Black Sheep on an empty stomach, but either way I began to indulge in some shameless trail one-upmanship. I reeled off the Pennine Way's overall height gain; described the natural wonders of Malham Cove and High Cup Nick; listed some of the top-of-the-range gear essential for a Pennine Way attempt; and stressed the trail's pre-eminence in the history of the outdoor access movement. It was a bit over the top, but also great fun.

It transpired that I was outnumbered 9 to 1 by Coast to Coast walkers around the dinner table that evening, but according to my landlady the overall ratio among the guests is more like 20 to 1 in favour of the Coast to Coast. Despite my heroic and largely futile defence of the Pennine Way, in the battle between the two heavyweight trails it was clear who was on top.

7

KELD – MIDDLETON-IN-TEESDALE

The Pennine Way's eccentric side

The next morning I followed a winding path out of Keld, past some of the noisy and spectacular waterfalls for which this upper part of the dale is famous, and across the rising moorland. All of a sudden, the Yorkshire Dales seemed to be over. After the comparative bustle of Keld and the animated trail conversation of last night, which continued in the bar at Keld Lodge with the trio of Pennine Way walkers from Great Shunner Fell, it all felt a little flat. The weather was grey and a bit drizzly and the moorland was dull and lifeless.

The sense of a changing landscape was reinforced when I arrived at Tan Hill an hour later. Ahead, the ground fell away to the Stainmore Gap, a low expanse of rather featureless moorland described very fittingly as a 'shapeless swell' by Sir Walter Scott. It has been an important crossing point of the Pennines since ancient times. Agricola marched his Roman soldiers this way in the first century AD between their garrisons at Carlisle and York, building forts at Brough and Bowes on the way. It was also the scene of the Battle of Stainmore, when Eric Bloodaxe, the last Viking king of Northumbria, was slain. Today, it was the turn of the A66, and already the speeding vehicles were in sight, while beyond lay the high, dark outline of the North Pennines and some serious hill country.

More immediately, though, there was a pub to inspect, and not just any old pub. At 1732ft above sea level, the Tan Hill Inn is famous as Britain's highest public house, and as a genuinely unique selling point it does a jolly good job of telling everyone about it. But it's also one of the most remotest in England (the nearest inhabited building is 4 miles away and the nearest town 11) and perhaps because of this it has gathered itself quite a reputation over the years, much of it appearing to surround a succession of eccentric landlords and at times an equally diverse clientele – including, of course, Pennine Way walkers.

It was late morning and already there were a few ramblers, cyclists, bikers and curious tourists milling about. Although I had a lengthy distance to cover before reaching Teesdale that night, I wanted to take a look around inside the pub so I went in for a coffee. It's a long, traditional two-storey stone building, gradually extended over the years and obviously robust enough to keep out the elements. You enter by the main bar, a dark but spacious low-ceilinged room whose flagged floor has doubtless received plenty of dripping rucksacks over the years as Pennine Way walkers collapse into chairs with a collective sigh. There's a large open fire at one end which, according to Steve and Viv, who were in charge when I visited, is lit every single day of the year. 'Except for when the chimney sweep is due to come,' added Viv, 'but then we get it going straight away afterwards.'

It's a comfortable and welcoming place and a far cry from the days when the customers were mainly drovers, pedlars, farmers and miners. The hillsides around the pub were once extensively worked for coal, and miners' cottages used to stand nearby. Back then, conditions at the inn were considerably more basic; and even in the early days of the Pennine Way, walkers described finding a gloomy, run-down inn full of peaty smoke. In 1945, when John Wood walked the length of the Pennines before the Pennine Way was even designated, he described how 'motor-coach parties may in summertime swarm into the scanty accommodation and raise bedlam with their vociferous demands for beer and fancy drinks, but for the greater part of the year there are few callers other than the more thirsty of the sheep-farmers of Arkengarthdale and the last fastnesses of Swaledale.'

Even then, landlords and landladies came and went with regularity, no doubt challenged by the isolation and loneliness. In his book *Mountain Trail*, John Wood mentions in particular the legendary Susan Peacock, whose family ran the pub from 1902 to 1945. 'If she liked the look of you she would serve a good meal for a shilling, or one-and-three if you had an egg. But if she did not take a fancy to you – and she could judge the character from the face – you would have to depart unfed.' She got through two husbands while at the pub and it's said that her funeral was so well attended that the procession stretched as far as Keld. JHB Peel is equally forthright in his 1972 book *Along the Pennine Way*:

'Mistress Susan Peacock was, as we say, a card who wore the pants, and would, if required, remove the same garment from unruly miners.'

However, the constant through all of this was that the pub was then, like now, at the mercy of the weather. In his guidebook *The Pennine Way*, Kenneth Oldham describes how, after the huge snowfalls of 1947, landlord Harry Earnshaw is said to have wished 'Happy New Year!' to a shepherd who called in for a drink in April – the first customer they had seen that year. There are framed photos on the walls of the bars showing the pub peeping out from underneath massive drifts of snow, as well as newspaper cuttings from the many times that the Tan Hill Inn has made the headlines for all sorts of bizarre reasons. My favourite is the spat that the previous landlady had with KFC in 2007, when the fast-food giant threatened her with legal action for using the trade-marked term 'family feast' to describe the pub's traditional Christmas meal. 'They are a multi-million-pound international organisation and I am just a little lady up a mountain,' she told the *Daily Telegraph* indignantly. Sensing a bucketful of bad publicity coming their way, KFC hurriedly backed down and punters at the Tan Hill Inn were allowed to tuck into their turkey dinners unhindered.

The pub's location and altitude are certainly a challenge to any landlord, but in the past they have also proved its salvation. In the early 1980s, the new landlord, Neil Hanson, desperate to find some money for renovation, saw an Everest double-glazing advert on TV and wrote to the manufacturers to suggest that the Tan Hill Inn would be an eye-catching location to promote their product. It obviously struck a chord, as executives from the company arrived by helicopter to inspect the pub and promptly installed new windows. They filmed a now famous scene where the late Ted Moult, a Derbyshire (not Yorkshire!) farmer, dropped a feather inside the window to show that the new draught-proof fixtures could withstand the fiercest Pennine gale. For reasons that I still find inexplicable, the advert became so well known that even now, 30 years later, it recently featured in a Channel 4 poll of the most popular adverts of all time. Neil left the pub after several years in charge and went on to become a successful author, writing among other things two entertaining books about his experiences at Tan Hill called *Inn at the Top* and *Pigs Might Fly*.

For many years, a framed photo of Ted and the actual feather he used hung on the wall next to the window that was featured in the advert (which, for the record, is the one to the right of the front door as you enter). Apparently many visitors to the pub asked to see the feather and the window, but unfortunately in 2010 one eager punter couldn't resist taking away a memento, and the photo (including the feather) was stolen. 'The picture and feather are Tan Hill's version of the Crown jewels and we are desperately saddened by their loss,' said the pub's manager at the time. There are unconfirmed rumours that the stolen items have since resurfaced at a rugby club not a million miles away.

There was little wind in evidence as I contemplated the long march north from Tan Hill, but ahead of me was Sleightholme Moor and a section notorious for bog. The official National Trail Guide warned that in bad weather it can be a 'dangerous place', while Wainwright is typically more down to earth, describing the moorland crossing as 'like walking through porridge' and saying that 'after heavy rain it is like walking through oxtail soup'. Such an interesting mix of food similes made me wonder if AW had written up his notes while dining at the Tan Hill Inn, perhaps indulging in a family feast? The same thought must have struck the pub's management, as the two relevant pages from *Pennine Way Companion* are framed on the wall of the bar. Let it serve as a warning if you are heading north on a wet Pennine Way!

Back at Keld, I'd stuck up for the Pennine Way in the face of a small but very affable army of Coast to Coast walkers and seen how Wainwright's route now led the pack of long-distance trails in the popularity stakes. But before AW's Coast to Coast Walk guidebook caught the imagination, it was his Pennine Way guide that was in fact the best-seller. Of all the many guides to the Pennine Way published over the years, Wainwright's *Pennine Way Companion* remains one of the most influential. Although the idiosyncratic author, who died in 1991, is perhaps as well known for his superbly original pictorial guides to the Lake District fells, it was his Pennine Way guidebook, published by the Westmorland Gazette in 1968 and preceding Tom Stephenson's official guidebook by a year, that for many people became the classic of Pennine Way literature.

However, Lancashire-born Wainwright had an association with the Pennines that went back much further. In 1938, the year that the Pennine Way Conference was taking place, the 31-year-old took a fortnight's holiday from his job at Blackburn Town Hall and walked from Settle to Hadrian's Wall. It was to become the subject of his first proper full-length book, originally called 'Pennine Campaign', although it wasn't actually published until as late as 1986 when it was renamed *A Pennine Journey*. His walk took in Horton, Keld, Bowes and Middleton, loosely following the route of some of what would later become the Pennine Way.

In *Pennine Way Companion*, Wainwright fully acknowledged Tom Stephenson's role in inspiring the trail and made clear the debt of gratitude that walkers owed him; but it was Wainwright's pocket-sized title, produced in his inimitable pen-and-ink style, that for many people became the essential guidebook to the trail. Questionnaire surveys carried out by the Pennine Way Management Project in the Peak District in 1988 and 1989 found that, of the walkers who used a guidebook, 71 per cent had Wainwright's and 26 per cent Tom Stephenson's, while 3 per cent used other titles. Indeed, such was the influence and popularity of Wainwright's guide (it sold more than 120,000 copies between 1968 and 1991) that when publishers Michael Joseph revised the original text in 1994, they incorporated a number of map and text amendments agreed with the (then) Countryside Commission in order to bring the guidebook up to date.

Earlier in my walk, when I chatted to Melanie at the Pen-y-ghent Café in Horton-in-Ribblesdale, she mentioned that she had recently heard a group of Pennine Way walkers discussing Wainwright's *Pennine Way Companion*. 'They were all in full agreement that it's a book to read at home, in comfort, and that nobody would actually take it on the walk any more,' she said. 'And yet, there was a time when everybody walking the Pennine Way had a copy. It was referred to as "the bible".' (Rather ruefully, I thought back to Crowden and to the two men I met who had tried to buck the trend and had come a cropper.)

No doubt reflecting the innate eccentricity of the author, Wainwright's book is perverse in so many ways, not least in that it's presented back to front. It begins at the end – Kirk Yetholm – and proceeds to describe the whole route in reverse, including the maps, which have to be followed up the page instead of more conventionally down.

Researching the book, Wainwright walked the Pennine Way 'in bits and pieces' over 18 months and called on the help of four colleagues (Len Chadwick, Harry Appleyard, Cyril Moore and Lawrence Smith) to cover the more inaccessible legs that he couldn't easily reach from his home in the Lakes. The author prepared a typically detailed set of instructions for the four 'collaborators', as he called them, each of whom was given a specific section of the new 250-mile path to check. Wainwright himself took the middle section from Malham Tarn to Tan Hill Inn. These guidance notes are reproduced in Hunter Davies's biography of Wainwright and show just what a meticulous and at times painstaking exercise it must have been, as well as explaining why Wainwright's published work is so precise and authoritative.

Wainwright sent each member of the team the relevant 2½ inch maps of their section with the line of the Pennine Way highlighted by a faint green line. He also enclosed the 1 inch maps, just in case. In an uncanny echo of the instructions that the Pennine Way Association gave to their pioneering route-checkers 20 years earlier when they were plotting the original line of the Pennine Way, the four were asked to check and verify the path, consulting with ramblers' groups and local authorities, and even with farmers over whose ground the route passed. The precise route had to be marked on the maps provided, with different symbols depending on its nature (motor road, intermittent path, no path at all, and so on) and in 'black waterproof Indian ink'. Alternative sections also had to be shown in full and objects of interest within a mile of the route identified, such as tumuli, waterfalls and good viewpoints. They were given seven months for the task and instructed to return the completed maps by Christmas 1965, so that Wainwright could then 'go over *all* [his italics] the ground, a bit at a time, during 1966 and 1967' in time for publication by Easter 1968.

At first glance, AW seemed a hard taskmaster, but he could also be generous. His instructions to the four researchers ended with a reassurance that he didn't expect any of them to be out of pocket. He enclosed a cheque to cover travelling and subsistence expenses, ending with the message: 'Payments need not be accounted for; if there is any balance it may be spent in riotous living with AW's compliments.'

Despite the scrupulous research and of course expertly presented final product, the book still had AW's highly personal stamp all over it; and it was clear that he had not fallen in love with the Pennine Way. By his own admission, he encountered a great deal of rain and boggy conditions during those 18 months of investigation. At Easter 1966, for example, AW began rechecking the southern end of the Pennine Way, intending to cover the route from Edale to Crowden, but only managed to get as far as the top of Grindsbrook (barely two miles) before being forced back by rain and mist. This no doubt accounts, at least in part, for his wholly negative conclusions about the path. 'As you stagger over the finishing line,' he wrote, 'the bliss you feel is the bliss you feel when you stop banging your head against a wall – the day-to-day performance is tedious. It is very interesting as a study of the geography of northern England, but the perambulation itself is dull … You won't come across me anywhere along the Pennine Way. I've had enough of it.'

How paradoxical that the very same book became such a 'bible' for would-be Pennine Way walkers. And the ultimate irony, today, is that a framed photo of this gifted writer, illustrator and draughtsman, an aficionado of the hills, but who ultimately disliked the Pennine Way, now hangs on the wall in the bar of the Border Hotel in Kirk Yetholm. Presumably it has something to do with the fact that for many years those ending the Pennine Way at the Hotel could, as he instructed, present a copy of his guidebook and receive a free pint of beer.

In 1997, as Mike Imrie set out on his own north–south walk along the Pennine Way, he asked the then landlord at the Border Hotel about Wainwright's famous 'free pint' and recounted the story in the Pennine Way Association's newsletter that summer. Apparently, at its peak, around 2000 walkers a year were signing the Border Hotel's Pennine Way visitor book and claiming their free pint on Wainwright. By 1986 this had dropped to half that and by 1995 it was down to about 500. Even so, as Wainwright's bar tab mounted, the pint became a half pint, and it is said that it ultimately cost the author something in the region of £15,000. Not that he was probably too bothered, as the *Pennine Way Companion* continued to sell in large numbers. By all accounts, Wainwright lived a very modest life and much of the income from his walking books went to a local animal rescue centre that the author quietly supported. In a typically quirky and old-fashioned way, Wainwright used to send a cheque for £500 to the Border Hotel – in advance – and trust that the landlord wouldn't be out of pocket and Pennine Way walkers would be properly catered for.

When Wainwright died in 1990, the solicitors administering his will wrote to the landlord and said that there was no provision for continuing the free drinks. Several companies sensing good PR opportunities offered to step in, but AW's widow (Betty) refused to allow such a blatant commercial approach. Instead, she persuaded his publishers, the Westmorland Gazette, to cover the tab for a little while longer; but then they were taken over by new publishers, Michael Joseph, who were even less keen on the arrangement. As both book sales and Pennine Way walkers dwindled in number, fewer and fewer claimed their free drink (barely 100 in 1995).

Today, I'm pleased to say, all Pennine Way walkers (whether or not they have AW's famous book) can once more enjoy a free half pint at the Border Hotel. At the time of writing, it's courtesy of Newcastle-based Hadrian Border Brewery, which periodically supplies the landlord with an extra barrel for thirsty walkers. Given all his idiosyncrasies, I'm sure the teetotal Wainwright would have approved.

In the end, I had no real problems with Sleightholme Moor. Yes, it was very sticky in places and certainly not the finest section of the Pennine Way, but unless you actually become marooned in the stuff, you plod and squelch onwards in a semi-automatic state. As one grizzled Pennine Way veteran said to me, when you've seen one Pennine bog you've pretty much seen them all.

Eventually I joined a firmer, semi-surfaced track and I think at that point I must have switched off. I'd now crossed into County Durham where they are evidently less generous with their waymarks and signposts, certainly compared to what had gone before in the Yorkshire Dales. I didn't realise this until, just beyond Sleightholme Farm, I found myself in an overgrown field with the beck nearly at my feet and a high, craggy bank opposite. I stumbled through some

Above The Dalesman Café at Gargrave has been a welcome sight for weary Pennine Way walkers since the 1960s. (photo: Chris Sainty)

Below The Pennine Way approaching Malham Cove.

Above The official launch of the Pennine Way on Malham Moor took place on 24 April 1965. (photo: Tom Stephenson/ Ramblers' Association)

Below The official launch was organised by Yorkshire Dales National Park Head Warden Wilf Proctor (left), seen here talking to Fred Willey, Minister of Land and Natural Resources (second from right). (photo: Joan Proctor)

Above Tom Stephenson and Fred Willey, at the opening of the Pennine Way on Malham Moor. (photo: YPN Yorkshire Post)

Below Limestone pavement above Malham Cove.

Main photo Pen-y-ghent is one of the most recognisable hills on the Pennine Way.

Below left The peaceful village of Keld, at the head of Swaledale, is where the Pennine Way and Coast to Coast path meet.

Below right Pennine Way walkers approaching Tan Hill Inn in 1957. (photo: Mary Jephcott)

Above Tom Stephenson led a group of MPs along the proposed route of the Pennine Way in May 1948 in a publicity stunt. They are pictured here at Birkdale Farm, Upper Teesdale. Left to right: Barbara Castle, Fred Willey, Arthur Blenkinsop, George Chetwynd, Tom Stephenson, Hugh Dalton, Julian Snow. (photo: The Dalesman)

Above Above Cronkley Bridge the Pennine Way follows the wide banks of the infant River Tees.

Right A Pennine Way postcard from Langdon Beck Youth Hostel, circa 1960s. (photo: John Martin collection)

Left The waterfalls of Upper Teesdale are at their most dramatic at High Force, where in 2010 heavy rain created a second mighty chute. (photo: Mike Ogden)

SCOTLAND

WOOLER

ROCHESTER

BELLINGHAM

Otterburn

HOUSESTEADS

HEXHAM

NEWCASTLE ON TYNE

HALTWHISTLE

ALSTON

DURHAM

PENRITH

LANGDON BECK

MIDDLETON IN TEESDALE

BARNARD CASTLE

APPLEBY

DARLINGTON

BOWES

KIRKBY STEPHEN

RICHMOND

KELD

SEDBERGH

ASKRIGG

HAWES

HORTON IN RIBBLESDALE

SETTLE

MALHAM

SKIPTON

COLNE

KEIGHLEY

NELSON

HAWORTH

BURNLEY

BRADFORD

LEEDS

TODMORDEN

HALIFAX

HUDDERSFIELD

ROCHDALE

MARSDEN

OLDHAM

GREENFIELD

MANCHESTER

SHEFFIELD

CHAPEL-EN-LE-FRITH

EDALE

10   20   30

THE PENNINE WAY

YOUTH HOSTEL, LANGDON BECK

HIGH FORCE, MIDDLETON IN TEESDALE

LANGDON BECK

MIT.117   CAULDRON SNOUT

Above For many Pennine Way walkers, High Cup Nick is one of the highlights of the entire trail. (photo: Steve Westwood)

Left Before Dufton Youth Hostel opened in 1978, Pennine Way walkers had to stay in nearby YHA Knock, a former RAF station. (photo: YHA Archive)

Below The striking stone shelter on the summit of Cross Fell was restored to mark the 50th anniversary of the Pennine Way. (photo: © Laurie Lambeth)

rushes and slithered down the shingly shore to the water's edge, rather puzzled that a footbridge described in the guidebook as 'substantial' was nowhere to be seen. I paused by the burbling water and consulted the map, gradually becoming aware that I seemed to have lost the route. As this slowly dawned on me I got a little cross. I had now walked over 120 miles, across high moors and misty hillsides, and the first time I had really gone astray was in some innocuous pasture by a little river in County Durham. I retraced my steps through the field and there, on the far side, was a brand new gate (without a sign or waymark) and the path (obscured by thick clumps of newly mown grass) leading down to the bridge. Slightly chastened, I resumed the Pennine Way, aware that the next wrong turn might see me inadvertently take the Bowes Loop rather than stay on the main route. The Way divided by a farmstead called Trough Heads, where the Loop continued eastwards above the beck all the way to the small town of Bowes.

The Bowes Loop was originally introduced to provide more accommodation choices for those walking the Pennine Way. Unfortunately, in a sort of cause and effect reversal, dwindling numbers of Pennine Way walkers have probably contributed to the fact that at present there are very few places to stay in Bowes (although at the time of writing, the Ancient Unicorn pub has just reopened), so apart from inspecting the ruined Norman castle there's probably little reason to visit. Since there are very few castles on or even near the Pennine Way, I suppose it does have some significance, but whether it alone merits a four-mile detour on an already long day is questionable.

The Bowes Loop rejoins the Pennine Way at Baldersdale after a rather unremarkable crossing of Deep Dale and Cotherstone Moor, fringing a former military area (RAF Bowes Moor) where warning signs are a reminder that mustard gas and other poisonous materials were once stored here. Back on the main route, I crossed God's Bridge, a huge and natural limestone slab over the River Greta, then safely negotiated the busy A66 via a grubby underpass, provided for walkers in much the same way as alternative crossings for cows are provided. Beyond the road, the rather drab moorland continued, gently undulating in low ridges northwards. A mile further on, near the crossing of a stream, sat a shooters' cabin, a low black wooden building where one room at the end had been left unlocked as a shelter for passing walkers. I took a plastic office chair outside and sat on my own, in the middle of the moors, and ate my lunch. It felt rather surreal.

I didn't linger, though, since I was conscious that there was still some way to go before I reached the day's end at Middleton-in-Teesdale. The 21-mile stage had been forced upon me because of the simple lack of accommodation. Over the years, the choice of where to stay in this sparsely populated and relatively unvisited corner of the north-east Pennines has dwindled. Not only are there very limited choices in Bowes, but the youth hostel at Baldersdale has also disappeared. The YHA opened this converted farmhouse, called Blackton Grange, in 1979, with funding from the Department for Education and the Countryside Commission, another reminder that the National Parks and Access to the Countryside Act 1949 had empowered authorities to facilitate accommodation for official long-distance paths. According to the Pennine Way Council's newsletter of autumn 1979, it boasted 'the latest wooden bunk beds, thick mattresses and continental quilts'. Although it was a self-catering hostel, the members' kitchen was well equipped and the warden even baked his own bread, which you were advised to order in advance. 'With the warden's keen interest and pleasant manner, Baldersdale Hostel, at the halfway point on the way, should become one of the memorable halts for the footsore legions walking the Pennine Way.' (The warden's sociable cat, called Wainwright, also went on to become quite well known among regular Pennine Way walkers and even featured on the hostel's ink stamp.)

Unfortunately, overnight stays were simply not high enough to keep this isolated hostel viable, almost certainly a direct consequence of the declining numbers of Pennine Way walkers. Indeed, writing in the Pennine Way Council's newsletter in autumn 1986, Baldersdale's warden, Richard Megson, admitted that the hostel relied heavily on custom from the Pennine Way, reporting that 75 per cent of advance bookings were from Pennine Way walkers via the Pennine Way central booking bureau. Although its quiet, out-of-the-way aspect pleased some visitors, in part because of the lack of school parties, it did mean that there was little funding for repairs and renovation. And things could get very quiet, too. Richard was writing in April of that year: 'I've just been through the quietest open period I've experienced during my four years here, with only two people having stayed here in the past 11 nights! Two others did drop in to use the shop, but on the whole this wonderful British weather of ours seems to have brought an unusually complete halt to activity on the Pennine Way. (A couple came through in March skiing the PW. Has anyone considered an aqualung maybe?) Bookings remain very quiet for at least the next month here, and as usual there is not even a semblance of a really busy night until July and August.' Richard also gently bemoaned the fact that the hostel seemed to be overlooked by most guidebooks, including Wainwright's, and that the hostel's location was incorrectly shown in the official HMSO guidebook – by several miles!

Another possible explanation why relatively few walkers stayed at Baldersdale was suggested by Mike Imrie in the Pennine Way Association's newsletter of spring/summer 2007. 'My theory about Baldersdale is that the official two-part guide to the Pennine Way dealt it a terrible blow. The guide ends book one at Bowes, so a majority of walkers divert to Bowes despite it being an alternative rather than the main route. Logically if you go to Bowes you spend the night there and walk to Middleton the next, ignoring Baldersdale hostel.'

In 2001, the hostel's woes were compounded by the foot-and-mouth outbreak, which forced the hostel to shut down for the entire year. Perhaps unsurprisingly, the hostel was closed to individual walkers five years later, then was subsequently sold off and now offers private accommodation for large groups.

My guidebook suggested that, in addition to crossing the Stainmore Gap and one of the most notable trans-Pennine highways, I was also nearing another significant point on the walk. As the Pennine Way Council had noted in their remarks about the former Baldersdale Youth Hostel, now just a few miles ahead, I was approaching the halfway point on the walk. My guidebook said that I would have notched up 129 miles since leaving Edale. However, this left me slightly puzzled, because logically it meant that the Pennine Way was just under 260 miles long, rather than the 268 that is usually bandied about these days. More than that, after trawling through old Pennine Way guidebooks before I set off, I was curious as to why the official length of the path was formerly given as significantly less. My well-thumbed copy of Tom Stephenson's official guide to the path (second edition, 1980) clearly stated it was 250 miles long. Tony Hopkins' later National Trail Guide (1997 revision) gave the distance as 256 miles. I totted up my own estimated total mileage, based on the latest guidebooks in my possession: not allowing for diversions off the trail, getting lost or miscalculations, it still came in at significantly under 268 miles. And yet, at the start in Edale, the official plaque in the wall clearly said 268 miles – I even had my photo taken next to it to prove it. Out of curiosity, I turned to Wainwright to see what Mr Meticulous had to say about the Pennine Way's distance and discovered that his total was 270 miles!

At this point, I started to get concerned rather than merely puzzled. Had I been telling everyone back home a great big fib about how I was going to walk 268 miles to Scotland, and that it would almost certainly be more, given evening detours to pubs and fish and chip shops? It may even approach 300 miles, I had said rather rashly to one or two people. Was I now going to have to eat my words?

In order to get a definitive answer, after completing my walk, I went to see Heather Procter. I asked her, as the person in charge of the Pennine Way National Trail, to explain this apparent discrepancy in distances. 'The agreed figure we give for the Pennine Way is 268 miles,' she confirmed. 'That total covers every piece of path officially carrying the Pennine Way, including the Bowes Loop, the extension to the summit of the Cheviot, and both the high and low alternative routes into Kirk Yetholm.'

So unless you somehow manage to walk two additional, alternative sections as well as the main route, there's no way you'll be walking the full 268 miles in one continuous fashion? 'That's probably true,' she replied, 'but don't forget that most people actually walk the Pennine Way as part of shorter outings, so a day's circular walk could include both the Bowes Loop and the main route, of course. However, the shortest direct route for end-to-end walkers is probably around 253 miles, but given the overall length of the trail it's always likely you'll be walking significantly further. Not only will you usually divert to visit places or find somewhere to stay, but the actual walking line on the ground doesn't always precisely align with the official mapped route. Dodging a patch of bog or wandering slightly off the route on an open hillside means that you'll never stick exactly to the right of way or mapped route, so walked distances will vary.'

Even from the early days, there were in effect three separate Pennine Ways: the legal line originally approved by the minister; the mapped line shown on Ordnance Survey maps and in guidebooks; and the line actually walked on the ground. In fact, the more I looked into it, the more confusing it seemed to be – at least, to begin with. Condition surveys in 1989 and 1994 revealed that some legal rights of way orders hadn't been put into effect and there were mistakes recording the precise route, quite apart from shifts in the actual walked route on the ground as users chose the most convenient (and driest) walking line. For instance, the 1994 survey found that the official measured route over the Cumbrian fells (the Cross Fell section) was 4.2 miles shorter than in 1989, due to realignment work as well as the 1989 survey recording dual routes.

There were separate issues in Scotland, where work to complete the final leg of the route couldn't legally progress until the passing of the Countryside (Scotland) Act in 1967, and in fact it wasn't until as late as 1977 that the last seven miles of the Pennine Way from the English/ Scottish border to Kirk Yetholm were officially designated.

Rather inevitably, over the years, temporary diversions became permanent, 'wet weather' alternatives proved more sustainable, and errors in some guidebooks and maps needed correcting. Careful restoration work also meant that the opportunity was taken to subtly realign the route onto more durable surfaces. The Pennine Way Management Project that was set up in the early 1990s to tackle problems with the route in the Peak District included an 'Alignment Officer', who was employed solely to update the legal right of way of the trail (whether it was the walked line, diverted line or restored line) and to ensure it had legal status, as well as to check that abandoned sections of route were formally diverted. A 1989 condition survey of the southern part of the Pennine Way found that almost a third of its length was misaligned and didn't follow the official route of the trail!

Bit by bit, and in more ways than one, the Pennine Way gradually got back on track.

The route dropped down gently into Baldersdale to skirt Blackton Reservoir. Over to my left, below the dam of the much larger Baldersdale Reservoir, was the former youth hostel, but ahead was a small farmstead with an equally interesting story and a famous ex-resident. As the Pennine Way swept past the entrance to Low Birk Hatt (also spelt Birk Hat), I glimpsed an attractive, detached property, half hidden by trees. Today, a shiny modern vehicle sits in the well-kept drive and a notice says free-range eggs are for sale, but back in the 1970s this was the celebrated home of Hannah Hauxwell who, since the death of her parents some years earlier, had led a solitary and spartan lifestyle. It was subsistence farming with no mains power or piped water, a throwback to a past era with barely a nod to the modern world. However, the little human contact that this woman in her mid 40s did have was with passing Pennine Way walkers, and a conversation with one who happened to be a TV researcher sparked an idea for a story. The upshot was a TV documentary, *Too Long a Winter*, which was broadcast in 1973 and proved enormously popular, making Hannah Hauxwell an unlikely star. With a straight-talking but charming persona, she fascinated and entertained audiences in equal measure, explaining her own sincere and uncomplicated approach to life. Several more TV documentaries followed, plus books, speaking engagements and foreign trips. It was a far cry from the austere little farm at Baldersdale, and although Hannah's propulsion to public fame raised questions about media exploitation, she never complained or resisted and seemed to enjoy the experience. 'If it wasn't for television, I'd have been unknown,' she once said in her typically matter-of-fact way.

I followed the Pennine Way up the hillside away from Low Birk Hatt, past a meadow that Hannah used to manage and is now named in her honour. Its rich spread of wildflowers is a direct legacy of Hannah's traditional farming methods, which left the ground 'unimproved' and free from artificial modern fertilisers and pesticides. At the top of the field is a barn, which has been turned into a simple visitor centre and useful walkers' shelter. I'm sure Hannah would have approved of me stopping for a moment to enjoy the scene. Describing what it was like to live there on her own in the early 1970s, she once said: 'Talk was limited. That's why I enjoyed chatting with walkers on the Pennine Way.'

Before I set off once more, I gazed over this remote and unfashionable corner of the North Pennines and thought how remarkable it was that the Pennine Way – a mere walking route – could on the one hand see off a purpose-designed and funded youth hostel, but on the other hand be the making of an extraordinary farming woman who would otherwise have remained entirely unknown.

The remaining miles to Middleton-in-Teesdale seemed to take forever. My legs were feeling heavy and energy levels definitely flagging as the path rolled up and down the endless hillsides. I looked in vain for an ice cream van in the car park of Grassholme Reservoir, but instead was met with suspicious glances from surly fishermen unloading rods and tackle from their cars.

After a short but steep stretch of lane and a cautious crossing of a particularly scruffy farmyard, I struck out across more fields and spied a walker ahead. He was approaching at some speed, a man in his 50s with a mop of blonde hair, bounding along towards me with a fair-sized pack on his shoulders. I decided I would stop and talk to him, whether or not it was in his own game plan, because I needed both a rest and a distraction. Mind you, my track record of flagging down Pennine Way walkers heading in the opposite direction lately hadn't been good. In popular outdoor locations like the Yorkshire Dales and Peak District, it was hard to work out who was walking the Pennine Way (or any trail, for that matter) and who was simply rambling about for the day. Over the last few days, one or two likely PW walkers had sailed past with a nod and grunt before I could barely open my mouth, and this one already seemed in overdrive. But I needn't have worried. He stopped abruptly with a big grin and flashed me that 'Pennine Way look' that I was beginning to recognise. It mingles ambition, determination and pluck together with genuine warmth and camaraderie, once you realise you've met one of your own. And Mark was clearly enjoying his solo north–south walk, so fit and relaxed it seemed as if he'd just started out. So why was he doing the trail that way round?

As he talked, we took off our packs, sat down and got out drinks. He told me how he had first walked the Pennine Way with four friends when he was 17, camping each night from Edale to Kirk Yetholm. Then, after 16 years working in the US and raising a family, he had returned to Britain and now, exactly 30 years after that original walk, he was back on the trail, but this time heading north to south and planning to camp most nights. I asked whether he had thought about getting his four pals together for a reunion walk, but no, they'd gone their separate ways over the intervening years. So why walk the Pennine Way again? And on your own? 'I just felt it was something I had to do,' Mark replied. 'I can't explain it. It's deep and very personal.'

We chatted a bit more, both wanting each other to know why walking the Pennine Way mattered. I mentioned how the path and I had turned 50 together and made a weak joke about resolving our middle-age crises together. He laughed and nodded sympathetically.

'It was such a formative thing, I suppose,' he added rather suddenly after a pause, resuming where he had left off, as though he had been trying to find the right words. 'That first Pennine Way walk. I remember it was such an adventure first time round, with incredible highs and lows. I've never forgotten it – the bogs, the amazing views, the pubs, feeling so shattered, the four of us together through thick and thin. Coming back to do it again is another adventure all over again, although this time on my own and in a totally different way. I've been thinking about that trip a lot, but also everything else that's happened in between and also the future.' He paused and smiled broadly. 'So maybe more reflective this time and just a little less gung-ho!'

We parted very warmly, shaking hands and wishing each other well. A few paces later, we both glanced round at more or less the same time and waved farewell, two complete strangers and their entire lives momentarily crossing on the same path.

MIDDLETON-IN-TEESDALE – DUFTON

Waterfalls, wildflowers and wilderness

For a trail ostensibly following a chain of hills northwards, the Pennine Way throws something of a wobbly after Middleton-in-Teesdale, lurching westwards across the grain so that in terms of progression I would actually be finishing further south than when I set off this morning.

As members of the original Pennine Way Association laboured hard to develop the route idea in the 1940s, they had been clear that the trail wouldn't simply seek out the shortest distance between the start and finish points, nor stick slavishly to the highest ground for the entire length. Instead, it would strive to link up places of scenic beauty and historic interest, even if that meant the occasional kink. To include the Upper Teesdale waterfalls and High Cup Nick, as well as a chunk of Hadrian's Wall, required a pronounced lateral movement, but a Pennine Way without these highlights would now be unthinkable.

Despite this being the second of three long days, I felt reasonably fit and strong. There had been overnight rain but it was a bright and fresh morning as the path picked its way along the shady bank of the River Tees, making its way steadily upstream into the hills. It was easy going, like a lowland ramble for a change. Before long I arrived at Wynch Bridge, a slender metal suspension bridge strung high above the surging water. The present bridge dates from 1830 and replaces one built a century earlier for use by local miners, which apparently was held by rudimentary chains and consisted of planks of wood and just one handrail. Claimed to be the first ever suspension bridge, few strangers dared use it. Unfortunately one day it collapsed and a man was drowned.

Water was the theme for much of the day, in particular the noisy and peat-brown Tees, gushing and frothing its way across a succession of gentle rocky drops at Low Force. However, the Tees really came to life a little further upstream at High Force, one of the natural wonders of the Pennine Way, where the river forces its way between a cleft in the dark dolerite rocks to plunge 70ft with an almighty 'whomp'. For Pennine Way walkers, there's a useful viewpoint high on the south bank just before you get to the fall, and there I sat for a few minutes, gazing and listening to the spectacle before me. It was mid morning and still relatively few people were about, which is unusual for what is one of the most popular locations on the entire trail.

Most casual visitors access the waterfall via the northern bank; but it can be a dangerous place if you get too close. There have been numerous fatalities over the years as people get into difficulties swimming and are pulled under and drowned by the fast-flowing water, or else fall from the slippery and unguarded edge of the rocks. In 2007, a man from South Tyneside fell to his death while attempting to collect rocks for his new tropical fish tank. However, two years earlier there was a miraculous escape when a man lost his footing and fell 70ft into the crashing water below. With a broken shoulder and semi-conscious, he was pulled to safety by a brave ice cream salesman who dived into the water to rescue him (who turned out to be an Iraqi Kurd, recently given asylum in the UK – just to give the story another twist). The *Daily Mirror* report said that the victim, a 55-year-old man from Nottingham, was 'walking the Pennine Way' and was trying to take photos of the waterfall when he slipped and fell. It's believed to be the first time that anyone has fallen from the top of High Force and survived. The item concluded: 'More than 80 people have died in the waters, and a Durham Police spokesman said: "All this gentleman suffered was broken bones." '

Water inevitably plays a significant part in many people's Pennine Way walk, usually in terms of how much falls from the sky, or what it does to the state of the ground underfoot. There are reservoirs aplenty to walk past in the South Pennines, of course, but because the path is usually high level and often (but not always) adjacent to the watershed, there are relatively few significant riverside sections. Most rivers are usually crossed (like the Calder and Ure) or followed in an infant state for a few miles (the Aire and South Tyne). There were one or two moments, high up on the Pennine watershed, when, should I have been minded to empty my water bottle to the left, its contents would have ended up in the Irish Sea and the Atlantic, while poured the other way they would have eventually issued out into the North Sea.

Although the Tees is really the only waterway that the trail follows closely for any appreciable distance, it doesn't mean that a walk along the Pennines can't still celebrate its rivers and streams. Among the many products generated by the trail, there is – quite wonderfully – a set of three MP3 albums released in 2013 featuring the sound of water that you can hear on or near the path. Nothing else, just the tinkling and splashing of running water. *Rivers of the Pennine Way* (volume 1) features Kelsocleuch Burn, Dove Sike and the River Nent, while volume 2 includes Ridge End Burn, the River Tees and Harwood Beck. Volume 3 has Sleightholme Beck, Meadowgrain Clough and a full 25 minutes of Scaleber Gill in full flow. The River Tees was clearly recorded somewhere other than High Force, as it sounds particularly benign, but my favourite is probably Kelsocleugh Burn, which rises on the northern slopes of Windy Gyle in the Cheviots. Listening to the plops and gurgles, you can almost picture the youthful stream tumbling down the hillside.

By now a few other walkers were appearing, each of us giving a little nod and a smile of understanding to acknowledge how lucky we were to be walking in Teesdale that morning.

A mile above High Force, the river opened out as the hills pushed back and the valley suddenly took on a whole new shape. I sat by the bank on the far side of Cronkley Bridge for a few minutes and let myself absorb this subtly different landscape. Ahead of me, the shallow but insistent river meandered across the wide valley, ringed by rigid green hills and darker moors beyond. There were plenty of clouds massing but, for now, a bright blue sky stretched overhead and the sun shone fiercely. Upstream on the far bank was a prominent whitewashed farmstead, elsewhere a few small barns dotted here and there, but otherwise the gentle meadows and bare rising hills gave the impression of an altogether more crisper, fresher and uncluttered scene.

The distinctive whitewashed farmhouses and cottages of Teesdale are deliberately kept that way by the landowning estate. Although there are different explanations for this, the most popular tells how the landowner, Lord Barnard, found himself stranded in Teesdale one night. Given overnight shelter and touched by the hospitality he received, Lord Barnard told the farmer to carry out any necessary repairs to his building and to send him the bill. When a large invoice duly arrived, he discovered that the farm in question was not actually part of his Raby Estate, so as a result his lordship ordered that all his tenant farms be painted white and kept that way so they could be identified in future.

As I walked through Upper Teesdale, I was struck by a landscape becoming wilder by the footstep, as the Pennine Way ventured into the unpopulated heart of the Pennines. No wonder that Tom Stephenson had been vocal in his support for its designation as an Area of Outstanding Natural Beauty (AONB), which finally happened in 1988. Tom was already in his early 90s when he appeared as a witness for the Ramblers' Association at the hearings in Durham, summarising as eloquently as ever what the Pennines meant to him: 'I believe that there is no area in England better qualified to rank as an Area of Outstanding Natural Beauty than this region in the Northern Pennines. It includes the most extensive area of wild moorland in the Pennines; the nearest approach in England to what might be termed a wilderness; mile after mile of uninhabited moorland. Eyes accustomed to softer scenes may see in these landscapes only a grim desolation. There are, however, many people today who may find a great satisfaction in these places of silence and solitude, places where they can feel they are in a world of their own.'

Tom's evident passion for the North Pennines is something that many share today, not least because it seems to embody so much of what the Pennine Way is all about: space, solitude, spectacular landforms and wildness. Covering 765 square miles, the North Pennines AONB is the second largest after the Cotswolds and is in fact bigger than most of the national parks in England and Wales. Not only that, but in 2003 the North Pennines became our first official geopark, an international designation that recognises the importance of a region's geology and landscape.

To understand more about this intriguing place, I spoke to Chris Woodley-Stewart, Director of the North Pennines AONB Partnership, who started off by explaining what it wasn't. 'The North Pennines isn't a wilderness. It's been shaped by people even on the most isolated felltops, but it does have a sense of relative wildness, remoteness and tranquillity with few equals in England. You can walk all day without crossing a road or meeting another human soul, and that's a very rare quality on these crowded islands.'

Quite apart from its geological importance, well-known rivers and famed dark night skies free of light pollution, it's the wildflowers of Upper Teesdale that make this area renowned. The North Pennines AONB contains 40 per cent of the UK's remaining upland hay meadows, and Moor House–Upper Teesdale National Nature Reserve in particular is famous for its concentration of rare arctic–alpine plants, which colonised the area after the last ice age. Factors including location, climate, grazing and soil type all conspired to provide an almost unique habitat, where not just arctic–alpine but also some more unusual continental plants could thrive undisturbed. However, in the late 1960s, this didn't stop the construction of Cow Green Reservoir a little further upstream, which flooded a two-mile stretch of the valley and with it the valuable habitat for many of these rare plants. A desperate campaign was fought by conservationists, which provoked national headlines; but, despite a public enquiry, it was to no avail, and the need to supply water to ICI's chemical works downstream at Teesside triumphed over the desire to safeguard irreplaceable plant life upstream in the Pennines.

Despite this, a walk through Upper Teesdale today in late spring or early summer remains a colourful spectacle and the Pennine Way is a surprisingly good vantage point. Rebecca Barrett is the Biodiversity Lead for the AONB Partnership and she explained to me that you simply have to take your time and use your eyes. 'When you sit down to rest or have lunch beside the path, examine the turf beside you. There are likely to be lots of tiny flowers dotted about the grass, which in turn supports rare insects and key pollinators like bumblebees. Perhaps the best known is the spring gentian, a tiny, delicate plant that flowers a vivid blue between April and early June. Also look for alpine bistort, yellow globe flowers by the riverside, mountain pansy and the white flowers of grass of Parnassus. And from early summer there are simply masses and masses of orchids, including heath spotted and northern marsh. Even non-botanists can't fail to be wowed by the display.'

There's a waymarked nature trail alongside the Cow Green Reservoir access road, pointing out some of the flowers; but in truth, the national trail and the public footpaths radiating off it are just as good.

Wildflowers aside, the Pennine Way also has a special relevance for Chris Woodley-Stewart, who walked it in the summer of 1983. 'We took 13 days of a flaming hot school holiday,' he explained. 'That year, when I was nearly 18, it never struck me that one day I'd be working here in the North Pennines, promoting parts of the route as the basis for local walking trails or helping to repair stretches of it with a helicopter.' But he says his fondest Pennine Way memory is walking the path with poet Simon Armitage in 2010. 'We watched fell ponies infuse through the mist and disappear like a spectral band. When I later read the poem he wrote about that moment, I was pleased that a lifelong memory for me had been captured so beautifully for others to share.'

I paused at Saur Hill Bridge, which the Pennine Way crosses to veer westwards towards Widdybank Fell and an increasingly wild, narrowing Tees valley. To the right, a short footpath led up across the fields to the road and Langdon Beck Youth Hostel which, since the beginning of the Pennine Way, has been a popular stopping-point for trailwalkers. In fact, there's been a youth hostel at this remote location in Upper Teesdale since 1938, one of the very first in the YHA network. It was built with public funding as part of a national scheme to alleviate urban poverty during the Depression years, but it soon became a popular summer destination for ramblers and cyclists looking to explore the North Pennines. The original building was a simple affair with a brick middle section and two wooden wings (male and female, of course).

Unfortunately in 1958 a fire destroyed the entire building, which was luckily unoccupied at the time, but such was the determination of a band of hard-working volunteers (including, it was reported, some coerced contributions from passing hostellers) that seven years later a new building was completed. Some stones were salvaged from the earlier building and a plaque of a phoenix was attached to the wall, symbolising the hostel rising from the ashes.

The new hostel opened in the same year as the Pennine Way and went on to become one of the best known on the entire trail; but just as the path itself fell on lean times, so the hostel needed refreshing. In the 1990s, it was decided to remodel and refit the entire hostel on modern environmental lines, in many ways befitting a rural building in the sensitive Upper Teesdale landscape. This included a 2.5kW wind turbine, a natural reed-bed water treatment system, recycled newsprint loft insulation and individual room thermostats. The hostel set its own carbon budget, measuring the reduction in the building's footprint, and among the YHA network it led the way in incorporating new technologies and a far-sighted sustainable approach. Pennine Way walkers and other visitors enjoyed better facilities, but also took away with them key environmental messages. Amid the struggle to make remote rural hostels viable, there clearly could be another way.

Beyond Widdy Bank Farm, the gentle riverside meadows disappeared and the young Tees squeezed through a gorge-like valley overlooked by the dark crags of Falcon Clints. The path became a jumble of rocks above the surging water and for a while it was rough going. Writing in his 1989 *Pennine Way North* National Trail Guide, Tony Hopkins warned of boulders polished smooth by countless feet, which can be a serious hazard for the unwary, particularly in wet weather. 'Twisted ankles and broken hips are regular mishaps on this section,' he advised. I also came across a photo of this location taken in the snowy depths of winter: it looks like something out of the remote Scottish Highlands, not the Pennines of County Durham.

The river slowly swung round to reveal the sight and sound of Cauldron Snout, the final grand water feature of the Tees. Rather than fall in one drop, like High Force, here the water is hurled down a series of rocky steps in a profusion of noise and spray. Following the trail, I clambered up the rocks to the right. Carrying a full pack, it was indeed something of a scramble, but this just added to the drama of the situation. Once over the top, it soon went quiet, and straight ahead was the high, grey dam of Cow Green Reservoir. Its rigid lines and brutal concrete appearance were in stark contrast to the otherwise open and natural landscape, and because the Pennine Way stays well below the dam, there was no sight of the two-mile expanse of water. Inevitably, outflow from the reservoir is carefully regulated, meaning that the volume of water running over Cauldron Snout is always controlled and so is no longer subject to drying up in summer or to sudden extra surges after winter storms. Cauldron Snout is still dramatic, but nature has been tamed just a little.

Still, if there is any sort of silver lining to be had in the damming of the Tees and the building of the reservoir, it may be that Peg Powler was finally seen off. According to local folklore, the grotesque green-haired mermaid of the Tees used to live in the now flooded valley, and you could tell that she was about by the froth on top of the water, called Peg Powler's Suds. It was said that she had a particular appetite for children!

The reservoir was soon forgotten as the Pennine Way now struck boldly westwards across the deserted moors. The last visible human outpost was Birkdale, a farm that 'marks the end of the civilised world and a step into frontier badlands', according to Tony Hopkins. In truth, it's nothing more than a vast tract of bare, treeless moorland, but with a growing sense of height and isolation the further on your plod. Preceding Hopkins' National Trail Guide was Tom Stephenson's HMSO guidebook *The Pennine Way*. In it, Tom wrote that the stretch of path from Teesdale to the Eden valley was the 'wildest and loneliest crossing in the whole length of the Pennines'; and he described the moorland as 'swarthy' and 'shaggy'. They struck me as good descriptive terms for these harsh and rugged moors. Apart from the track underfoot, the only man-made intrusion was across the shallow valley to the left, where red flags marked out the edge of the MOD's Warcop military range, but all was quiet today.

Now the trail dropped down to the footbridge over Maize Beck, which at first glance looked a little over-sized for the job. It's a very long and solid structure made out of wood and metal, supported on one end by a sturdy stone base. On the day I crossed it, the water below trickled gently over the rocks, and you could have been forgiven for thinking that it would have been just as easy to hop over the boulders in the stream. The bridge has traditionally provided the so-called 'flood route' over the beck, since in the past walkers have jumped across the rocks or forded the stream further down and followed the path on the other bank; but when Maize Beck is in full spate, both options could be an extremely hazardous proposition. In March 1968, a party of walkers got into difficulties trying to cross the swollen beck on foot. The weather conditions were terrible, with wind, rain and snow. One man was drowned; and after the rest of the party divided and a specialist team was called in from Durham to help with the rescue, another man was later found dead, while others suffered from exposure. The tragedy led to the formation of Teesdale and Weardale Search and Mountain Rescue team, and serves as a continuing reminder not to underestimate the North Pennines. As Tony Hopkins observed: 'There is no real hazard along the Pennine Way unless the weather turns against you, when everything is a hazard.'

I paused halfway over the footbridge to glance at the plaque attached to the handrail. It commemorates Ken Willson MBE, former chairman and president of the Pennine Way Association, who died in 2003. The life and times of the association have inevitably been bound up with the life of the path – and it's been every bit a roller coaster. When the famous Pennine Way Conference was held in the Peak District in 1938 and, for the first time, there was a full discussion about a walking route along the Pennines, one of the upshots was the formation of a new body to further the work and realise the idea. It consisted of sub-committees of local volunteers, whose job it was to go out and survey the proposed route on the ground, section by section. Despite the interruption of World War II, the Pennine Way Association still managed to make a submission to Lord Justice Scott's Committee on Land Utilisation and helped to push the case for the Pennine Way and provide details of its likely route.

When the path was eventually opened in 1965, the association disbanded, its work done, but five years later there was a growing feeling that there should be some sort of body to keep the vision of the early campaigners alive and sustain the enthusiasm that helped create the path in the first place. So the Pennine Way Council was (re)established as 'a focus of public interest in Britain's first and most famous long-distance footpath'. Tom Stephenson was its president, and sitting round the table were all those responsible for the funding and maintenance of the trail, including the local authorities (district, borough and county councils) and the Countryside Commission, as well as voluntary bodies and pressure groups, such as the YHA, Ramblers' Association, National Farmers Union and the Council for British Archaeology. The Pennine Way Council's 1977 annual report stated that there were in fact 28 different affiliated organisations. Its full remit was wide-ranging: 'to secure the protection of the Pennine Way, to provide information about the Way to the public, to educate users of the Way and its environs in a proper respect for the countryside, to assist in the organisation of voluntary effort directed at maintenance of the Way and to provide a forum in which different interests connected with the Way and its use can discuss problems of mutual concern'.

In the early days, the Pennine Way Council was the definitive body for the path and it exercised real power over the route, for instance objecting to a proposal to reopen a coal seam south of Hadrian's Wall, which compelled representatives from the company to come out to present their case to members (planning permission was eventually refused). But as the trail's star waned, the organisation's pre-eminence also faded, with coordination becoming ever more focused in the hands of the centrally funded national trail officer. By 1990, most members were individual associate members and many of the early representative bodies had gone. In 1992, renamed the Pennine Way Association once again, the now much smaller organisation continued to liaise with the path manager and campaigned against threats to the path – from off-road vehicles and youth hostel closures to proposed wind turbines.

By 2000, it was run largely by and for walkers, and although it still provided a useful arena for news and debate, more and more information was becoming available through other sources, especially via the internet, in particular rendering the association's long-standing accommodation guide less vital. In addition, there was an ever dwindling number of new recruits to help run the organisation, so it was decided that the Pennine Way Association had run its course. Following the 50th anniversary of the trail in 2015, it was formally wound up. The association's newsletters and other archives, stretching back over four decades and such a treasure trove of news and information, are being digitised and made accessible via the charity Pennine Heritage (www.pennineheritage.org.uk).

In researching this book, I spoke to two of the association's retiring officers and Pennine Way veterans, Chris Sainty and Peter Stott, about the role and contribution of the organisation. Far from feeling a lingering sadness at its demise or regarding it as a step backwards for the trail, there was a feeling that it was symptomatic of the Pennine Way entering a new era. The path had grown up now, survived its various crises (some of them verging on the life-threatening) and received critical support when it was needed, and now it was a trail once more standing on its own two feet with a more assured future. Granted, fewer people were walking it than 30 or 40 years ago and they seemed to be walking it differently; but there was still an evident need for a challenging, uplifting and life-enhancing upland trail that provided physical and mental stimulation and quite simply allowed people to get away from it all.

On some of the long moorland stretches of the Pennine Way, I too was utterly content to get away from it all, comfortable with my own company and savouring the solitude. At other times, it was more enjoyable to walk with others. On the long haul across the core of the North Pennines from Cauldron Snout, I felt particularly sociable, so it was really rather nice to fall into step with a young couple who were backpacking the Pennine Way. We'd already seen each other a few times since Malham, passing and repassing on the trail, but now there was an opportunity to walk together and enjoy the synchronicity and rhythm of walking and talking side by side.

Neil and Alison, from Wellingborough, were in their mid 20s and softly spoken, even a little bashful. Both were slight in build, but were handling their large packs well and maintaining a steady pace. Heading south to north in a fortnight to fit in with holiday leave from work, they said this was a new experience for them and it was enjoyable, but hard work. So why had they chosen to walk the Pennine Way?

'We both love the idea of the long journey on foot and walking at our own pace through the landscape,' explained Alison.' Neil nodded in agreement. I asked them what other paths they'd walked.

'This is the first proper trail,' replied Neil, a little sheepishly. 'We're new to this kind of thing!'

I expressed some surprise that they'd chosen the Pennine Way as their first long-distance path, and carrying a tent and camping gear as well.

'Well, we had a practice walk along the Norfolk Coast Path,' said Alison, 'but it was too flat and boring. Apart from the length there was no challenge. For us it was either going to be the Pennine Way or the new Wales Coast Path. We want to have an adventure!' (How heartening to hear those words 'challenge' and 'adventure' from two people under 30!)

As we plodded on above Maize Beck, we chatted some more. Both Neil and Alison seemed to be enjoying their Pennine Way adventure, although they were understandably finding it tough. In particular, they spoke eloquently about the views, the hills and the general landscape around them and about how the Pennine Way had enabled them, as town dwellers, to have a close-up encounter with nature.

I remarked that I had expected to see rather more trailwalkers and that Pennine Way users seemed rather thin on the ground. 'I suppose so in terms of the actual numbers of us doing the whole path from one end to the other,' agreed Alison. 'But look at all the people we've met out on the Pennine Way for a short ramble today beside the Tees. I bet if you asked some of them to describe where they went they'd say "I walked the Pennine Way from Middleton to High Force and back", or "I did a circuit of Cauldron Snout and Cow Green from Langdon Beck via the Pennine Way". The path seems to be a means to an end, as well as an end in itself.'

I was pleased that Neil and Alison, newcomers to the Pennine Way, were with me at this location, for ahead was one of the Pennine Way's most memorable prospects. For those who imagine that the Pennine Way is simply a long and dull moorland trudge, devoid of any jaw-dropping moments, then try walking across High Cup Plain from the east. The Pennine Way approaches rather nonchalantly above the beck, then beyond a curiously flat and grassy area, like a high Alpine meadow without the flowers, the ground suddenly falls away at your feet in a simply vast and almost perfectly formed U-shaped valley. Neil, Alison and I stood on the rim of High Cup Nick and gazed at the spectacle in silent awe.

It's difficult to do such a place justice in simple words and explain what it's like to suddenly come across this huge glacial trench, almost one and a half miles long, after a long period of relatively level and uniform moorland. When you approach it on the Pennine Way from the other direction, from Dufton, you see it from further out and adjust accordingly; but from the east, it just appears at your feet as an almighty chasm. The long smooth slopes of grass and scree plunge over 600ft and are topped by a line of dark crags running around the entire valley like a dirty collar. It's another manifestation of the Whin Sill, that tough volcanic rock of the North Pennines that 295 million years ago was molten but now forms distinctive dark columns at such diverse locations as the Farne Islands, Hadrian's Wall and here at High Cup Nick.

Although everyone agrees on the stupendous view, there is an odd lack of consensus on the actual name. Some guidebook writers claim that the 'Nick' only refers to the narrow point at the very head of the valley where the stream flows; otherwise, they say, it should simply be referred to as High Cup. Either way, a pinnacle of rock below the northern edge is certainly called Nichol Chair and, according to local folklore, was once climbed by a Dufton cobbler who heeled a pair of shoes on top.

The descent to Dufton was long but gradual, down a track once used by miners. With the Eden valley spread out below and the Lake District fells in the far distance, it felt very much like coming off the edge of the Pennines. It had been another long day; but with some welcome afternoon sunshine, the tranquil village of Dufton seemed like the ideal place at which to finish. Overlooking the green in the centre was the Stag Inn, which I intended to patronise later since it didn't open until 6pm, and on the other side was the youth hostel. Compared with the hurly-burly of Malham Youth Hostel where I stayed a few nights ago (admittedly Malham is a larger and more popular destination), Dufton was altogether more refined and restful. It seemed to reflect the serenity of the unshowy, red sandstone building, with its elegant wooden staircase and comfortable lounge where, for many years now, a painting of Tom Stephenson has hung over the fireplace. Before it opened in 1978, Pennine Way hostellers had to walk a further mile to Knock Youth Hostel, now closed, which was housed in an old RAF station built for workers at the radar facility on the top of Great Dun Fell.

I chatted to Simon, Dufton's manager since 2010, who told me that he had previously managed Baldersdale hostel before it closed. Handfuls of Pennine Way walkers wander through his door all season, from March to October, he explained. 'Probably four or five days out of seven we'll have them in, but only in small numbers, although occasionally a party of four walking together will meet with another couple and we hit six! Although there aren't usually big numbers on any particular day, they are out there all year round.' He's aware that people walk the Pennine Way during the winter months, because they do occasionally interrupt him even though officially the hostel's closed. 'I think it was January time, and as I settled into my sofa for a cosy late night cuppa there was a knock at the door of my house. It was already dark and our doorstep light was off. I switched it on to see who was there and was greeted by an elderly man with a not insignificant trickle of blood running down his face. He was a Pennine Wayer who'd come a cropper on the way down from High Cup Nick. He was fine, he reassured me, despite his gruesome appearance, and was only hoping for a bed. Under the circumstances, even though we were closed, I made the exception of letting him stay for free as sending him on to the B&B seemed too unkind.'

So, I asked, what are Pennine Way walkers like, who stay at the hostel? Are they all experienced outdoor types? 'They seem to include a few folk who haven't necessarily done much, or even anything, like it before,' he replied. 'They've just got the idea from somewhere, perhaps are doing it for charity, and may not necessarily be outdoor types. The award for the best-dressed Pennine Way walker, who I think was only walking a section or two, goes to a fellow in a three-piece suit who, after a heavy night on the beers in the Stag with his companion the night before, set off up Cross Fell towards Alston in the hot summer sun! I was a little concerned that perhaps he didn't know what he was in for. But, when I tentatively enquired, they said they knew it was 20 miles over a big hill so I wished them good luck.'

In *The Shell Book of the Pennine Way* (1968), which rather bizarrely is a motorists' guide to exploring the Pennine Way, author Michael Marriott was also interested in the hostel's guests and singled out one in particular. 'Perhaps Dufton's most memorable visitor was the 91-year-old veteran who arrived one night a few years ago (having walked all the way from Edale, of course), spruce and sprightly, carrying only the most diminutive of knapsacks. His supper consisted of two biscuits and a glass of milk. He was in bed by 9pm. Breakfast was one slice of brown bread and honey (no butter), and a lightly boiled egg. On this he sailed forth to tackle the mighty Cross Fell. An argument, if ever there was one, for fell-walking and an abstemious diet as aids to longevity.'

In many ways, Dufton is in an enviable location on the Pennine Way, with two outstanding if challenging legs north and south, as Simon recognised. 'Unless people are unlucky enough to get bad, low cloud – and I've checked in a few folk who, despite knowing High Cup Nick is there, arrive here not having seen anything of it – there's still good walking in either direction. When I was at Baldersdale this wasn't always the case, as the leg before us could be pretty wet, bleak and boggy, and walkers would be glad just to have completed it.'

There was the usual cross-section of guests staying at the youth hostel that night. A couple of families, one or two solitary and untalkative male walkers, a trio of women who seemed to be walking some but not all of the Pennine Way (they weren't entirely clear about it) and the predictable oddball that hostels just seem to attract. This one wasn't a walker but an overweight man with a very short haircut and a faintly menacing air, who was travelling round Britain on a vintage scooter. He was from the London end of Essex, with a pronounced Cockney accent, and I fancied he might once have been a mod, or a hit man, or perhaps both. He said he'd never stayed in youth hostels before but was a bit strapped for cash, so he thought he'd give it a spin. What was I doing? he asked. I explained that I was walking the Pennine Way, describing the challenge of its length, terrain and weather. He shook his head firmly and said it didn't sound like his idea of fun. I was tempted to say that driving round the country on an old Lambretta wasn't mine, but I thought better of it. His parting remark, as he left to see whether there was anything in the members' kitchen he could eat, was that he could drive from Derbyshire to Scotland in less than a day. 'You could save yourself all that grief,' he advised me, shaking his head a little sadly. Just for a moment, but not for the first time, I wondered who was the real oddball.

9

Close to the sky: overcoming Cross Fell

It seemed to take a long time to get into gear on that calm, mild morning in Dufton. I hadn't slept well and felt lethargic and creaky. In the youth hostel bedroom, I'd had to sit down to pull on my socks, which is always a bad sign. Maybe it was the long stages that went before; perhaps it was the prospect of Cross Fell ahead, although the conditions seemed benign from where I was down below.

The route was straightforward enough, except it just seemed to go up and up. As I slowly followed the rising path, weaving its way across the unending slopes of Knock Fell, I could see a figure high up above me. Another walker, the same bulky pack and steady tread, but too far away to make out any detail. They didn't seem to be getting any nearer, and when I eventually got to the cairn at the top they were already some distance away, crossing the high open ground towards Great Dun Fell. I paused by the square stone currick, known as Knock Old Man, and regained my breath. Some light cloud had drifted in ahead when I wasn't looking, temporarily covering the top of Cross Fell, but otherwise it was clear and remarkably still. The North Pennines stretched out to the east, miles and miles of endless moors and smooth, rounded hills, with Cow Green Reservoir finally revealed. The River Tees began life in earnest somewhere nearby, the South Tyne and Wear not too far away. It looked boggy and rather uninviting, so I was pleased to be up high looking down.

Mind you, the tops were rather damp in places too, but thanks to a few slabs and some judicious footwork I managed to dodge the worst of it and reached a surfaced road intact. This was the vehicular approach to the radar station on the top of Great Dun Fell, which was just above me now: the huge white golf-ball structure (called a radome) and antennae are used in the management of air traffic across northern England and southern Scotland. The road to the radar station was originally an unmade miners' track up Knock Ore

153

Gill, but after it was surfaced the Pennine Way was slightly re-routed around the top. I paused briefly by the brutal modern structure at the very top of the hill. It was ugly but it was there, so I took a photo and scampered on, cheered by the view first of Little Dun Fell and then of Cross Fell beyond, both clear of mist and within a few minutes' reach. The other walker was still ahead of me, closer now but evidently keeping up a good pace, an intermittently slabbed path allowing both of us to make decent progress.

Despite everything I'd read about Cross Fell, all the warnings and premonitions, I walked up onto the summit plateau and could hardly feel a breath of wind. Far to the west, the higher Lake District peaks were cloaked in white cloud. When John Wood walked the length of the Pennines in summer 1945, he wrote in his book *Mountain Trail* that Cross Fell provides 'the grandest one way view in England and, on an exceptionally clear day, you can make out not just the Lake District's fells but also the Solway Firth, Criffel and the Galloway hills'. He also wrote that, in the 1830s, political demonstrations were held on the summit, with large crowds coming from considerable distances away: 'Besides the serious business of demanding reforms, wrestling and other sports took place, and there was dancing to music provided by brass bands. Great supplies of refreshments were brought up on horseback.' And he went on: 'Political organisers of today would give a lot to be able to arouse such enthusiasm, but only keen ramblers would now climb anything more than a flight of steps to attend a meeting, and then only if it were to demand access to mountains.'

The top of Cross Fell was surprisingly broad but entirely bare, made up of wispy turf and a few rocks. Given the height and the reputed ferocity of the wind, I was surprised that even a few blades of grass managed to cling on in this tundra-like environment. The only visible structures were made by human hands: the ubiquitous trig point half-surrounded by a low, protective ring of boulders, and nearby a handsome stone shelter built in the shape of a giant cross, with a sturdy stone pillar in the middle. This open and roofless construction had been restored by Laurie Lambeth and the North Pennines AONB Partnership's stone-walling trainees, with funding from Natural England, to mark the

Pennine Way's 50th birthday. No doubt it provides welcome shelter from the wind in more extreme conditions.

There was one other walker in sight, presumably the person who had been ahead of me since leaving Dufton. I went over to say hello, since I wanted to tell someone else just how pleased I was to be on the top of Cross Fell without any wind and rain. That person turned out to be Hazel, a 30-something Pennine Way walker from Bristol, backpacking on her own and camping as and where she saw fit. She looked strong and determined, a tall woman with sharp features and piercing brown eyes. She seemed happy to talk for a moment. I told her how I had followed in her footsteps all morning, but didn't seem to be able to make ground on her. 'Yes, I looked back and clocked you early on,' she replied with a grin. 'But there was no way I was going to let you catch me up.' I smiled back, ever so slightly disconcerted.

We shared a little small talk about the trail, about bogs, hills and other walkers we'd both met. So why was she walking the Pennine Way? I ventured, trying not to sound too nosy. 'Personal challenge,' she replied, with a shrug that seemed to indicate that this cross-examination by a complete stranger on the top of Cross Fell was now over. We parted cordially and agreed we'd probably bump into each other somewhere between here and Kirk Yetholm. I watched her as she strode off purposefully towards Alston. Only if I can catch up with you first, I thought ruefully.

I was loathe to leave Cross Fell, which I'm sure is not a sentiment shared often by Pennine Way walkers, given the horror stories in books and blogs about the more usual weather at the summit. Tales abound of violent wind speeds, thick mist and driving rain, and the high slopes often hold snow until well into late spring. Not only is it literally the high point of the Pennine Way, but at 2930ft it is also the highest top in England outside the Lake District, and loftier than such notables as Coniston Old Man, Pillar and Blencathra. Strange, therefore, that it is omitted from the old Pennine saying: 'Ingleborough, Pendle Hill and Pen-y-ghent are the highest hills between Scotland and Trent'.

It might also have something to do with the fact that Cross Fell seems rather detached, standing guard above the Eden valley; or maybe it's because of its sheer bulk – it really does feel big, like the roof of England. Geoffrey Berry describes how you feel close to the sky on the top of Cross Fell, while William Atkins says that it has 'the hugeness of something meteorological'. Certainly the weather has a lot to do with it, since Cross Fell is unique in having its own named wind. The Helm Wind is a fierce and destructive phenomenon that periodically roars down the East Fellside flank of the North Pennines. It's distinguished from other strong winds that routinely batter Cross Fell because the Helm Wind only blows from the north east; it forms a 'cap' of cloud over the fells; and it also produces a 'bar' of cloud that hovers in front of the fells. It's a windy stretch of the Pennine Way, whether you're on the bottom or on the top. In the storms of January 1968, the wind speed on Great Dun Fell was measured at 134mph, and it was only a shade less in 1993. Apparently, the weather station on this summit holds some other equally dubious records, including the highest number of foggy days and the most prolonged frost.

After refuelling, I reluctantly left the top of Cross Fell, now a cooler and darker place as a menacing but high cloud bank passed over the mountain. Wainwright suggested a more direct route off the summit north-eastwards, but the official route heads north down a bumpy and featureless slope without any clear sign of a path. No wonder people go wrong in the mist, I thought, grateful for unhindered visibility. Eventually I turned right onto a clear track and trotted eastwards across the open hillside. I pulled on another layer as the wind became noticeably chillier, then for a few moments I was pelted with small hailstones. Cross Fell was evidently toying with me.

As I walked off Cross Fell, there was evidence all around of historic mining activity. There had been a scattering of workings along the Pennines so far, including a huge limestone quarry at Horton and long-redundant coal mines at Tan Hill, but over the last couple of days I had walked through an area once worked for its lead. The current size and shape of both Middleton-in-Teesdale and Dufton owes much to the activities of the London Lead Company, which in the late 17th and 18th centuries worked the important North Pennine orefield around Teesdale and Weardale. The company was run by Quakers, who ensured that their workforce was well cared for, providing not just decent accommodation but also schools, chapels and libraries. A lasting reminder of this is the prominent water fountain that can still be see on the green in the middle of Dufton, one of four taps established by the company to provide free drinking water.

Ahead of me, the hillside was pockmarked by pits and spoil heaps, great chutes of rocks that spoke of hard and unforgiving work. A couple of miles back, just below Great Dun Fell, I had crossed Dunfell Hush, a deeply eroded groove in the hillside, where miners once created an artificial dam and then released a torrent of water to literally scour the hillside and hopefully reveal riches beneath.

Another legacy was, until fairly recently, several open and dangerous holes in the ground, as Mike Imrie recounted in the Pennine Way Association's newsletter of spring/summer 2007. 'On my first successful Pennine Way expedition I was walking with a companion in early April 1984 on Cross Fell and much of the way down was covered in snow. We took Wainwright's alternative route off the top (it saves a good half mile) when we saw a brightly coloured rucksack leaning against the fence. We were stumbling through snowdrifts which totally obscured the ground and I walked round a hole to reach the pack. We couldn't see any reason for it being there – it clearly hadn't been there long – so we ploughed on down to Alston. Later that evening we heard that two lads had been walking down the Way when one of them broke through the snow cover and fell 200ft down a disused mineshaft. He died of course. That was the hole that I skirted round. It could, so easily, have been me. There are slabs of concrete over the hole now.'

Another relic of this bygone age of lead mining was an old stone hut by the side of the path, originally built as a blacksmith's shop and to accommodate miners during the working week. After a long period standing derelict, it returned to use as a maintained shelter for hillwalkers and occasionally for local shepherds and mountain rescue teams. Known as Greg's Hut, it is named after John Gregory, a popular climber killed in the Alps in 1968. It is the highest bothy in England and is looked after by the Mountain Bothies Association in collaboration with Greg's Hut Association.

Greg's Hut is one of the few proper bothies on the Pennine Way. (There's also a small one adjacent to Top Withins, Haughton Green Bothy in the Kielder Forest just north of Hadrian's Wall, and the two wooden refuge huts in the Cheviots.) I went inside and looked around. The simple two-room building has a stove and a raised wooden sleeping area; although new windows make it weatherproof, it was dim with a faint smell of wood smoke, a little damp and not particularly enticing on an early afternoon. However, I imagined that once it got dark, and the stove was lit and the kettle on, this would be a cosy place to bivvy for the night; and certainly it's used by plenty of Pennine Way walkers.

On the windowsill was a visitors' book and I couldn't resist glancing through some of the entries. There were a surprising number of people walking from Land's End to John o'Groats, as well as one adventurous soul running the Pennine Way, but most seemed to be walkers for whom a shelter this high up on Cross Fell was evidently something of a lifesaver. 'A welcome respite from the wind and rain' was the usual comment. Among the most recent to show their gratitude was Edward, who I had first encountered at Hawes attempting to stuff a bulging bag of bolognese into his rucksack while regaling me with eye-popping tales of poisoning and extreme camping on the Pennine Way. According to his scribbled message, he had finally located Greg's Hut in the late evening gloom as the weather worsened. 'My angel guided me,' he wrote rather sweetly. The little I knew of Edward made me suspect that it was a very busy angel.

The Dufton to Alston stage is long, as well as high and remote. Unless you wild-camp, bivvy at Greg's Hut or find somewhere to stay at the village of Garrigill towards the end, this is a strenuous day's walking, whatever the weather decides to do. In many ways, it typifies the Pennine Way experience, which is probably why as many people like this section as loathe it. One of the former is Paddy Dillon, author of over 70 walking guidebooks, including the popular Cicerone guide to the Pennine Way, and one of our most respected outdoor writers. Born in Burnley, Lancashire, just six miles from the route, he has a long association with the path and told me that he prefers the emptier and higher stages, like Cross Fell and the Cheviots. I wanted to know what an experienced guidebook writer really thought about such a well-known and arguably overexposed route. When did he first become aware of the trail?

'I think it was the early 1970s,' he said. 'I was a young teenager when I stumbled across a Pennine Way signpost with one of my pals, while we were camping near the route. We knew what it was, and that it went all the way to Scotland. We had a bit of a discussion about how long it might take us to get there. We spent a few minutes walking briskly along the route, figuring that if we could keep up a good pace, we'd get there quicker.'

When he was 16, Paddy embarked on his first long outing on the Pennine Way, following it northwards from his home as far as Cross Fell, then cutting cross country to the Lake District, before returning home through the Yorkshire Dales. 'It was my first long-distance walk. I made plenty of mistakes, including getting horribly lost between Knock Fell and Cross Fell. I had really heavy, mouldy and useless kit, and wore all the wrong sort of clothes. My cheap PVC overtrousers were sucked off my legs in a horrible bog on Great Shunner Fell. No doubt they are still buried beneath the flagged path! I left home with only £17.33 in my pocket, although at that time campsites were about 20p per night. Soon after that trip, I spent a few weekends following the Pennine Way southwards to explore the higher parts of the Peak District. In short, I used the Pennine Way as a springboard to a series of early adventures, and the early adventures are always going to be firm favourites.'

Paddy finally walked the whole route for the first time when he was 21, and he says it snowed for the first five days! Altogether he's completed the entire trail three times, although he's since followed some parts many times over. On one of those early outings, he responded to a challenge set by Peter Bayes at the Pen-y-ghent Café in Horton-in-Ribblesdale: Peter asked Pennine Way walkers to submit log sheets of their walks, the prize being £10 and a badge. Being a creative sort, Paddy produced a hand-drawn, spoof newspaper page called 'The Daily Peatbog', which reported on the trials and tribulations of his epic walk. It promptly won the café's competition, and they in turn informed the local press, who beat a path to Paddy's door for further comment. He says they didn't appear to quite understand what it was all about. 'One question was "How far is it?" I told them it was nearly 300 miles. Then they asked "How much did you win?" I told them £10. Stunned silence, then: "You walked 300 miles for a tenner?"'

Now that he's been walking the Pennine Way and writing about it for over 40 years, I suggested to Paddy that he must have seen quite a few changes in that time. 'I've seen parts of it trodden quite literally to death,' he replied. 'It wasn't pleasant to find huge swathes of bog trodden to soup, and to see them get worse with every visit. When the route was being repaired, I generally kept away from where the work was taking place, because I knew it would look like a building site.' However, when Paddy began to update Cicerone's guidebook to the path in 2009 and returned to what had been some of the worst sections, he was pleasantly surprised by what he found. 'Places that I remembered as nasty, eroded scars turned out to have been flagged and I've been delighted to see how new paths have bedded in and the ground alongside restored. It shows that with a little help, nature is a great healer.'

It's now over 40 years since Paddy first walked the Pennine Way in earnest. I asked him how, from his standpoint, perceptions of the Pennine Way had changed during that time, quite apart from the physical state of the ground.

'When I was a teenager, people would ask me "Are you walking the Pennine Way?" If I said yes, then I could tell that they were impressed, and if I said I was just following part of it for the day, it was clear that they were less impressed. Basically, quite a few folk were using the Pennine Way as a measure of how serious you were about walking. And people would also ask "Have you walked the Pennine Way?" as if they were trying to get the measure of you, according to how you responded.'

In the 1970s, there were only a handful of long-distance walking routes, but four decades on and Paddy recognises that there are now hundreds to choose from, including 'exotic' overseas trails that are now comparatively easy to reach. 'However, it doesn't change my perception. I love the Pennine Way, and when the time comes I'll cheerfully walk it again and again. But I know of very few in the outdoor media who have any great love for the Pennine Way and there appear to be plenty who would cheerfully dismiss the trail. I do think a lot of the perceived difficulty of the route dates from its early years, when you had to flounder among featureless bogs in some parts, and they're so much easier now. Mind you, Cross Fell in bad weather can still be challenging. Try it in a winter gale with −26°C wind chill. I have a photo in my guidebook and it looks lovely! I just don't understand why anyone would be negative about the route. I've had great times on the Pennine Way and I'm looking forward to even better times in the future.'

The Pennine Way had now swung eastwards for the long descent to the village of Garrigill in the South Tyne valley. A glance at the map suggested that a more obvious route would be to continue north along the watershed to reach the A686, still true to the high Pennines, but this is an exposed and largely pathless country and after conquering Cross Fell it felt like it was time to descend. The long, wide track that led down from Greg's Hut has evidently been used for centuries. I passed a young farmer speeding uphill on a quad bike, a sheepdog tucked under his arm, but looking around me at the traps and other signs of gamekeeping activity, I thought it likely that on another day I'd have met a gamekeeper instead. In years gone by, there would have been lead miners heading for the upper slopes, as well as the occasional funeral party, since the route was also a corpse road between Garrigill and Kirkland (in the Eden valley). A corpse road or coffin road was an everyday route used by funeral parties to transport the newly deceased to the nearest church for burial in consecrated ground. Most were very short, but occasionally in the Pennines and Cumbria these tracks could stretch for miles across exposed hill country, and the route from Garrigill was one of the longest and most punishing.

It was strangely reassuring to know that, high on this desolate Cumbrian hillside, my feet were simply the latest to tread a historic path that had been used by such a variety of people, all of whom were intent on their own purposeful journeys. Recreational long-distance walking might be a relatively new phenomenon, but the notion of journeying on foot into the unknown, moving independently over long distances, is a romantic adventure that seems to resonate. It's as if the endless Pennine horizons offer a succession of new discoveries, a long and methodical journey with the growing anticipation of arrival. In his 1982 guide to walking in the Yorkshire Dales, Colin Speakman sums up this deep-seated desire for movement very well: 'It is good, too, to be totally independent of any mechanical contraption, to measure yourself against a substantial distance: "I walked there" is, in an age of instant mobility, no mean boast. It is an age-old primitive wanderlust, the illusion of freedom, of the open road, a pleasure as acute as it was for our migrating ancestors crossing the primeval forests and forbidding wastes of Europe.'

Indeed, for some people today, walking a route as long, remote and challenging as the Pennine Way has the definite ring of a pilgrimage about it. The long trek, unexpected encounters, physical hardships, meeting fellow companions, seeking new shelter every night, self-discovery and realisation – all of this would be familiar to pilgrims on any number of well-used long-distance routes stretching back to medieval times. The sense of going on a journey (including spiritually) and testing yourself is not new to the Pennine Way.

After a couple of days of empty hills and quiet moorland, the town of Alston seemed a busy place; in particular, the noise of traffic running across the cobbled main square was thunderous, like someone frantically thumping a child's drum. Luckily for footsore Pennine Way walkers, the youth hostel is directly on the trail as it enters the town, so you don't have to run the gauntlet of raucous traffic until you venture out for an evening pint. The hostel was developed by the YHA in 1975 to serve the Pennine Way, but in 2006 it was sold to private owners, who then struck a franchise deal with the YHA. It's a welcoming place where you can soothe aching legs, dry wet gear and watch the family of red squirrels feeding in the trees outside; but more than anything, its story reflects the YHA's close but changing relationship with the Pennine Way.

In the years following the Pennine Way Conference in 1938, when the trail was still on the drawing board, the provision of facilities for walkers required some careful thought. Tom Stephenson and his colleagues were well aware that for some deeply rural and isolated sections of the proposed route, accommodation was either thin on the ground or entirely non-existent. In his 1950 book *Youth Hostel Story*, Oliver Coburn reports that 14 youth hostels were identified on the line of the proposed route. It was reckoned that seven more would be required, of which three were already planned.

From the outset, YHA groups played a pioneering role in the development of the trail, and in subsequent years youth hostelling and the Pennine Way became synonymous. After its birth in Germany earlier in the century, the youth hostel movement took hold in Britain in the 1930s and its development mirrored the growing enthusiasm for and participation in rambling and outdoor recreation, including the drive for greater access to the countryside. Youth hostels provided basic, low-cost accommodation, especially for active young people exploring the great outdoors. They provided a bed, sometimes a hot shower and a meal, but then as now there was still an element of independence and self-sufficiency.

Mary Jephcott first joined the YHA in 1942 and has remained an active and enthusiastic member ever since. In August 1957, she was part of a group of 14 young men and women who walked the Pennine Way on an organised YHA holiday. After my walk, I visited 92-year-old Mary at her home in Derbyshire and she showed me the original three-page letter from Mr Darby, the walk leader, typed on yellowing flimsy paper and sent to her on 27 June 1957. It set out the itinerary for the walk and offered some advice on what to wear and what conditions to expect. He had walked the route the year before and clearly felt he could pass on a few tips regarding kit and the weather of the Pennines. 'A scarf and a pair of gloves if you suffer from cold hands is useful. A scarf will also absorb some of the rain running down your neck when it rains, but when it rains in the Pennines you will get wet whatever you wear. Don't bother with a heavy cape – a lightweight plastic mac or Army gas cape is preferable.'

Mr Darby had some other useful information: 'I hope you don't object to drinking water from hill streams with your sandwiches. If you do, or feel the need for something hot, you'll need a Thermos flask and something to go in it. Wherever possible we lunch inside but it's not always possible, and the new Catering Act is making "Tea places" more difficult to find.' There was good news at Twice Brewed Youth Hostel, where a choice of supper had been offered: corned beef and chips, or eggs, chips and beetroot, or sausage, chips and beetroot, or meat and salad, or stew and potatoes.

There was also a note about the route. 'Where we diverge from the Pennine Way we do so usually because of accommodation difficulties. Some small deviations occur because we feel that our route is more interesting than the Pennine Way just there. We are also throwing in the famous Yorkshire Three Peaks for good measure, but taking two or three days over it instead of one.'

So much for the instructions, but what was the Pennine Way actually like to walk in 1957, still some years before it was officially open?

'There was no path to follow,' recalls Mary. 'I reckon we walked it in! We were often going across completely open and unwalked hilltops and moorland.' She showed me a photo of her posing alongside a new Pennine Way fingerpost at Tan Hill, one of just a handful that existed. 'It was a jolly good walk, but an absolute sweat at times. The advert for the holiday had said "strong walkers only should apply", so we had a fair idea of what it was going to be like. I remember quite a lot of rain and that many of the hostels had very basic facilities. You often had to put wet things back on in the morning because nothing would dry.' She has clear memories of the Pennine Way youth hostels she stayed at then, quite a few of which have since disappeared. 'There was Stainforth, where we had the most delicious bacon. Keld is now closed, of course, as is the wooden shack at Bellingham. And then there was Wholehope Cottage, up in the Coquet valley in the Cheviots near Alwinton, a cold and filthy old stone building!'

The hostels of the Pennine Way each had their own character and charm, occasionally verging on the quirky; but if the buildings themselves were memorable, then it was nothing compared to some of the wardens who ran them. Writing in the Pennine Way Association's newsletter of spring/summer 2007, Mike Imrie had colourful memories of Keld Youth Hostel: 'For some years there was a curious warden who had a tame rabbit and a cat – he maintained that the rabbit was the real warden, he was only the assistant. He did, however, have a large pot of tea waiting for tired hostellers. Then, for a while, there were some energetic new-age wardens very much into heavy metal rock and their cooking seemed biased towards oatmeal and solid vegetarian fare.'

In a subsequent Pennine Way Association newsletter, fellow committee member John Needham shared his memories of the old youth hostel at Once Brewed when he walked the Pennine Way in the year it was opened. 'It was a three-sided building which suggested something from the Roman period. In charge was Mac the famous one-legged warden and his cats – all of course named after the Emperors. In the Common Room a stag's head graced the wall over the fireplace and in its mouth a cigarette nonchalantly drooped.'

Not all the tales of youth hostelling in the early years of the Pennine Way were quite so positive. Alan Binns recalled walking the trail in the early 1960s and at one point falling into step with another hiker. 'We walked together for several days,' Alan told me. 'I was not to know until later that he was a Roman Catholic priest. We arrived at Mankinholes late in the evening. The warden told us clearly that the kitchen was closed and we had to go to bed without a hot drink. The place was full of "suitcase hostellers" and a lot of kids. In the morning, for our customary chore, we were given a kitchen fork and told to weed the cobbled yard, a wide expanse. I enquired as to how much we had to do and was told to get on with it until we were told to stop! I jibbed at this and was prepared to object, but my companion quoted scripture. He said: "If a man takes your coat give him your cloak also, and if a man makes you go a mile, go with him two. It will heap coals of fire on his head." As we departed he told me his calling. I was worried what I might have said!'

At Crowden, one of several hostels that were either specifically built or adapted to provide accommodation for Pennine Way walkers, the warden came to the rescue of many footsore and beleaguered first-day Pennine Way walkers by keeping a store of cardboard boxes for walkers to send home items of unwanted gear. As well as being the author of an early guidebook to the trail, Christopher John Wright attended the opening of the Pennine Way as a representative of the YHA and afterwards continued as a voluntary warden in the Peak District. In his 1967 book, *A Guide to the Pennine Way*, he relates how Crowden Youth Hostel was unveiled on 4 June 1965 by the Rt Hon Fred Willey, Minister of Land and Natural Resources, who less than two months earlier had opened the actual trail. The hostel was converted from six cottages and built on the initiative of the Peak District National Park Authority with government funding. Michael Marriott's 1968 guidebook, *The Shell Book of the Pennine Way*, waxes lyrical about the hostel's private double rooms, the good food, charming common room and fine library, as well as 'footbaths in the toilets and copious supplies of hot water'. Clearly there was both enthusiasm and an impetus to provide a proper network of hostels to ensure that the route was properly walkable.

In 1983, the Pennine Way Package (later renamed the Pennine Way Bureau) was initiated by YHA Northern Region, allowing you to centrally book all your YHA accommodation in one go. 'It would save members a lot of letter writing', they helpfully explained. 'The booking fee is £1. This saves you £3 on postage costs alone.' To begin with, the package deal ran from 16 July until mid September, with a few places reserved from late May onwards. At that time, there were 18 hostels along the trail, with three gaps in the chain covered by privately owned B&B and bunkhouse accommodation. The Bureau's booklet guide described the experience you could expect: 'Everybody we talked to – even those who had to drop out – said how much they had enjoyed it, and the euphoria of those who had actually "Gone all the Way with the YHA" was wonderful.' In its first year, the Pennine Way Package was used by 233 members; but by 1986 this had risen to 923.

Back in 1971, and probably reflecting the relatively youthful age and budget of most users, 41 per cent of Pennine Way walkers camped and 30 per cent used youth hostels (the figures were reversed for groups), while 17 per cent stayed in hotels and B&Bs and 8 per cent in farmhouses (4 per cent accounted for 'other', such as sleeping rough in a barn or a bivouac in the open). Tellingly, half the long-distance walkers surveyed in 1971 wanted to see more hostels on the trail. By the time of the next full Pennine Way Survey in 1990, 35 per cent of long-distance walkers said that a youth hostel was their main type of accommodation, compared to 29 per cent camping and 11 per cent bed and breakfast.

Over the last week of my walk, I'd learnt a lot about the rise and fall of the Pennine Way, from its opening in 1965 and popularity in the 1970s and early 80s to its subsequent decline in the face of problems of overuse, erosion and competition from other trails like the Coast to Coast Walk. This was mirrored by the plight of the YHA's small hostels along the trail, many of whom owed their viability to a sufficient number of trailwalkers. Since hostels like Crowden, Baldersdale and Alston were specifically established to plug accommodation gaps in the Pennine Way, it was perhaps inevitable that they would be vulnerable to a significant drop in user numbers.

Fifteen years after that 1990 Pennine Way Survey – when youth hostels were apparently the most popular form of accommodation for path users – the world looked a very different place for the YHA. Holiday habits and recreational patterns were changing, especially with more and more people enjoying cheaper holidays abroad. Overseas adventure, even treks into seemingly remote and exotic locations, appeared to be more in reach.

Then there was the outbreak of foot-and-mouth disease in 2001, which was devastating for farmers but no less calamitous to the income of the YHA's network of rural hostels. The organisation reportedly sustained losses of over £5 million and visitor numbers dropped by a third, while for some individual hostels it was simply catastrophic. As I'd discovered earlier in my walk, Baldersdale hostel was in a quarantine zone and was forced to close for the entire year. The YHA chief executive, Roger Clarke, called it 'the worst disaster to hit the YHA since the War'; and the slump in overnight stays on the Pennine Way was bound to eventually take its toll on the viability of some out-of-the-way establishments. Dufton had been earmarked for closure but was reprieved following a vociferous public campaign and newly found sources of funding. However, in 2006, YHA head office announced plans to close 32 hostels across England and Wales, including a significant number on or near the Pennine Way. Earby, Stainforth, Baldersdale, Keld, Alston, Greenhead, Bellingham and Byrness would all go. Crowden was later handed over to Rotherham Metropolitan Borough Council to be run as an outdoor education centre and was restricted to groups of ten or more. Some, like Alston,

Earby and Greenhead, became part of the YHA Enterprise scheme and were run on a licence basis; and the Scottish YHA's Kirk Yetholm hostel also re-entered the network on a similar footing. Others, like Keld and Byrness, were sold but reopened as privately run establishments. However, for Pennine Way walkers, the days when you could go all the way with the YHA were over. Explaining their decision to rationalise the hostel network, YHA said they were 'withdrawing from unpopular locations and looking to relocate to new and better sites' and that they 'want to provide good accommodation in good locations that people want to visit'. It was proof, if it were needed, that the Pennine Way wasn't the path it once was.

10

ALSTON – ONCE BREWED

In the footsteps of history along the Roman Wall

After the stiff climb out of Dufton yesterday morning to the top of Cross Fell and the long march back down in the afternoon, I fancied a rather easier outing, so a wander through the valley of the South Tyne from Alston was ideal. But although this narrow green corridor provides the obvious and direct link to Hadrian's Wall, it's a stage that many northbound Pennine Way walkers seem to find unsatisfying. Paddy Dillon laments what he calls the 'fiddly field paths' of this section, since the official route weaves this way and that around the hillside. I decided that I couldn't be doing with intricate route-finding this morning and so instead I would follow the general direction of the Pennine Way for the first few miles by walking along the South Tyne Trail next to a very small railway line.

As I'd found over the previous fortnight, there have been some inevitable and significant changes in terms of route and infrastructure along the Pennine Way, not only since it was first plotted over 75 years ago but also after it was opened five decades ago. One of the earliest Pennine Way guidebooks to feature detailed mapping alongside route description was Christopher John Wright's 1967 title *A Guide to the Pennine Way*, which preceded both Wainwright's and Stephenson's books. It's fascinating to leaf through the pages now and note the Pennine Way passing Windy Hill in the South Pennines without any sign of the M62; or visiting Cauldron Snout before Cow Green Reservoir was built.

The stage north of Alston along the South Tyne valley also features a railway still *in situ*, the former branch line from Haltwhistle that was first opened in 1852 and ran from its junction with the Newcastle & Carlisle Railway for almost 14 miles to its terminus at Alston (it was originally planned to go on and serve the lead mines at Nenthead). Closed by British Rail in 1976, it was partly reopened as a narrow-gauge heritage line in the 1980s. At the time of writing, the South Tynedale Railway extends three and a half miles from Alston as far as Lintley, but it will soon be extended to Slaggyford and possibly further still. However, the good news for walkers is that, presumably because of its gauge, the line can presently accommodate an adjacent footpath and so the South Tyne Trail (already concurrent with the Pennine Way from Garrigill to Alston) now provides a scenic walking route from the town centre northwards through the valley. In fact, because the entire track bed was retained in public ownership, the line is a permitted path used by the South Tyne Trail all the way to Haltwhistle, including across the spectacular, nine-arched Lambley Viaduct, soaring over 100ft above the river. If this direct, elevated and traffic-free walking route had been available all those years ago, might some more of it have been included in the Pennine Way's official route?

Although there was some early morning activity around the engine sheds at Alston, it didn't appear that I would see any trains in action. Instead, there were a few amiable dog walkers and ramblers heading out on the trail. One of the latter was a deeply tanned and very fit-looking mature woman (I never learnt her name) wearing Lycra shorts and what I took to be expensive trailrunning shoes. Her rucksack was compact, sporty and included a built-in hydration system with drinking tube. It all looked rather serious for the South Tyne Trail. She seemed to be heading northwards with purpose so for a few minutes we walked together. After ascertaining her views on the weather (hopeful) and narrow-gauge heritage railways (disinterested), I remarked that she looked like she should be running a marathon instead of idling along the South Tyne Trail. Rather inevitably, it turned out that she ran plenty of marathons and took part in regular challenge walking events, but she also liked walking long-distance paths. She had completed the Pennine Way twice ('once each way, for different views') and from her northern England home regularly set out for two- or three-day walking expeditions along her favourite parts of the trail. The North Pennines and Hadrian's Wall happened to be two such areas, and currently she was heading from Alston to the Roman Wall to complete a three-day outing along the Pennine Way from Middleton-in-Teesdale. She seemed confident that she would make Haltwhistle by teatime so that her husband could collect her by car. Before she left me in her wake, I wanted to know why she kept returning to walk the Pennine Way when there were plenty of other routes to choose from.

'I walk other paths and trails as well,' she replied, 'but I like the Pennine Way because it joins together so many stunning places. I suppose I also like the people that walk the Pennine Way. You know, sitting on the top of Cross Fell eating lunch and chatting with complete strangers, but who I know will be on my wavelength. They also want to be up there, like me, they "get" the hills and all these wild open spaces.'

I couldn't see her carrying any map or guidebook, so I asked her what she used. 'I do have a few torn-off sheets of an Ordnance Survey map somewhere in my pack, but I also like walking sections of the Pennine Way so often because I know it intimately by now. I don't have to check where to go any more or think about directions. I just switch off and immerse myself in all this.' She made a gesture with both arms as if she was conducting the hills. I knew what she meant.

So why, I enquired politely, was she walking the South Tyne Trail and not the exact route of the Pennine Way through the adjacent valley? She smiled and gave me a wordless look that I took to mean she went where she pleased, so I didn't pursue it any more.

At a trackside halt beside the railway, I stopped at a picnic table, ostensibly to get my flask out and have a coffee, but I sensed she wanted to speed up, so I said goodbye and wished her well. A brief conversation with this experienced and confident Pennine Way walker reminded me again just how completely a familiar and much-loved walking route like the Pennine Way can become part of your life. It was self-evidently the case for me, too, although I couldn't pretend to know the walked route as well as others. Still, the Pennine Way and I were more or less the same age; it had been lodged in my walking subconscious (if there is such a thing) ever since footpaths and the outdoors first registered with me at an impressionable young age; and although I'd never walked the trail in one go until now, I clearly felt a deep compulsion and a longing to tread this illustrious path northwards. Several times on the walk, I even had the odd sensation of almost knowing what was round the corner – the view, the path direction, the layout of a hamlet – even though I'd never physically set foot on that particular patch of ground.

At one point, I did wonder whether I was getting ever so slightly obsessed with the Pennine Way, but my conversation that morning on leaving Alston convinced me that the path really did exert a positive power, embracing personal motivation and inspiration, belonging and companionship. Indeed, its magnetism for some people is quite remarkable, not least because it keeps drawing them back.

The Countryside Commission's survey in 1990 revealed that a quarter of Pennine Way walkers said they returned 'again and again – some up to five times a year – while a third of day visitors do likewise.' Writing in *The Dalesman* magazine as far back as April 1965, Kenneth Oldham offered the following analogy. 'The Pennine Way has the peculiar fascination of a good book: the more you read, the more certain it is that you will not give up before the final chapter is complete. Unlike reading, however, you can tackle it from either end or sample random sections from the middle.' But what drives some people to read that book over and over again?

It was at Crowden that I'd first come across Mike Imrie's investigation into the physiological effects on the human body of an exceptionally long walk. Mike has walked the Pennine Way a dozen times. Why? I asked him. 'Sometimes we find a place that resonates for us, somewhere we feel we really belong,' he told me. 'The Pennines have that effect on me. Each time I feel the excitement of meeting an old friend, of "coming home". Some parts more than others; indeed there are parts I'm not fond of, but I still feel like saying "It's me, I'm back, sorry to have been away so long."'

Someone else for whom the Pennine Way has become a way of life is Chris Sainty. For 20 years he was the honorary secretary of the Pennine Way Association (previously the Pennine Way Council), before becoming its newsletter editor and then chairman. His guidebook to the path that he'd walked 10 times was published in 2014; and he had already embarked on his 11th Pennine Way outing when I met up with him at Hebden Bridge after my walk.

I began by asking him which was his favourite section of the trail. It turned out that he, like Tom Stephenson, preferred the Cheviot

Hills. 'I've always loved the Border Ridge, it's proper fellwalking,' he explained. 'The scenery is fantastic and when the sun is shining there is nothing on the Pennine Way, apart from High Cup Nick, to match it. I always look out for the wild goats that graze on the ridge. As a south to north walker, there's the excitement of the last section, too.'

Feeling just a little like a doctor (or psychiatrist) with a patient, I asked Chris to describe his first attempt on the path. 'It was in September 1975,' he recalled. 'I was about 20, totally inexperienced and unprepared. I wore jeans, a bright orange cagoule and Spanish fell boots which were made of a sort of felt material, totally impractical for the Pennine Way.' He had to give up at Alston because of blisters, but the Pennine Way bug had bitten. 'The Pennine Way is a sort of illness,' he said, stretching the medical analogy a little further than I'd anticipated, 'and the only cure is by taking a vaccine that is the Pennine Way.' So he went back better equipped, fitter and wiser, and successfully completed the whole distance in April 1977.

But why go on and walk it so many more times? 'Initially it was because the walk was very popular and as a solo walker I could always tag on to a small group and travel with them on their Pennine Way journey. After that, I fell in love with the Pennine Way countryside and the history of the place.'

Indeed, part of the pleasure is clearly familiarisation. 'I find I can switch off and really enjoy the walk because I know the route so well,' he explained. 'And because of its length and sheer variety there is always something new, something I want to go back for. For instance, only on the fifth walk did I finally experience the summit of Cross Fell without cloud!'

I suggested to him that, after 10 or 11 times walking the trail, his knowledge of the Pennine Way must be approaching encyclopedic. 'Well, I once walked it without taking my guidebook out of the pack,' he admitted. 'And on another occasion, when chatting after "lights out" in a youth hostel, a group of us managed to name the location of every trig point on the Pennine Way. After a while you get to know the B&B and youth hostel wardens, too, and they greet you by your first name.'

However, even on his latest walk, he was looking forward to discovering something new about the Pennine Way. 'There's the beacon guard's grave off Pinhaw Beacon, which I've only just learnt about and never visited,' he explained. 'Enlisted men were stationed by hilltop beacons in case they needed to signal that Napoleon was invading. Unfortunately the guard on top of Pinhaw Beacon froze to death near his shelter in the severe weather of 1805 and there's a simple stone in the ground where he was found. I'll try and find it when I walk the path this autumn.'

The more I talked to Chris, the more it became apparent that this wasn't a head-down-for-the-line sort of guy. It wasn't about finishing at all costs. Four decades on from first setting foot on the Pennine Way, for him it's now as much about the countryside, history and heritage of the Pennines. 'I enjoy booking a cottage along the route and going out for a series of circular day walks,' he said. 'During my various Pennine Way walks I've come across many UK and overseas walkers, mainly Dutch and Australian, and they love it. I don't know of any other footpath where some walkers would simply turn round at the end and walk right back to the start.'

In a way that many of us can probably understand, Chris described how the Pennine Way – despite the physical and mental challenge – has helped him de-stress and mentally recharge after a hectic time at work; but he talked about the Pennine Way with not just great feeling but also a real sense of intimacy. 'It's a love story, really,' he admitted quite candidly. 'The Pennine Way is my mistress in a way, but luckily I can take my wife with me as well.'

Eventually the little railway line came to end, but the cleared vegetation and piles of ballast beyond showed that plans to extend it further were well in hand. However, for now, the walking route continued alone via the hamlet of Slaggyford as far as Burnstones. It was time to resume the official route of the Pennine Way, and for the first mile or so there was good progress along a typically direct and no-nonsense Roman route called the Maiden Way, which linked the Eden valley with the Roman fort of Carvoran near Greenhead. But after dropping down off the open hillside, the path started to get fussy, weaving this way and that as it crossed Hartley Burn. As if to add to the vague sense of uncertainty and lack of direction, there was even an official-looking sign nailed to the top of a wooden stile beside the path saying 'NOT Pennine Way' (apparently the route did go this way once). A little further on, and rather more helpful, was a small wooden sign with an arrow and 'Pennine Way' painted in crude black letters; then when I did at last reach a stile exhibiting an official national trail disc and formal yellow footpath arrow, it was marooned and unused in overgrown vegetation beside an open gateway.

Signposting the Pennine Way is not as straightforward as you might think. Quite apart from the fact that there is an awful lot of ground to cover, a number of different highway authorities share the responsibility, and man-made structures and signs don't necessarily last long in such a punishing outdoor environment. Then there is the much bigger question of whether or how far the Pennine Way should be signposted in the first place. As an officially designated national trail – the premier league of long-distance paths in England and Wales – the Pennine Way has to meet certain standards when it comes to waymarking and path furniture (as stiles, bridges and signs are rather quaintly called). You would expect to see the national trail symbol, for instance, the familiar white acorn on a black background that adorns the likes of the Offa's Dyke Path, Cleveland Way and so on, but in the case of the Pennine Way you might not necessarily expect to see quite so many.

From early on, the Pennine Way's designers were keen that the essential wildness of this upland route should be kept as intact as possible and not overburdened with signage. It was, after all, designed to be a strenuous and adventurous trail where the walker should be confident of his or her own navigation skills and enjoy uncluttered vistas. The Pennine Way Association's submission to the Scott Committee in 1942 was clear about how it saw the path on the ground: 'Some indication of the route would probably be necessary. Waymarking is a controversial subject, and it may be mentioned the Pennine Way Association does not favour the idea of marking the way with splashes of paint as was the pre-war practice in some continental countries. On the higher ground, stone cairns could be erected as is done in the Lake District, Snowdonia, and other mountainous parts of Britain.'

In the end, there were proper signposts and waymarks, of course, but they tended to be more numerous in the lowland sections and around farms and villages. Few cairns were actually built, but one area where this did happen was on top of the Cheviot Hills. It was the late 1950s, and more and more ramblers were out exploring the much-talked-about Pennine Way. On the bare and remote slopes of the Cheviots, where navigation could be tricky at the best of times, earlier wooden signposts had quickly vanished, so the decision was taken to erect a series of 12 stone-and-turf cairns between Chew Green and Windy Gyle. Northumberland County Council agreed to provide the tools, equipment and materials and the Ramblers' Association's Northern Area would supply the volunteer labour. One of the latter who was instrumental in the project was Les Herbert, and he recounted what happened in a fascinating series of articles for the Pennine Way Council's newsletters in 1982–83.

Les explained that the locations were carefully chosen to guide walkers so that they would provide confirmation of the correct route in good weather or reassurance in bad, with plenty of reconnaissance taking place beforehand to work out the optimum sites. However, erecting the structures 2000ft up on a string of remote, rough and inaccessible hilltops proved quite a challenge and wasn't without the odd mishap, including minor injuries, marooned vehicles and plenty of bog-splattered clothing; but eventually (and with the help of a surprisingly enthusiastic party of what might today be called young offenders from a nearby special school) they were completed and a further dozen followed.

In *Pennine Way Companion*, Wainwright's sketch of one of the structures shows a low mound with a short post and a small sign that simply reads 'PW'. However, Wainwright goes on to report that many of the posts had been 'wantonly beheaded'; and although some of the cairns are still recognisable today, others have all but vanished, which seems to be a repeating pattern with official signage in this remote location. Geoffrey Berry's 1975 guide to walking in the hills of northern England shows a photo of himself standing by a huge, official-looking Pennine Way information board and map (easily 8ft high) at the top of Clennell Street, a remote and historic border crossing on the trail between Windy Gyle and King's Seat. Even Berry is rather perplexed by its presence, commenting that it seemed a strange place to have put such a prominent construction. Needless to say, it's not there now and instead there's a simple directional fingerpost. In fact, 20 official 'map boards' (as they were called) were installed at locations along the path not long after it opened, and although they weathered over time and some disappeared or were replaced, a copy of an original one still exists by the bus stop at Kirk Yetholm.

Despite the enormous effort it took to build two dozen cairns in such a difficult location, Les Herbert was sanguine not only about their purpose and effectiveness but also about their potential shelf life. He recalled how he had been guided by a much earlier conversation with Tom Stephenson. 'He told me, as he must have many others, that once the cairns were built, walkers would use them, and before long the track between the cairns would become so well defined that a map would hardly be necessary thereafter; one could even assume (I assumed) that the cairns could eventually be allowed to lapse into dignified redundancy; or be kept in token being by the occasional stone dropped as an offering by grateful followers of the beaters-out path.'

At about the same time, in the Yorkshire Dales, they were also contemplating putting in extra signs and waymarks. Head Warden Wilf Proctor (who, at Malham, had organised the Pennine Way's opening ceremony) was quoted in the *Evening Post* as saying that the original idea was for the new trail to have as few markers as possible 'and thus create a sense of achievement for those who managed to follow the Way. But there has been an increasing tendency for Mum, Dad and son to come out for the day in the car.' Wilf went on to explain the problem in more detail. 'Dad and son leave the car and follow the Way while Mum drives the car round to the next point where the route crosses a road. There is some danger of people like this getting lost and we must guard against that.'

Today, the Pennine Way's signage and waymarking on the open, wilder sections remains low-key, if it exists at all. Back on Bleaklow, I'd seen a few small and unobtrusive stone markers with yellow-painted arrows, maintained (somewhat reluctantly, I felt) by Pennine Way Ranger Martyn Sharp, who had only installed them where walkers keep going wrong; and just the day before, on Knock Fell, there were similar short stone posts with gold-painted arrows. As Martyn had said to me rather wistfully, if you need to rely on signposts to walk the Pennine Way then perhaps it's not the path for you.

The Scott Committee submission from the Pennine Way Association, made (it should be remembered) some 23 years before the trail was officially opened, also suggested that footbridges over moorland streams 'need be nothing more elaborate than a single plank adequately secured against flood waters'. It also had a sensible suggestion regarding drystone walls: 'However careful one may be, it is not always possible to scale these without dislodging some stones. To avoid this annoyance to the farmer, wooden ladder stiles could be erected where required.'

Today there are whole chapters in illustrated manuals devoted to the construction of footbridges, as well as a British Standard for gaps, gates and stiles (BS5709, in case you are interested). According to the Pennine National Trails Partnership Manager, there are 402 Pennine Way signposts featuring the national trail acorn along the length of the path. The trail also has 427 gates, 120 bridges, as well as 260 stiles and 27 sets of steps, which probably goes some way to explain why you are likely to finish the Pennine Way with considerably stronger legs than when you started.

I scaled one of those 260 stiles to gain access to Blenkinsopp Common. Like the preceding Hartleyburn Common, it was a depressingly soggy and wholly unremarkable patch of land. There was a token section of boardwalk, but after that it was a question of hopping from tussock to tussock and trusting that you wouldn't sink in too far. To cap it all, the white cloud and patchy sunshine had been blown away to be replaced by some fierce-looking shower clouds, one of which let forth a short but violent deluge.

At the end of the afternoon, I had to walk off the route by several miles to find accommodation, as it was Saturday and most of the places in and around Greenhead were booked up. I was now in Hadrian's Wall country, where tourism is taken seriously; and I was reminded again that for the solo walker looking for a bed in a private establishment, there are two words that really end up grating: 'single supplement'.

However, the B&B I stayed in was comfortable and friendly, if rather expensive, plus it was close to the Wall which meant that in effect I left one national trail (Pennine Way) for another (Hadrian's Wall Path). Quite apart from waking up and looking out of the window at a wall that was getting on for two thousand years old, it was interesting to rub shoulders with other guests walking different paths and learn about their journey – which often shines a light back on your own. Mind you, it didn't start too promisingly. Guests at the B&B were invited to take breakfast together at the same time, and at one large table. I'm generally not at my most talkative at such an early hour and the prospect of polite chit-chat round the table over bacon and eggs always fills me with a sinking heart. Each guest had been given a sheet on which they had to tick their breakfast order: tea or coffee, full English or continental, and so on. I stared at the form and wondered whether I could add an extra section at the bottom, with tick boxes. It might run something like this:

Do you want to engage in conversation with your fellow guests over breakfast?
☐ Yes please, the more inane and pointless the better!
☐ Measured cheerfulness with a few polite asides
☐ Occasional one-liners only
☐ Don't even look at me

In the end I needn't have worried, since the other guests were charming, not least because it was such an international mix. There were three couples (English, American and Australian), together with a young and good-looking Dutch family of four – fit, sporty and implausibly radiant.

Everyone apart from me was walking the Hadrian's Wall Path. I thought back to Keld and began to experience a Coast to Coast Walk déjà vu, but soon it became clear that the Hadrian's Wall Path was an entirely different proposition from the Coast to Coast and Pennine Way routes. The elderly Australian couple explained that the Roman Wall, rather than the path itself, was the attraction, and that they had actually found the undulating trail surprisingly hard work. With the exception of the family from the Netherlands, they were all on organised walking holidays and were having their luggage transferred every day, so they only had to walk with a light daysack. Even so, the elderly Australian lady complained that her knees were giving her so much trouble that she might catch a bus to Carlisle for a day off instead. But what, she wanted to know, was the Pennine Way like? She said that it sounded like quite a challenge.

I puffed out my cheeks and thought for a moment about my shameful boasting at Keld and how I'd mercilessly put down another long-distance path.

'Yes, it is quite a challenge,' I agreed. 'And if it's any consolation my knees hurt a bit, as well.'

Everyone laughed. The kindly Australian lady leant forward, patted my arm in a way that only grandmothers can, and said: 'Hadrian's Wall or the Pennine Way, we know it's worth it in the end, don't we?'

From Greenhead, the Hadrian's Wall Path and the Pennine Way run together eastwards for around nine miles. For walkers, it's probably the most exciting and scenic section of the whole Hadrian's Wall Path National Trail, even if the undulating route over the Whin Sill outcrops is also the most exacting, as some of my breakfast companions had found. At 84 miles, the trail is a much shorter coast-to-coast alternative to Wainwright's route further south, which is well over double the length and crosses much higher ground; but as I'd heard that morning, it's the World Heritage Site that is the main draw. The Roman Wall itself is not continuous, since it's had almost two millennia to decay and be deliberately dismantled (in the past, stone has been plundered for local buildings), but there are still sections that are reasonably intact, especially along the more remote and inaccessible middle sections that lay before me now.

The Wall originally stood up to 15ft high, although today it's much less than that. There were forts every five miles, such as Carvoran and Housesteads, and between them were milecastles. If these come up a little sooner than expected, it's because a Roman mile was slightly less than a modern mile. Altogether, Hadrian's mighty edifice took the best part of a decade to build, which isn't bad considering something in the region of two million tons of stone had to be quarried and cut. In fact, it was about the same length of time as it took to develop Hadrian's Wall National Trail, from its designation in 1994 to its opening in 2003. From the early second century AD, the Wall represented the northern frontier of the Roman empire for almost 300 years, separating the Romans from the barbarians (in the words of Hadrian's biographer Tacitus) and providing a bold and visible statement of Roman authority.

On that mild July afternoon, dry and reasonably clear, it was a great path to walk. The Roman Wall crested up and down ahead of me, over bare grassy hilltops interspersed with small, dense clumps of trees, but overall with a feeling of rugged open country. To the south, there were far-reaching views over the bare moors, rising steadily upwards as the North Pennines took shape. In the other direction, towards Scotland, the horizon was filled with rough pasture, forests and a few lonely farmsteads. Immediately ahead, however, the path was beginning to get busy, with a mix of walkers and weekend day trippers.

Since it opened in 2003, the Hadrian's Wall Path National Trail has allowed the public to enjoy much better access to this incredible feat of Roman engineering; and in doing so, it has generated almost £20 million for the local economy, according to a 2010 report commissioned by Natural England. At the other end of the country, a survey published in 2012 suggested that the economic impact of walkers (mostly day walkers) on the 630-mile South West Coast Path National Trail totalled a whopping £436 million a year, supporting an estimated 9771 jobs. By contrast, the official Pennine Way Survey of 1990 (entitled 'Use and Economic Impact') found that long-distance walkers on the trail spent an average of £10.70 per day, and day walkers £5.50. Total spend was just under £2 million, which created or supported around 100 jobs. Given its largely out-of-the-way rural route and bearing in mind that, unlike the other two trails, it doesn't generally embrace mainstream tourism, that's still an impressive total.

As I'd been finding out over the last fortnight, even with a much reduced footfall, the Pennine Way is still indirectly supporting village pubs, B&Bs, walking holiday and baggage transfer companies, not to mention the outdoor publishing industry. This suggests that, although the recent fate of small, Pennine Way-dependent youth hostels is still a reminder of the precariousness of this market, the Pennine Way's economic impact is still significant and that walking trails generally make a much underrated contribution to local rural economies.

The trail billowed up and down before me, and people were visible for some distance ahead. The popularity of the path, combined with the fact that two national trails run in tandem here for a short while, was clearly throwing up its own issues of footpath wear and tear. The parallels with the Pennine Way were interesting, even if the resulting approach was entirely different. In a handful of places there were the familiar slabs, as well as stepped paths on some of the sharp ascents, but elsewhere the instruction to walkers was *not* to walk in single file and to *avoid* walking along established lines on the grass. In other words, spread out and walk side by side so as not to create or perpetuate a defined walking route in the ground.

When the government gave the go-ahead for the Hadrian's Wall Path, it was a condition that the surface of the path would remain a green sward, give or take a few exceptions. A voluntary code of conduct called 'Every Footstep Counts' encourages walkers (and other visitors) to spread out and walk on healthy grass in order to reduce the likelihood of creating a visible walked route, which it was thought would detract from the setting of the Wall. In addition, when the general route of the trail was being decided, it deliberately avoided as many of the lumps and bumps in the ground as possible, in case they might be buried archaeology.

After so many days of variously keeping to narrow lines of slabs or being careful not to stray from a walked route and exacerbate erosion by widening the path, this seemed at first a little counter-intuitive; but there again, I thought, if a national trail is aligned to a World Heritage Site, then its long-term management is likely to require some unique approaches. Concerns over the fragility of the Roman Wall also mean that people are prohibited from walking on top of it (which early Pennine Way walkers sometimes did); and in the wetter winter months, walkers are encouraged to follow circular routes in the vicinity of the Wall rather than a linear walk along the actual trail.

When the Hadrian's Wall Path was formally opened, it became the 15th national trail in England and Wales (Scotland has its own equivalent long-distance paths, such as the West Highland Way and Southern Upland Way). In total, they cover over 2500 miles. Latterly, the Wales Coast Path has been launched, with its English equivalent slowly taking shape. I mention this for two reasons. First, because it shows just how far our official long-distance footpath network has developed since the Pennine Way blazed the trail in the 1960s, putting the grand old path into context but also partly explaining why its appeal has been diluted. Second, because that night I stayed at Once Brewed Youth Hostel, just off Hadrian's Wall (which has since been redeveloped as part of The Sill National Landscape Discovery Centre), and there I happened to come across a leaflet called *The Best Trails in England and Wales*, produced jointly by Natural England and Natural Resources Wales in 2013.

The leaflet was a general overview of all the national trails, full of glossy photos and peppered with facts (for example, you're never more than 50 miles away from a national trail). I gazed at the dark-blue line of the Pennine Way, which made its way boldly northwards across the map of England, splitting the country in two, and so long that its name had to be repeated at both ends. However, what really caught my eye was a quote from the trail officer for the Pennine Way, who said that walking it was 'the journey everyone should make at least once in a lifetime'. It sounded almost like a pilgrimage, a call to Mecca. And then I realised that it was speaking to me. This was my journey of a lifetime, of course. This was the walking adventure that decades of exploring footpaths had built up to, the culmination of my trailwalking career to date. I stared at the small photo of High Cup Nick, looking ruggedly beautiful, and thought 'I've been there, I've done that.' And all of a sudden, I felt really good.

After I finished my walk, I met the author of that quote, Steve Westwood, who between 2000 and 2015 was the Pennine Way National Trail Officer. So did he mean it as a pilgrimage or a penance?

'I actually nicked the "Once in a Lifetime" bit from the Talking Heads song,' he admitted with a laugh. 'I'd met lots of serious walkers who had said that they were going to complete the Pennine Way one day, as if it was something that they aspired to and spent their life working towards.' Steve first walked the Pennine Way in full when he was 16, setting off with two fellow Scouts who eventually fell by the wayside. 'Looking back at my scribbled notes from the time, it seems I got by on Coca-Cola, cheese and onion crisps, and Alpen,' he recalled. 'I don't remember having any money and it seems incredible that I managed to do it at all.' Steve not only went on to backpack it again, but much later, as the path officer, surveyed the whole route on foot eight times; then latterly has even completed the Spine Challenger competition.

Given that he knows the path so well, does he think the Pennine Way's hard-hitting reputation is deserved? 'Even now, it still carries its reputation before it,' he said. 'As far as British walking trails go, it's certainly tough, but there's an almost mythical element to it and I think some of those who have completed the Pennine Way probably perpetuate this, whether deliberately or not. After all, if it's commonly believed to be such a challenge and you manage to do it, then you're hardly going to do it down afterwards.'

However, Steve was keen to get away from concentrating simply on physical endeavour. 'The magical thing about the route of the Pennine Way is that it links almost every important designated landscape in northern England, including some like the North Pennines and Northumberland away from the Wall that are not heavily visited. Over 80 per cent of the Pennine Way passes through sites that are designated for either their landscape, biodiversity or heritage value, and over a third is internationally recognised. A continuous walk allows you to thread them all together and get a good grasp of northern England – where the Dales end or the watershed lies, for instance – which you simply don't get hurtling along in a car.'

So what are his favourite sections? 'The Cheviot Hills for the wildness and sustained uplands. Also Teesdale, especially when the flowers are out. And High Cup Nick, surely one of the most remarkable natural features in England. But I admit there are some rather dull bits of moorland in between.'

We talked about how the Pennine Way had suffered some dark days in the 1980s and 90s but since then had been through a period of gradual repair and recovery. So how did he see its future? Steve started by recalling a walk he had taken along the path with a government minister in 2005 to celebrate the Pennine Way's 40th anniversary. 'The conversation got round to public funding and he asked me how much the Pennine Way cost over the course of a year. When I told him, he nodded and said that was the equivalent of locking up a single young offender for 12 months.'

The amount spent on national trails, and access and the public rights of way network generally, may have seemed derisory then, but over the last decade it has worsened. 'Funding for a national trail like the Pennine Way covers staff and day-to-day maintenance,' said Steve, 'which is all very well, but the real investment and capital spending needed for more fundamental work and improvements on certain sections is simply not there. I worry that as time goes on, the overall quality of the path will slowly deteriorate.' Steve paused and shrugged. 'Still, the Pennine Way's fortunes have always gone up and down, I suppose, and probably always will. Whatever happens, the Pennine Way will always be there for people to walk, a line on the ground, embedded as a part of our history like no other path.'

As the Pennine Way celebrated its 50th birthday in 2015, I was a little surprised at how such a relatively little-walked path still managed to generate so many headlines. Apart from organised activities, such as exhibitions, readings, guided walks, a music and dance show, and a new online Flickr group sharing Pennine Way photos, there were numerous magazine and newspaper articles, as well as a four-part BBC TV series. Five decades on, the Pennine Way still seems to register in our national consciousness in a way that no other footpath does, especially (it would appear) among those who are never likely to set foot on it. What other long-distance path, I kept thinking, could spawn over 50 books, a three-volume downloadable recording of streams and rivers encountered along the route, and a cross-stitch Pennine Way map for embroiderers? Even more remarkably, there are two schools named after the path: the Pennine Way Junior Academy in Derbyshire, and Pennine Way Primary School in Carlisle, Cumbria.

Frank Zappa reputedly said that you can't be a real country unless you have a beer, an airline and a football team. To take his words slightly out of context, if you're judging the seriousness of a path in terms of its beer, look no further than the output of the Yorkshire-based Pennine Brewing Company. They have produced beers with names such as Kinder Scout mild, High Cup IPA and a blonde ale called Pennine Challenge, as well as a golden beer simply called Pennine Way, described as 'mellow bitterness with a hint of subtle spices followed by a pleasant dry and refreshing aftertaste'.

It is abundantly clear that the Pennine Way is a path with a story, a character and a life; but measured simply on dwindling user numbers, it's perfectly reasonable to argue that the Pennine Way has, in fact, become rather peripheral. With so many trails and waymarked ways criss-crossing Britain, legal access to much of the uplands and a signposted public rights of way network, the *need* for the Pennine Way is much diminished. Perhaps, too, the popularity of some walking routes naturally ebbs and flows? Just look at the Lyke Wake Walk, a challenge walk across the North York Moors: in its heyday, it drew tens of thousands, but after negative publicity about mounting erosion and overcrowding, its star waned.

As the first official long-distance footpath, the Pennine Way not only put a marker down for all that followed, but it whipped up a huge public interest in trailwalking and stimulated the subsequent and rapid growth of the wider network. Now, radiating off the Pennine Way spine, you can link to the Trans Pennine Trail, Calderdale Way, Ribble Way, Dales Way, Coast to Coast Walk, Teesdale Way, Eden Way, Hadrian's Wall Path and St Cuthbert's Way, not to mention the parallel Pennine Bridleway and a whole host of other waymarked routes. Trailwalking in Britain today is unrecognisable from how it was just a few decades ago, and it all began with the Pennine Way. However, given the explosion in recreational walking that followed, maybe it was inevitable that the Pennine Way would be eclipsed by more accessible and trendier routes like the Coast to Coast Walk, with all its Wainwright baggage and the appeal of a glossy walking magazine. But I couldn't help feeling that to simply judge a national trail, or any long-distance path for that matter, on user numbers alone was to miss the point. The bean-counter approach would have written off the Pennine Way long ago. It was the quality and depth of the experience that mattered; and for those who walk the Pennine Way, it's certainly a trail that leaves its mark.

Perhaps a little surprisingly, it was an official review of national trails carried out by Natural England that really put its finger on it and in a simple sentence summarised why the Pennine Way still matters: 'National Trails, and the Pennine Way in particular, offer experiences at the wilder end of that spectrum and are important in raising people's horizons.'

In many cases, this raising of horizons that the Pennine Way provided, especially for younger people, turned out to be a springboard for a lifetime's love of walking and the outdoors. The likes of Paddy Dillon and Chris Sainty had already confirmed this. Another was John Manning who, aged 22, walked the Pennine Way with two mates in the summer of 1986. His brother and sister had already completed the trail and he had a vague idea of what was in store, but the 15-day trek was so absorbing and enthralling that when he got to Kirk Yetholm he just wanted to keep walking. 'It was life-changing,' he said. 'It not only gave me a residual fitness but a mental attitude that prepared me for other walks and an enduring love of the outdoors.' He went on to become a volunteer countryside warden for eight years – the Calderdale stretch of the Pennine Way was part of his patch – and an outdoor journalist, spending 13 years as deputy editor of the walkers' magazine *The Great Outdoors* and subsequently being appointed editor of *Lakeland Walker* magazine. The passion for walking instilled in him by the Pennine Way culminated in him walking the entire 2650-mile Pacific Crest Trail through North America, in 2004. 'I treated it as ten Pennine Ways, back to back, in order to break the walk down into psychologically manageable chunks,' he explained. 'The approach, attitude and level of commitment needed to complete that massive walk all stemmed from my original Pennine Way journey. The desire to walk and explore the outdoors has never left me.'

11

ONCE BREWED – BYRNESS

A question of motivation
in Northumberland's woods

The Pennine Way left Hadrian's Wall at Rapishaw Gap, a small dip in the undulating line of dark crags. I knew I it was time to head northwards into the forests of Northumberland and make for Scotland, but on that damp, grey morning it didn't look particularly enticing. There was drizzle in the air, with the threat of something more significant to come; and the ground was sodden from last night's rain. Immediately below the Roman Wall was a belt of rolling, dreary pasture and grubby moorland, and beyond that dark lines of conifers filled most of the horizon. This was Wark Forest, part of the much larger Kielder Forest; and with a darkening sky and the mist swirling around the densely packed treetops, it looked almost Tolkienesque. I trudged over the squelchy ground towards this Mirkwood, keeping an eye open for roving goblins or other unpleasant creatures.

The trees opened up to reveal a wide forest drive and for a while I made good progress. All too soon, a Pennine Way signpost pointed me onto a narrow path through the trees and what was, in dry conditions, no doubt a perfectly pleasant little grassy strip between the spruces. After last night's deluge, it was a slippery trail of mud with long wet grass and thigh-high vegetation. There was no alternative route, no way of penetrating the tightly packed trees either side, so I sploshed my way onwards, hoping for firmer ground ahead. It started to rain in earnest by the time I reached the edge of the plantation, but ahead lay Haughton Common, an area of open moorland and what I assumed would be firmer ground. How wrong I was.

Less than five minutes later, both lower legs had taken it in turns to be submerged in the bog. Within ten, I'd gone in above the knee. In the annals of Pennine Way journeys, this was no big deal, I told myself – plenty of walkers have been immersed up to their waist, or fallen full-length, or lost items of footwear or clothing in the bog. However, both my boots were now full of water and, despite my gaiters, my trousers were soaking, plus the rain was trying to get in at various other places on my upper body. It really was quite disagreeable. In one place, a small burn crossed the route (it couldn't be called a path) and for a wide margin either side it was evident that the ground was spongy, at best, or near liquid, at worst. This extended left and right for as far as I could see. There seemed no other option than to simply head straight on, either jumping in vain from one clump of rushes to the next, or ploughing straight through the middle of the marsh. From the churned wet ground, skid marks and bubbling depressions, it seemed that neither option had been particularly successful for previous walkers, so I simply waded in and resigned myself to the inevitable. I reasoned that since I had probably reached the point of maximum saturation, it probably didn't matter any more. On the far side of the common, the Pennine Way re-entered the forest, although this time down a slightly firmer track between semi-cleared plantations. When I finally arrived at a deserted metalled lane, I threw off my rucksack, removed my boots and wrung out my socks. A steady trickle of warm peaty water dribbled and steamed its way across the tarmac.

Is there a part of us, I wonder, that in fact quite likes to talk up this wretchedness, valiant in the face of adversity and all that? Pennine Way veteran Keith Carter wrote about his own experiences for the Pennine Way Association's newsletter in autumn 2003. 'I first walked the trail in 1986, before the bogs were tamed by the miles of slabs which now ensure a rather drier passage through the worst areas of slutch which used to characterise the Pennine Way. One of my abiding memories was of my companion sinking up to his waist in a hole, having wandered off the path at Redmires after crossing the M62. I recall thinking of us like the First World War infantry, weighed down with huge packs, slogging up the line, head down into the withering fire of the slanting rain.'

Keith went on to walk the route again in 2002. He suggests that talking up 'the Pennine Way experience' is just as important as walking it. 'Pennine Way walkers seem to thrive on horror stories, of days spent adding unnecessary miles to an already long day due to losing the way, pubs refusing to serve food when nowhere else is open, blisters as big as golf balls and toenails turning black, soaking wet gear and nowhere to dry it – the stories are told and relished wherever Pennine Way walkers get together. Wherever walkers gather they delight in outdoing each other's war stories, including me. I wonder if recollecting those times of hellish struggle against the elements, blisters, tired legs, aching back, heavy sack, etc is more fun than the actual doing of it?'

In many ways, it's to be expected that long-distance walkers share their tales of struggle and woe with each other, although perhaps in the case of the Pennine Way – as Steve Westwood had suggested – it usefully serves to heighten the sense of challenge, of facing up to insurmountable odds, and so makes the eventual achievement all the more praiseworthy. Despite this, Keith Carter finishes his article on a wholly upbeat note and encapsulates how the Pennine Way experience can also enrich: 'My recollections are nearly all good ones. Of meeting like-minded walkers and spending time with them in the pub, the German beer in the Lister Arms in Malham, the snack caravan at Bleakedgate Moor where the bacon sandwich tasted like a gourmet meal, Pen-y-ghent on a brilliant June day with views as wide as the sky, the walk along the Tees with the meadows in full bloom, a family of partridge chicks frantically shepherded away by their mother on Ickornshaw Moor, inquisitive cows near Gargrave, trooping behind me as if I were the Pied Piper, drying my gear in front of the fat-bellied stove at the bunkhouse in Baldersdale, the taxi driver in Haltwhistle who went the extra mile, the hostel in Malham who wouldn't charge because new carpets were being fitted, waiting in the White Swan at Hebden Bridge for a companion who was waiting for me in the White Lion, watching the World Cup match at Keld and enjoying a pint at breakfast at Tan Hill – the experiences are what makes the Pennine Way, not the walking. The walking is good and bad, easy and hard, memorable and forgettable, all these things rolled into one.'

Keith describes how it was sad to meet some people for whom getting to the end was the only thing that mattered. 'There's far too much to see and absorb to let getting to the end worry you. Some of the established sections are too long. Parts of the route are frankly awful.

The main thing is to take it as a whole and put it down to a treasured part of your life's experience.'

Writing in a walking anthology in 1988 (John Hillaby's *Walking in Britain*), Hugh Westacott also had a clear view on how to walk the Pennine Way (which he had personally completed six times). 'The unfortunate truth is that too many people walk it for the wrong reasons. Instead of appreciating it for its very real scenic merits and diversity, many regard it as a challenge and attempt to walk it as fast as possible just to prove how tough they are. In the process they may gain nothing but a few blisters, some injury to their pride if they fail, and a lasting prejudice against walking long-distance paths in particular.' In other words, they had the experience but missed the meaning. He went on: 'But if you're tough enough it makes for a very rewarding expedition.'

From its very early days, the Pennine Way become shorthand for personal challenge, as poet Simon Armitage observed in *Walking Home*: 'In many ways, the Pennine Way is a pointless exercise, leading from nowhere in particular to nowhere in particular, via no particular route, for no particular reason. But to embark on the walk is to surrender to its lore, and to submit to its logic, and to take up a challenge against the self.'

In the 1971 Pennine Way Survey, the two overriding reasons given by 'whole way' walkers for walking the Pennine Way were 'challenge' (stated by 86 per cent) and 'unique experience' (51 per cent). Scenery and peace and quiet were the main motivations for day walkers. Two decades later, the 1990 survey results were broadly similar, although long-distance walkers now cited 'wild country' and the prospect of 'getting away from it all' as the principal answers, with 'challenge', 'scenery' and the opportunity for 'good walking' as other reasons. For day walkers, 'scenery' and 'fresh air' were still the two key motives.

Today, the findings and conclusions of the 1971 Pennine Way Survey still resonate: 'The qualities of the scenery that most appealed to walkers were the wildness and openness of the countryside, and its unspoilt nature … the appeal of "peace and quiet" could be seen to involve not only a desire for "solitude" and "remoteness", but also a desire to escape from everyday life – "to get away from it all" … it seems that no quality could define the unique experience to which

Above Greg's Hut, over 2300ft up on the shoulder of Cross Fell, was originally built for lead miners but is now a bothy and provides shelter for Pennine Way walkers. (photo: Chris Sainty)

Below For a few miles the Pennine Way follows the glorious switchback route of Hadrian's Wall, via the remains of milecastles and forts.

Above A Pennine Way group in high spirits at Bellingham Youth Hostel in 1961. (photo: YHA Archive)

Right Simple guidance for Pennine Wayfarers on the deserted moors of Northumberland.

Above Wholehope Youth Hostel in the remote Cheviots was basic, to say the least, as Mary Jephcott's Pennine Way group found here in 1957. (photo: YHA Archive)

Below From Windy Gyle looking towards the Cheviot. (photo: Chris Sainty)

The Pennine Way spur to the Cheviot summit has been made easier by flagstones.

Main photo The last few miles of
the Pennine Way across the Cheviots
before the descent to Kirk Yetholm.

Right The Border Hotel, Kirk Yetholm, marks
the northern end of the Pennine Way.

Right inset The sign on the
Border Hotel, Kirk Yetholm.

THE OFFICAL START OF THE **PENNINE WAY**

KIRK YETHOLM 268 MILES/429 KM

SNAKE INN →

BLEAKLOW →

The Hebden Bridge Loop
on The Pennine Way

Pen-y-ghent CAFE on the Pennine Way

PENNINE WAY   PENNINE WAY

PENNINE WAY · PUBLIC FOOTPATH · www.northyorks.gov.uk

Pennine Way!

PENNINE WAY →

many walkers referred; this appeared to derive from the great variety of pleasures that the Pennine Way had to offer.'

'Getting away from it all' was a phrase that many Pennine Way walkers had used in conversation with me and was clearly an integral part of the path's appeal. Such a simple phrase, too, but such a loaded sentiment. The 1990 survey specifically picked up on this issue: 'Long-distance walkers and particularly whole-way walkers are a *select* group – predominantly young men with enough fitness and stamina to walk the route – who look for a measure of *exclusive* use of the route to enjoy solitude and "getting away from it all".'

Now, perhaps more than ever, the Pennine Way continues to give us the opportunity to step off the daily treadmill, to slow down and immerse ourselves in the natural environment. Connecting (or reconnecting) with green spaces is increasingly important and the Pennine Way, at times so close to large urban areas, allows us relatively direct access to the hills and moors, the big skies and endless horizons, the dreaming room – whether for a few minutes or a fortnight. We need High Cup Nick or Malham Cove or Kinder Scout or the Three Peaks or the Cheviot Hills to stop us in our tracks so that our mouths hang open and we are lost for words. We simply seem to have less and less time or opportunity for it these days, but the Pennine Way still offers us that chance.

I carried on walking. More dull forest, more damp pasture, more wet moorland. It continued to rain on and off, and all remained resolutely grey and sombre. Don't forget this is all part of the Pennine Way experience and about getting away from it all, I told myself. Yeah, right. I crossed one lane then briefly joined another, but they were empty. The scattering of farms all seemed deserted. Where did everyone go in the middle of the day? And then, seemingly out of nowhere, I bumped into a small Dutch man called Wim. He appeared over the hilltop ahead of me, young and smiling and full of life, bounding along the Pennine Way from north to south. As he paused to chat, his warmth and enthusiasm were immediately uplifting. When I grumbled about the rain, he laughed and said it was good Pennine weather. I warned him of the bog and swamp behind me, but he simply responded by turning round and showing me a line of mud that stretched from his boots to his waist. 'Oh, I slid all the way down the hill. But no harm!'

Over the years, the Dutch have had a long association with the Pennine Way. I'd already come across author Gerard de Waal, who in 1982 published a Dutch-language guide to the path called *The Pennine Way Ten Voeten Uit* (which I gather means 'The Pennine Way full-length'). He followed it up five years later with an English language version, *Going Dutch: The Pennine Way*, a highly original and enjoyable account of how he and his companion Nico braved the rain and bogs to successfully walk from Edale to Kirk Yetholm.

Wim said he came from a small town (which I couldn't pronounce, let alone spell) somewhere near Utrecht, and that he had been over before to walk in northern England. So why this fascination with the Pennine Way? Was it, I asked tentatively, in case I appeared either rude or stupid, because the Netherlands was so flat? After all, Gerard de Waal had finished his own book with the comment that, coming from a flat country, he found going uphill 'exhausting and an almost impossible job to cope with'. But like the few Dutchmen I'd ever met, Wim seemed pretty fit to me. He pretended to look serious for a moment at my question, then grinned from ear to ear. 'Of course, that's part of it. I love the big hills, the trail just going on and on, with great views all the time. It's just a really big adventure. I don't understand why more people in your country don't do it.'

Wim explained how he'd walked quite a few trails on mainland Europe, including the Camino de Santiago across north-west Spain; but for him, as for many of his countrymen, the paths of northern England held a particular appeal. 'The Pennine Way has always been easy to get to from the Netherlands,' he explained, 'and the people here are really friendly and welcoming. I love walking in your hills. I've already done the Coast to Coast Walk, but the Pennine Way ... hey, this is the big one!'

As recently as the early 2000s, the Pennine Way was actively marketed in the Netherlands. Steve Westwood told me how the national trail team used to go over each year to a popular Dutch walking festival to promote the path and other northern England national trails. 'We even translated some of our official path literature into Dutch,' he explained. 'They love coming over here. I've always found the Dutch really well travelled and highly knowledgeable. They tend to be very fit and properly kitted out. You can tell a Dutch walker on the Pennine Way from some distance away!'

The rain gradually eased as the day wore on; but even though the weather slowly improved, there was still no one around. I spied an occasional tractor trundling around in a distant field or a quad bike zooming down a lane, but otherwise the Pennine Way passed a succession of farms and isolated houses that seemed devoid of human life. However, one of them, at least, extended a visible welcome to walkers via some distinctly home-made signs. On the back of a large plastic lid nailed to a gatepost was scrawled: 'Refreshments Up Hill. WC! Shower! Kettle. Fridge.' Intrigued, I followed the signs to Horneystead Farm, where there was indeed a basic room for walkers to use as they pleased, whether for a brew, a wash or simply shelter from the rain. A note explained that it was returning the generosity and care shown to the owners and their family on their own travels. I wanted to seek out someone to discover more, but apart from a frantically barking dog there seemed no one about and I didn't want to enter the main farmhouse unbidden.

As I left the farm across more empty fields, I reflected that once upon a time a rambler would have had no hesitation in knocking on a farmer's door. Sixty years ago, the countryside was a rather different place and attitudes weren't as hardened, polarised or even as suspicious as they are now. In the spring 1979 edition of the Pennine Way Council's newsletter, Ken Willson shared his memories of leading a Holiday Fellowship walk along the Pennines in July 1949.

A former chairman and president of the Pennine Way Association, Ken was also involved in the Yorkshire Dales Society and Campaign for the Protection of Rural England, and was a member of the Yorkshire Dales National Park Authority. Back in 1949, he and his wife led the 12-strong party from Alston via the Roman Wall and the Cheviots to Kirk Yetholm, and in a fascinating article he began by setting the scene. 'It may be interesting, I think, particularly from the standpoint of younger walkers, to look back on the Pennine Way in 1949. To begin with, there were no guidebooks, signposts or maps of the Way as such. For myself, I had only the vaguest idea of where the Way was supposed to go. When a bulky package arrived from the H.F. I thought it would provide all the answers but when I opened it, out fell nine 1 inch maps, a first-aid box and a list of the places where we were booked for night accommodation – but no route. So, one merely decided, from an inspection of the map, which looked the most likely route and off one went.'

He went on to explain that of course they had difficulty in finding little-used footpaths through what was unfrequented countryside in the first place, but trespass wasn't a major concern. 'Farmers were all so very friendly in those days. There were so few walkers around that they seemed to be genuinely welcome and if, whilst off the path, one bumped into a farmer, he first put one on the right route and then spent the next 30 minutes chatting about the weather and his stock and the state of the nation.'

In 1949, not only were there still, as yet, no national parks or official long-distance paths, but the hardships of World War II were still all too evident, as Ken reminded readers. 'Food rationing was still in force, particularly tea and sugar, so that the addicted tea drinker set off without his ration book at his dire peril. We decided that mid-day and afternoon tea was almost an essential and in those days most farmers' wives were happy to provide it. Consequently, if around lunch-time a farmhouse were to be seen on the horizon, we would make a bee-line for it and always, as leader, I came out with the same set piece – "please could you make us some tea – we have our tea and sugar rations with us". We were never refused tea and if I remember rightly, no one ever accepted our proffered rations, for country dwellers seemed always to be better off than townsfolk when it came to food and drink. We were often asked if we would like something to eat. One farmer's wife gave us a jar of rhubarb jam and another invited us all into her spacious kitchen and told us to boil ourselves some eggs whilst she went off to take the hay-makers their tea. All this now sounds very trivial but in those days, when so much was rationed, to be given extra food was a noteworthy event.'

Ken's narrative, and that of Mary Jephcott and Peter Stott, who had also walked the route many decades before, reminded me yet again that the Pennine Way is not just a one-dimensional path or a line on a map, but has in fact played an important part in our social history for over a generation. Since the 1930s, the notion of a Pennine Way had inspired ramblers and access campaigners, and in those immediate post-war years, with a crusading and confident new agenda, it was the driving force that opened up the hills and wild country and made outdoor recreation mainstream. And, quite simply, it shows how different it all was then. For instance, Ken Willson goes on to mention how his group successfully forded Wark Burn to reach Bellingham, then ate supper at the Temperance Café in the town, before subsequently staying at Alnham Youth Hostel, a historic pele tower that's now a private residence.

It seemed a long, hard pull up to the top of Shitlington Crags, although in truth it wasn't really that high and not terribly difficult. I dodged a herd of sullen-looking cows who refused to get out of my way, hurried over the exposed summit of Ealingham Rigg as the rain intensified again, then momentarily lost my way across the rather featureless Ealingham Rigg Common by not noticing which way the direction arrow had pointed. But by now Bellingham was in sight in the valley below and, quite frankly, I was glad. It hadn't been the best of days on the trail, some miserable weather matched with some indifferent scenery. I was realistic enough to know that two and a half weeks' walking on the Pennines wouldn't be rain-free, and I was still grateful for a clear day on Cross Fell, but by now I was ready for a cup of tea and a hot shower.

I slithered down the hillside into the valley of the North Tyne, then sploshed along beside the main road past a wet-looking campsite into an even wetter-looking Bellingham. Opposite the filling station, I found a bench under a tree, which offered some sort of shelter from the rain, and heaved off my pack. I sat back and let out a weary sigh. My feet were still uncomfortably wet and my legs ached. I unclipped my soggy gaiters and threw them on the ground, then I unlaced and removed my boots. I peeled – there is no other word for it – my two pairs of socks from my feet and, for the moment, discarded them in an unpleasantly warm and soggy pile; then I stared down at what was revealed. They didn't look like my bare feet, at least not the pair I had last seen when I stepped out of the shower earlier that morning. The two pale, shrivelled soft specimens staring back put me in mind of a scene in a TV crime drama, where a detective inspects a corpse dragged from two weeks' floating in a river. I half expected that my little toe would have attached to it a tag, reading 'Pennine Way walker. Found Wark Forest bog. Male, early 50s. Identity unknown.' To complete the forensic examination, I then bent over to take a close-up photo of the lifeless limbs. If nothing else, it would later entertain my 8-year-old daughter.

The afternoon ended in a suitably bizarre fashion with me sitting inside a railway carriage drinking a cup of tea. It was not what I was expecting when I followed the road up to Bellingham Heritage Centre, but if you decide to house a visitor attraction in an old railway station then you may as well theme the café accordingly. In fact, the renovated 1957 Mark 1 train carriages standing at the platform looked really quite smart, far too smart for a bedraggled Pennine Way walker, but it was almost closing time and I was both thirsty and a little curious. I learnt that in 2011 the two 66ft-long carriages were brought all the way to Northumberland from Okehampton in Devon on the back of low-loaders, a 418-mile journey that took 14 hours and which is chronicled in an entertaining YouTube clip ('Railway coaches return to Station Yard, Bellingham, Northumberland', parts 1 and 2). It's worth watching the first couple of minutes to appreciate just how completely a 32-ton railway carriage on the back of an exceptionally long lorry can fill a narrow country road (you can only guess the reaction of queuing motorists). Now fully restored and repainted in the Border Counties livery of maroon and cream, replacing the British Rail blue, the carriages feature the original seats and many of the original fixtures and fittings from when the train was last in service.

That evening, I sat in a Bellingham pub and chatted to two other Pennine Way walkers. One was a young lad on his own heading southwards, already complaining of sore toes and the weight of his pack. It didn't seem like he was enjoying it very much so far and I hadn't the heart to tell him what was in store for him tomorrow. My other companion was Hazel, the fast-paced solo walker who I had briefly encountered on the top of Cross Fell. Since today had been one of her planned rest days, I had now caught up with her; but from Bellingham she was aiming to finish in two days, camping at high level, so it was unlikely I'd see her again.

However, now I had a chance to talk to her and it seemed clear that Hazel was motivated by the sheer physical challenge of walking the Pennine Way, as well as by an appreciation of the hills and the outdoors in general. Like so many others, male and female alike, there were also hints, but only hints, at deeper currents – of family and relationship changes, the value of independence and self-assertion; but as so often with my snatched conversations along the way, I was wary of barging into the intimacies of someone else's Pennine Way journey.

Hazel told me that she had previously walked the South West Coast Path but felt that the Pennine Way was, for her, the ultimate British trailwalking adventure ('it's mentally the toughest, which counts for a lot'). This led to the usual conversation about other long-distance paths we'd completed or would like to explore.

We'd had a couple of pints by now and were all getting on well, so I felt a bit bolder with my questions. So what's your real motivation for walking the Pennine Way? I asked. And why are you walking on your own?

She shrugged and looked away for a moment. 'To spend a bit of time with myself, I suppose, and to go at my own speed and all that. You can take in so much more when you're on your own.' She sipped her drink and regarded me over her glass with just a hint of a smile. 'And to get away from men asking me those sorts of questions.'

We laughed at the time, but three nights later, after finishing the walk at Kirk Yetholm, I was sitting on my own in the bar of the Border Hotel, idly leafing through the book signed by those Pennine Way walkers completing before me. As expected, Hazel had passed through the day before and her elation at finishing was evident from her entry ('I've made it! Yes!!'); but she went on to write that, for her, walking the Pennine Way was not just a personal challenge but an act of remembrance for a very close friend who had passed away. I wasn't sure whether I was more pleased that Hazel had finished or ashamed at pressing her so directly.

Later that evening, as I wandered back through the drizzly town to my B&B, the conversation with Hazel helped me think once more about my own journey. I was now within a few days of the end; and despite being a bit wet, and notwithstanding some unforeseen calamity, I knew that I would finish this epic walk. I'd tamed the bogs of the Peak District and mastered the giddy heights of Cross Fell; I'd learnt why the Pennine Way was created and found out about the long struggle to get the dream realised, and then about the fluctuating fortunes of a path too popular for its own good; and I'd spoken to a lot of people about this complex, enthralling and infuriating phenomenon that is the Pennine Way. So surely, by now, I must have figured out what it was all about and exactly why was I walking it?

Certainly there was the physical and mental challenge, for me the midlife test. Was I up to it, could I push myself all the way? Now I could answer 'yes', especially if the extent of my discomfort was simply wet feet and a few aching joints. Then there was the trailwalking ambition and the 'once in a lifetime' completion of the country's premier long-distance footpath, the Route 66 of my imagination for so many years. But there was something else that was becoming apparent as I strode through the hills of northern England for a third week. It was less tangible than the more obvious motivation of challenge or ambition, not easy to articulate, but the *experience* of walking the Pennine Way was taking me not just to Scotland but also to somewhere else entirely. It was bigger than me, happening on a different level, and it could only be felt and not simply done. This extended, measured walk through the hills was giving me the time and space for quiet and prolonged introspection. I found myself reflecting on so many things, including who I was (or thought I was) and what was important to me. I hadn't necessarily found any clear answers yet; perhaps they wouldn't all come and maybe it wasn't even necessary to find them – just contemplation alone was enough. Nevertheless, the experience of journeying at length along this path and the repeated interludes of solitude had the effect of elevating me above the humdrum, the hectic and the everyday to a place where there was calm, space and time. How often in my adult life had I experienced that?

Steve Westwood, during his time as national trail officer, also discovered the transformative effect that walking the Pennine Way has, at least on some people. He recalled that as part of the path's 40th anniversary celebrations in 2005, he invited the public to send in their own memories of walking the Pennine Way and to explain what it meant to them. 'I was amazed that for some people it seemed to change their entire lives,' he told me. 'A few said they packed in their jobs when they got home, others made similar life-changing decisions. Perhaps walking for two or three weeks through the hills simply gives you time to think and reflect on what really matters in life.'

In particular, Steve emphasised how the human body attunes to the rhythm of walking day after day and the benefits this brings. 'We are designed to walk and our bodies work a lot better when we do,' he explained. 'Getting into this daily routine of simply putting one foot in front of the other, amid the fresh air and wide horizons, is a great way of dealing with stress and ordering the mind. If nothing else, it gives you thinking time.'

Arguably, you could have this experience on any long-distance footpath or protracted walking journey through wild or remote places, and many of course do, but I suspect that the complex and high-profile nature of the Pennine Way, with its reputation bordering on mystique, draws more people in and perhaps heightens the experience – for good or for bad.

It was raining heavily again the next morning and from my breakfast table I could see the huge raindrops bouncing off the car roofs outside. My host had helpfully used the kitchen stove to dry out my boots overnight. They looked a little bit sorry for themselves, and after a ten-hour bake at gas mark 6 were almost certainly incapable of repelling the mean Northumberland rain that awaited them. I thanked him nonetheless and he gave me an extra sausage.

There was another couple at breakfast, a very pleasant, early-retired husband and wife from the Midlands, who were doing the Pennine Way 'here and there'. For this holiday, they had booked a handful of guest houses along the northern half of the route and were enjoying a series of circular day walks along the Pennine Way, which struck me as a really good idea. They also confided, with just a little suggestion of smugness, that some days when the weather was really bad they didn't walk at all. And, they said, today looked like being one of those days.

In order to leave Bellingham, the Pennine Way, rather uncomfortably, follows a narrow and twisting road uphill, but immediately north of the town is a lovely wooded valley that was once the site of a 19th-century ironworks. It now boasts ancient woodland and a string of waterfalls, culminating in Hareshaw Linn, and is owned by Northumberland National Park Authority, who promote a popular path up to the falls. In the very early days of the Pennine Way, walkers took this course, then struck out eastwards onto the open moors; but following objections from the landowner, the trail was re-routed away from Hareshaw Dene. For some years, the Pennine Way Council pressed the authorities to reinstate the route through Hareshaw Dene and include this famous local beauty spot that was originally intended to be part of the trail, but the difficult terrain and cost of constructing a sustainable new route proved too much, so the plans never got any further.

Beyond Whitley Pike, the Pennine Way meets a deserted moorland road. Originally the route followed this road via the isolated farmstead of Gibshiel into the forest; but, as Wainwright noted in *Pennine Way Companion*, the Northern Area of the Ramblers' Association were keen for a superior route that stayed on the high and open ground to the east of the trees. They were partly successful, so that the Pennine Way now skirts Padon Hill (with its 'pepperpot' monument to Alexander Peden and his fellow Covenanters, who attempted to evade religious persecution by worshipping in remote outdoor locations) and then goes on to Brownrigg Head. From here, the Ramblers wanted the route to continue northwards via Kelly's Pike and Blackwool Law, before following the southern bank of the River Rede westwards; but instead, the Pennine Way veers into the conifers to join long forest rides to Blakehopeburnhaugh. The short section from Brownrigg Head into Redesdale Forest is notoriously boggy and, rather ironically, is today often bypassed by walkers, who take the drier Gibshiel road for an easier passage. The southbound Pennine Way walker I had briefly met the night before had reported seeing abandoned and mud-drenched walking socks hanging from a fence beside the eroded path.

I didn't see any socks, probably because I was concentrating more on where I put my own feet as I slithered slowly and awkwardly along. Finally I entered the trees and reached a broad forest ride that was undulating, direct and thankfully firm underfoot. There were a couple of very short, signposted diversions either side of the track, seemingly pointless excursions that judging by the overgrown vegetation were little used. Northumberland's conifers, it has to be said, don't get a very good press from Pennine Way walkers. They grumble about the midges and about the huge logging trucks that sometimes tear along the tracks at speed, but mostly about the aura of the dense and regimented lines of trees, planted as a cash crop with little regard for scenery or landscape. Maybe it's also the general lack of wildlife (indeed, any form of life) that can make walking through the forest such a lonely and deadening affair. Certainly, the sheer number of trees is overwhelming. In addition to Wark Forest, Kielder Forest Park also comprises the forests of Redesdale, Kielder, Falstone, Kershope and Spadeadam, covering 250 square miles and making it the largest in the UK.

More than anything else, though, walking through the seemingly endless conifers is simply monotonous and uninteresting. It forces you to retreat deep into your thoughts and, as the miles mount and weariness sets in, you end up switching on what JB Priestley first referred to as the 'skull cinema', a whirl of random and nonsensical thoughts that play in your mind, sometimes a single reel over and over again. For long-distance walkers, it really seems to kick in above 20 miles, as physical and mental tiredness join forces. Most memorably, long-distance walker John Hillaby wrote about his own skull cinema in *Journey Through Britain*, when among other things he imagined being sucked down into a Dartmoor bog. Hillaby described skull cinema in more general terms in an article in the *New Scientist* in December 1977, suggesting that it was the inevitable by-product of very long walks that suffer from 'persistent ordinariness'.

With a few exceptions, so far the Pennine Way had been anything other than ordinary. Some moorland stretches were undeniably dull, but they had seldom lasted more than a few hours; and their sheer open space, combined with the changing and sometimes dramatic scenery that surrounded them, had provoked expansive and largely positive thoughts – hence the irresistible feeling of journeying on another level and freeing the mind. Half a day wandering amid a few million dripping Sitka spruces and lodgepole pines quickly dispelled that feeling.

Drawing on his own experience, John Hillaby explained that while the skull cinema's flow can always be turned on, it cannot so easily be diverted or turned off; and unless attended to, it has a tendency to become morbid and follow patterns of discontent. He recounted a conversation he'd once had with a wise old innkeeper in the Alps, who said that when people walk alone they live through their lives backwards and forwards, and the thoughts that emerge are usually kept from their friends, which wasn't always a good thing. 'But with company, he felt, you were obliged to live largely in the present and that was much easier and entertaining.'

Later that afternoon, pausing as I approached Byrness, I jotted down what played on my own loop during those long and solo miles through the forest. It wasn't so much a reel as a series of seemingly random and unconnected thoughts. Inevitably I dwelt on my feet, and I see that I spent a few moments speculating on the symptoms of trench foot and whether I was showing early signs. Prompted by the sight of a barn owl that morning, and a superb close-up view of a short-eared owl a few days before on the slopes of Knock Fell, I spent a short time thinking about owls, which don't usually register highly in my thought processes. As John Hillaby's innkeeper predicted, I went backwards and forwards a few times, but not really in any maudlin kind of way. In fact, more than anything, I recalled all the B&Bs and pubs I'd stayed at on the Pennine Way so far and rated them in order of beer, food, comfort and so on. This, as I'd found on other long-distance walks, is an entertaining game that you can play on your own and with others. On this occasion, it was also enlivened by including amusing place names, since the present forest ride ended by a house called Blakehopeburnhaugh, which is not only the longest place name on the Pennine Way but also, it is claimed, the longest in England. Less than a mile later, Cottonshopeburn Foot tries to outdo it, especially when some maps join the 'Foot' to make it all one word. For a reason that is now lost to me, probably fatigue or dehydration, I found this really quite absorbing and I even made up some names of my own and practised them aloud on the trees around me as I marched along. Two and half weeks of walking the Pennine Way alone can do funny things to a person.

12

The testing home stretch through the Cheviots

There are a number of establishments on the Pennine Way that over the years have become something akin to trail institutions. Myths have almost developed around them. The Old Nags Head at Edale, May's Aladdin's Cave Shop near Hebden Bridge, Pen-y-ghent Café at Horton-in-Ribblesdale, Tan Hill Inn and the Border Hotel at Kirk Yetholm all come to mind. Also now on that list is surely the Forest View Walkers Inn at Byrness. It was previously a YHA hostel, but when this closed in 2006 it was bought by Colin and Joyce Taylor, who used their experience in the hospitality industry to turn it into bespoke walkers' accommodation.

Sometimes referred to as the last village in England, Byrness is located on the A68 a few miles south of the England–Scotland border at Carter Bar. It's probably true to say that most motorists don't give the rows of plain, terraced houses much of a second glance. They were originally built to accommodate forestry workers, and the walkers' lodge occupies two of the houses, with Colin and Joyce living next door in a third. It doesn't look much from the outside, but with only a few miles left of the Pennine Way who really cares? However, as soon as you step across the threshold, you realise what this place is all about: a large conservatory where you can remove your wet gear, dump your stuff and make a brew; a good drying room (Colin will clean your boots for you without asking and is a little put out when you do it yourself); packed lunch and evening meals; a small bar with proper hand-pulled local beers; a tuck shop at the foot of the stairs to stock up on goodies; a library of walking books and maps; and en suite rooms throughout. You can even camp in the back garden and use all the facilities, so long as you come in and eat.

Given that it's at the beginning of the last stage for those heading south to north, I presumed Colin and Joyce would know the ins and outs of Pennine Way walkers. So what state did they tend to be in at Byrness?

'Most say to us that they're both excited and sad to finish,' said Joyce. 'It's clearly very personal to them. We quite often have grown men and women in tears because they're at the end of their journey. It doesn't matter whether they're raising money for a charity in memory of a loved one or perhaps realising a lifetime's dream after being made redundant, we really get a sense of the tremendous personal challenge that people are going through. The Pennine Way is clearly not just any old path.'

It's also true to say that Colin and Joyce have seen some, well, unusual Pennine Way sights over the years.

'There was a young Canadian lad,' remembered Colin. 'He'd been walking on his own, camping along the way, and was proud of the fact that he hadn't showered the entire route. Anyway, he wanted to eat with us, but his smell was so overpowering that I told him "no shower, no meal".' (Apparently they then had trouble getting him out of the shower, he was enjoying it so much.) Colin also recalls the army colonel who walked the route supported by his 'bat man' and two others going on ahead in a 'flashy Volvo estate'. Apparently they set up tables and chairs for lunch on the trail each day, bringing out a tea service and prepared sandwiches. 'They all stayed here two nights and had a ball,' remembers Colin. 'If that wasn't memorable enough, just a fortnight later we had a young, single man turn up, having walked from Edale in an old T-shirt and cargo pants. No rucksack, just some spare underwear, a water bottle stuffed in his pockets and a waterproof tied round his middle. Said he had loved every minute of it!'

Then there was the man they fondly nicknamed 'Slowcoach', who first walked some of the trail aged 16 but gave up because of blisters. Over the years, he went back and completed a couple more sections, but his trailwalking stopped when he got married and had children. He finally returned to finish the path nearly 40 years after starting it.

'There's something about the Pennine Way,' says Joyce. 'I don't know why but for some people it's a compulsive path. If you don't finish, it nags away at you so you have to go back, and for those that do they start thinking about doing it in the other direction. We regularly have people coming through who have walked it several times, a few even into double figures, and they've become firm friends.'

Joyce says that the numbers of Pennine Way walkers staying at Forest View, since it opened in 2006, have risen slowly each year. 'Maybe it's gone up lately with all the publicity surrounding the path's 50th anniversary, but from talking to walkers we get the sense that after being lured away by the fanfare surrounding other routes, like Julia Bradbury's programme about the Coast to Coast Walk and the opening of the Hadrian's Wall Path, people are gradually coming back to the Pennine Way.'

Like the Forest View Walkers Inn, the final stage of the Pennine Way has also developed something of near-legendary status, mainly because it's an exceptionally long and challenging hillwalk – the Pennine Way in microcosm, in fact. Depending on whether you tag on the detour to the summit of the Cheviot, it's in the region of 26–28 miles, with no obvious break for accommodation; and given that it's along the top of a very high and exposed range of hills, this can be extremely taxing. Rather typically, Wainwright didn't mince his words: 'Make no mistake about it. This is a long, hard walk. Damned long. Damned hard. Especially in rain.' On the other hand, so the argument goes, after two and a half weeks on the trail, walkers should be fit and strong; and given an early start and favourable conditions, there's no reason why you shouldn't traipse into Kirk Yetholm in a fairly reasonable state by early evening.

For northbound walkers, it's like one last hurrah, as if you have to pass the final exacting test before you can call yourself a true Pennine Wayfarer, just as the opening day's walk across Kinder Scout and Bleaklow is designed to weed out the uncommitted and ill-prepared. However, plenty of walkers now seem to be putting enjoyment over endurance and splitting the last day by using Colin and Joyce's pick-up/drop-off service halfway along (a B&B at Kirk Yetholm offers a similar service for north–south walkers). I also rather fancied sauntering rather than staggering into Kirk Yetholm at the very end, as well as visiting the Cheviot summit; so I booked a minibus pick-up below Windy Gyle for later that afternoon, in order to break it into a two-day walk, and set off for the final push.

Getting out of Byrness and its narrow valley that morning was a bit more tricky than I'd envisaged. I slithered up the steepening path among the trees and the ever-higher bracken, then finished off with an undignified scramble among some rocks, but eventually I was on the top and it felt good. The weather was at last more promising, fresher and clearer with plenty of energetic cloud but occasional glimpses of sun. Showers were still forecast, but I could live with that. A concrete base on the hilltop indicated the location of a former fire lookout tower, and back across the valley towards Bellingham the view took in dark ranks of trees that crested up and down across the hills for as far as the eye could see, arbitrarily broken up by light-brown strips and gaps where individual plantations had been felled. It was as if a demented barber had shaved random patches of someone's head. Further up Redesdale, the bright reflections of Catcleugh Reservoir broke up the near-uniform green landscape. However, the views that really grabbed my attention were directly northwards – the Cheviot Hills – the final uplands.

At the beginning of my walk, I'd pondered the whys and wherefores of the Pennine Way starting in Edale; but just as there's been speculation over the route's southern terminus, the northern end has also come in for scrutiny. Northbound walkers on the Pennine Way experience three distinct east–west breaks or gaps in the hills. The first is Craven, dividing the moors of the South Pennines from the Yorkshire Dales, then comes the Stainmore Gap, separating the Dales from the North Pennines. The final break is more or less along the line of Hadrian's Wall, from Carlisle to Newcastle, sometimes called the Tyne Gap. Andrew Bibby, in his excellent book *Backbone of England*, exploring the Pennine watershed, chooses this third geological divide to end his own journey. Wainwright also felt strongly that the Pennine Way, after traversing Cross Fell and reaching Cold Fell, should then finish at a point loosely east of Carlisle. It was here, he claimed, that the Pennines as a distinct group of hills came to an end, so the trail should really be known as 'a Pennine Way and a Cheviot Way combined'. Tom Stephenson, though, was adamant that the Cheviot Hills should be included in the Pennine Way proper. Here, like the Peak District, were some outstanding hills that too few ramblers knew about or walked. Accommodation aside, in the end the Cheviot section of the Pennine Way was fairly straightforward to develop and didn't involve the bitter and protracted fight for access that was necessary in Derbyshire.

However, if the Cheviots were to be included, where precisely should the Pennine Way end? When the route was first proposed, the early maps that emerged didn't show it crossing the Scottish border to finish at Kirk Yetholm, but instead continuing north-eastwards beyond the summit of the Cheviot to end at Wooler in Northumberland. We can get a clue to the likely direction from a very early, if undated, leaflet entitled *The Pennine Way Association* (price 2d). Its contents were reproduced in the Pennine Way Council's newsletter of spring 1977 and suggested this route: 'From the north-east cairn on Cheviot go north-east and then alongside the fence over Scald Hill. Go through dip between Broadhope Hill and Preston Hill, and descend by way of Broadstruther, Reastead, and Wand House to Wooler Hostel.' The Pennine Way Association's submission to the 1942 Scott Committee also stated that the route would end in Wooler; and as late as 1947, John Wood's book *Mountain Trail* reached a similar conclusion.

We can only conjecture why the original route was altered, since on the face of it Wooler, with its youth hostel and bus connections, had a lot going for it. Trevor Hardy was one of the original committee members of the Pennine Way Council and spent many years with Northumberland National Park Ranger Service. 'The switch north-westwards to Kirk Yetholm changed what was originally destined to be an all-English Pennine Way into a cross-boundary walk and gave it a Scottish ending,' he told me. 'But in so doing it extended the glorious ridge walk along the border and took in Hen Hole, the Schil and Black Hag, all of which would have been missed on a direct descent into Northumberland.'

Trevor suggests that perhaps the real answer lies in the fact that when the 1938 Conference first considered an outline route, the far northern part of the proposed trail was, for the most part, an unknown quantity. Indeed, as the minutes from the Conference show, the sub-committees of the Pennine Way Association that were formed to survey the likely route had various rambling federations, YHA and Holiday Fellowship groups already pencilled in to cover the southern and middle sections, but for Hadrian's Wall northwards there were a lot of blanks. 'Enquiries to be made in Newcastle area for possible assistance' was all that the Conference organisers could say about investigating the entire route north of Hadrian's Wall. Compared to the already much more well-known and accessible moors of Derbyshire and Yorkshire, the Northumberland part of the route, including the Cheviots, was little more than a line on a rather empty map.

The path bounced along the broad ridge, with wide-ranging views in almost all directions. On a low summit there was a cairn, perhaps one of those erected all those years ago to guide Pennine Way walkers. Rather more brutal, in both appearance and message, was a large modern sign indicating that I was now in the vicinity of a Military Firing Range. It warned me not to touch any military debris, since 'it may explode and kill you'. The MOD's training range extends over a vast area to the south and east of the Pennine Way – well over 20 per cent of Northumberland National Park, in fact – and it's unlikely that you'll get through the Cheviots without hearing or seeing explosions or firing (although I was told they're only blanks). It doesn't always make for the most tranquil of journeys and is particularly jarring given the simple physical beauty of the landscape with its national park designation.

I came across another sign stating that this was an archaeological area and that digging and vehicles were prohibited. Rather more puzzling were occasional metal discs in the shape of the Star of David, attached to posts. I learnt afterwards that they are old Ministry of Defence markers that denote an archaeological site. Perhaps they were reminders to the soldiers not to blow them up?

From the very early days, the vast military no-go area, as well as the Cheviots' sheer remoteness, proved a challenge to organising accommodation on this section of the Pennine Way and led to some inventive solutions, including the conversion of a former shepherd's cottage six miles south-east of Windy Gyle into a simple walkers' hostel. Wholehope Cottage (pronounced 'wool up') was basic, to say the least, and as I learnt from Mary Jephcott it wasn't to everyone's tastes. At 1300ft high and two miles from the nearest road, it only opened on Saturday nights to start with and relied on a volunteer warden who would catch a bus from Newcastle on the Friday evening then walk up to the remote bothy. The building had no toilet or washing facilities and offered the opportunity for only rudimentary cooking; but despite this, it had a small but enthusiastic following. 'Wholehope YH is a challenge to the ambitious and opens up some of the finest Cheviot country,' reported the YHA's *Rucksack* magazine rather candidly in 1949. In the early 1960s, the building of a new road made Wholehope more accessible and it began to attract some less desirable visitors. It finally closed as a hostel in 1964 and the building was subsequently demolished.

There was a smoothness to the rounded hills, bare whaleback slopes radiating this way and that. As the clouds scudded over, the light kept changing, so that the hills continuously went through subtly different hues of greens and browns. This sense of perspective and distance, an overwhelming feeling of openness and freedom, was what had been lacking in the last couple of days. There were constant glimpses into secret side valleys, as well as views across wider Northumberland and into Scotland, since for much of this final stage the Pennine Way follows the border fence. Writing about the Pennine Way in *Across Northern Hills* in the 1970s, Geoffrey Berry reported that 'both sides are well trodden over considerable distances so that strong nationalists may follow their own inclination'.

I'm not sure what I was expecting, but I was ever so slightly disappointed that there wasn't a grander barrier separating the two nations. John Wood sums it up quite neatly in his book *Mountain Trail*, describing how he walked alongside 'this ignobly weak wire fence that follows the frontier line'. A local at Byrness had also made a good job of pricking my bubble the night before. Don't get too excited, he said, it just looks like any other post and wire fence. He also let on that the border tends to shift just a little every few years when the farmer relays the fence and chooses a new line.

I was surprised how many Pennine Way walkers said that the wild upland scenery of the Cheviot Hills made it their favourite section. I'd expected the Yorkshire Dales or the North Pennines to top the list, but I think the Pennine Way has introduced a whole generation of walkers to the relatively little-visited but glorious hill country of Northumberland. Certainly Tom Stephenson thought it was superb hill country, too. Quoted in a booklet produced by the Ramblers' Association in 1976 to commemorate his life and achievements, Tom spoke of 'standing on Windy Gyle in the late afternoon. Storm clouds were drifting along with a beautiful light spreading across the hills. Looking over the great expanse from Cheviot right away across to Lamb Hill and Carter Bar and beyond – those great rounded hills and deep winding valleys and the play of light over them, I think probably I would plump for the Cheviots as my favourite ground.' Indeed, Tom even took members of the National Parks Commission into the Coquet valley and up to Windy Gyle in the 1950s, in order to persuade them to include the Cheviots in the new Northumberland National Park – which they did, of course.

Whether it was championing a national park in Northumberland or pressing for the designation of the North Pennines as an area of outstanding natural beauty, Tom spent a lifetime campaigning for the public's right to access the hills and the protection of wild places. It wasn't simply about the creation of a single long-distance footpath, despite the importance of the Pennine Way and what it symbolised. He was passionate that everyone should be able to enjoy the pleasure, inspiration and enrichment that walking in wild places could bring, and he combined this deep-seated motivation with his skills as a writer and journalist, public speaker and all-round political operator to great effect, over many years and in lots of different situations. Although he left his job at the Ministry of Town and Country Planning after World War II, he continued to represent ramblers at every level and used his connections and influence to further their interests. In 1948, he became the national secretary of the Ramblers' Association, initially unpaid, a role that he held for the next 21 years before stepping down to become its president. During that time, he not only pressed for the National Parks Act 1949 and served on the National Parks Commission, but also campaigned for further legislation and improvements, including the Countryside Act 1968.

One person who knew him quite well in the 1960s was Andrew Dalby, who worked at the Ramblers' Association as assistant secretary alongside Tom. 'There was absolutely nothing of the "great man" about him,' Andrew told me. 'He was naturally friendly with a quiet sense of humour and a real depth of humanity. But behind his mild-mannered and gentle exterior Tom was totally uncompromising and believed passionately about his causes.' Despite that, he didn't wear his beliefs on his sleeve and often could be quite self-deprecating. 'He told the story of how, in the early 1920s, he attended a formal job interview,' recalls Andrew. 'Someone on the panel expressed surprise that a self-educated man was evidently so knowledgeable. So where on earth did he learn it? With a straight face, Tom replied: "Oh, I studied it when I was in prison."'

In his long life, Tom Stephenson was active until almost the very end. He continued to walk the hills into his early 80s; and even when he couldn't manage the hills any more, he enjoyed several motoring tours the length of the Pennines with his new-found Dutch friend, Gerard de Waal, who came over specially to present Tom with a copy of his own Pennine Way book. Together they visited many of the friends and acquaintances that Tom had made over the decades of walking in the Pennines, including not just fellow ramblers, access campaigners, journalists and footpath officers, but also local farming families who he had stayed with or simply dropped in on for a pot of tea and a chat. In 1985, aged 92, and two years before he died, Tom returned to Malham Moor to celebrate the Pennine Way's 20th anniversary, but despite being the VIP guest, taking the plaudits and once more being feted as a hero by everyday ramblers, he remained a supremely modest man. In particular, he was adamant that there should be no public memorial to him in relation to the Pennine Way. It was more important, he said, that people should simply walk the route and enjoy the hills.

Over the last two and half weeks, I had come to learn much about Tom Stephenson and about the story of this remarkable path: the inter-war surge of popularity for rambling and youth hostelling; the vision, determination and energy of those early campaigners; but also the sheer frustration that public access to the hills was so wilfully denied. As I researched the Pennine Way, I kept reminding myself that when the idea of the long green trail was first aired in the 1930s, there were no formal recreational walking routes, no right of open access, no national parks even. It was illuminating to discover that some of the young people I encountered walking the Pennine Way in 2015 seemed to take open access to our hills and moors as a given – understandable perhaps since they were still at school when the Countryside and Rights of Way Act 2000 ushered in the modern 'right to roam'. It must seem extraordinary to some of them that once upon a time there were actually ramblers for whom access to the Pennine hills was so important that they went to prison for it.

The Pennine Way story is tightly bound up with the long fight for access and landscape, the National Parks Act 1949 and all that went with it. It is no coincidence that the Pennine Way starts in Britain's first national park and like a golden thread weaves its way through a second and third, as well as through an area of outstanding natural beauty, which arguably could have been a fourth. It chronicles our outdoor heritage, the protection of special landscapes, and above all how common people asserted the right to walk among their own hills.

Well over half a century ago, in those black-and-white days when the country was still getting over the upheavals of World War II, there was a genuinely held belief that encouraging common folk to walk a long-distance footpath through the countryside could be a force for good and contribute towards moral and social improvement. This is an editorial in *The Dalesman* magazine from August 1952, a year after the Pennine Way was officially designated: 'It is hoped that with the achievement of the Pennine Way other walking ways will be opened up, along river banks, along our coastline, and through some of the remoter country which is at present inaccessible. Such walking ways will, under proper control, help the countryman and the townsman to find a common interest. They will help, too, to teach us all, in the best possible form, yet more of the geography and history and varied beauty of our native land.'

Despite a few brief, fast-moving showers, the conditions remained fresh and bright, just right for a high-level route across the hills. And once up, the Pennine Way stayed up. Ridge after ridge, the trail crested the Cheviots via a succession of soaring rounded tops: Houx Hill, Ravens Knowe, Lamb Hill, Beefstand Hill, Mozie Law, Windy Gyle – such evocative names, too! There were occasional crossing points, some no doubt once used by reivers and mosstroopers, the cattle rustlers and armed outlaws who made this deserted land such a lawless and dangerous place. Long before them, the Romans set up a signal station at Brownhart Law and a marching camp at Chew Green, on the route of Dere Street from York. You can still make out the grassy mounds and outlines that defined the small outpost at Chew Green, which must have been a lonely and inhospitable place.

After an altogether more comfortable night back at Forest View, I resumed the Border Ridge. Ahead of me now, from Windy Gyle to King's Seat and seemingly on towards Cairn Hill and the Cheviot summit, stretched a line of slabs. It weaved its way across the heather, rank grass and patchy bog; then where the ground became firmer, it ended, only to resume for a short while across another damp patch. Not since the first couple of days of the trail had there been such long and continuous stretches of hard surface, but like the Peak District this upland stage was once notorious for its difficult conditions underfoot. There may not have been the same footfall here as in the more accessible and popular national park at the southern end of the trail, but the Cheviot tops cut up just as badly and the bogs became infamous. However, even before this, it was an arduous section on foot. 'This is one of the hardest day's walking in the whole of our journey,' wrote Kenneth Oldham in 1960, 'for the twenty-seven miles of these high summits are tufted coarse grass and heather, much of which has grown leggy and requires knee high raising for miles on end.'

Nowadays, the walking route is much clearer and generally easier, with long sections of paving providing relief from the wettest sections. But, just as on day 2 of my walk as I left the Peak District, I wondered again whether the essential challenge and 'wild spirit' of the trail had in part been diluted by these lines of flagstones. Now, almost at the end of the walk, it was clear to me that the Pennine Way didn't need to be eroded and boggy underfoot to be a challenge. I knew from what my body was telling me that I'd walked a very long way and that it had been a challenge, slabs or no slabs.

Some have grumbled that the stones are slippery after rain, that they are always hard and unforgiving underfoot, so that rather than scanning the moorland vistas you find yourself checking ahead to get a proper stride or avoid tripping. Yes, there's some truth in all of that; but I thought of how I'd moved swiftly across Black Hill on day 2 and was now moving equally rapidly over the Cheviots, rather than splashing and wading at a snail's pace through the treacherous bog that so many walkers described years before. Aesthetically, the slabs seem to gradually blend in, too, just as the much older causey paths have now become part of the upland landscape and reflect our changing use of the hills.

Perhaps more than anything else, though, I was reminded of a comment made by virtually every trail manager and ranger I spoke to: the slabs have not been put down to make the Pennine Way easier to walk, but to protect the fragile upland habitat. The blanket peat bogs of the English Pennines might not seem a particularly sexy habitat when compared to the Amazon rainforest or Great Barrier Reef, but internationally they're surprisingly rare and the UK has around 15 per cent of the world's total.

Ultimately, as one Pennine Way walker said to me, you don't have to walk on the slabs if you really don't want to. If wading through streams and floundering amid spongy bog is your idea of walking the Pennine Way, then go ahead – but I didn't see anyone opting for it. But how much of the Pennine Way really has been surfaced? The latest data from the national trail office, which they admit isn't bang up to date for the entire path, suggests that there are around 21–22 miles of flagstones on the Pennine Way. In other words, approximately 8–9 per cent of the total length. It may be a little more; but given the scale, cost and complexity of this kind of capital work, it doesn't usually happen too readily. Put like that, and in the context of providing a sustainable path over a highly fragile and internationally important landscape, it's a no-brainer.

Approaching Cairn Hill, I branched off to follow the Pennine Way spur to the summit of the Cheviot. (I was told it was simply called 'Cheviot' by local people; and if you really want to prove you're in the know, it's apparently pronounced 'Cheeviot' not 'Chevviot'.) Much of the there-and-back route was along an almost continuous line of pale slabs which, in places, seemed to float just above the bare, semi-liquid peat.

One or two lifted and rocked slightly as I trod on them, returning to position with a satisfying plop or squelch.

As far back as the mid 1940s, John Wood summed up walking to the top of the Cheviots as 'much side-stepping on the hummocks, and slipping on the peat-banks, and squelching in the starry-mossed green swamp.' He also bemoaned the soft peaty summit plateau of the Cheviot, which because of its wide expanse effectively nullifies what you expect to be a commanding viewpoint (it's a lofty 2674ft high). I plodded to the very top and could see what he meant, but the views on the way up were expansive and the sense of elevation was still palpable. At the very top, the trig point was perched upon a stone plinth, a higher and bulkier version of what I had seen on the top of Black Hill all those miles back. The military first established a trig point here over 200 years ago, but since then two have sunk into the soft peat, hence the 10ft-high stone base.

Traditionally, many Pennine Way walkers tackling the Byrness–Kirk Yetholm stage in one go have shunned the add-on to the top of the Cheviot, being too focused on finishing, pushed for time or already exhausted (or a combination of all three). The additional distance to include this high point, quite apart from the extra height gain, makes for an exacting day's walking; but, there again, it is officially part of the Pennine Way and I had come an awful long way to get here. There were now a few other walkers beginning to assemble at the summit on that peaceful afternoon, although I appeared to be the only Pennine Way representative. They included a man in his 70s and (I imagined) his young grandson, who had walked up from Wooler and, like me (but for different reasons), were very happy to be standing on the summit of the Cheviot in the hazy sunshine. We exchanged a few cheerful words and congratulated each other. No, they hadn't walked much of the Pennine Way ('just a bit round here'), but the little lad thought it might be something he would like to do when he was older. His granddad smiled and nodded in quiet encouragement. 'It's a grand path,' he said softly, 'one of the best.'

I trotted back down the path with renewed vigour. Surely it was all – literally – downhill from here? At Cairn Hill, I rejoined the main

Pennine Way after my successful summit push (it sounded good described that way) and immediately dropped steeply down by a huge gash in the hillside called Hen Hole. No slabs or steps, just a very long and plunging slope. At the bottom, sitting all on its own on a bare ridge, was Auchope Rig mountain refuge hut. A small, one-room wooden structure, it resembled little more than a reinforced allotment shed; but 1600ft up a bare mountainside, it's a potential lifesaver in bad weather or if you become benighted.

The current hut, replacing an old railway wagon that served as the original shelter, was built in 1988 by members of the Northumberland National Park mountain rescue team and voluntary wardens. With no road access, the wooden panels (pre-cut and assembled in the head warden's back garden) and various materials needed to construct the concrete base were flown up to the site by a helicopter from RAF Boulmer. Like Lamb Hill refuge a few miles back, it's maintained by national park volunteers; and as well as providing an emergency shelter and somewhere out of the wind to eat your sarnies, it also allows the more intrepid Pennine Way walkers a place to bivvy and take a flexible approach to the final few miles of the trail.

Auchope visitors' book made for fascinating reading; and, with the end almost in sight for south–north walkers, the comments were mostly upbeat and encouraging, from the exhortation 'Keep going!' to the determined 'The wind is howling outside but not long to go. A late start because of the foul weather, but I will do it.' Another walker reflected 'what a journey … it's not been easy, but when has anything worthwhile been easy?' There were one or two more prosaic entries, including '1.09 and I need a poo', and a simple one-liner from Annie of Carlisle, who wanted it to be known that she stopped to make a brew.

Reading some of the entries in the refuge hut book simply added to the momentum and the growing, swirling mix of feelings inside me, now that the end of the walk was drawing close. I realised that this is what the Pennine Way was beginning to unleash in me now – an intensity of feeling that I presumed reflected the scale of the challenge. It was the steady build-up – literally, at walking pace – over two and a half weeks, rather than, say, an instant adrenaline hit after a sudden but short-lived burst of activity. It made the sensation deeper, richer and also unstoppable.

It was evidently a sentiment shared by others. A glance at some of the comments in the various Pennine Way guestbooks along the trail, or at the numerous online diaries and blogs from others who have completed the walk, shows that this strength of feeling is echoed: people either love the path or ultimately loathe it (Pennine Way Ranger Martyn Sharp calls it the 'Marmite trail'). I was surprised that people seemed to bare their souls in a rather un-British sort of way, expressing their profound sense of achievement and accomplishment, and just occasionally abhorrence, with surprising candour.

An anonymous entry from one of the Pen-y-ghent Café log sheets, reproduced in the Pennine Way Council's newsletter of spring 1989, gives a flavour of what lingers long after the walk: 'What I have to say about the Way is that it is one of the ultimate tests. And that I have completed the route, and survived, gives me, occasionally, a sense of achievement when life is starting to get me down and my superiors are being more than usually superior. I can look at them and think to myself, you've never tackled the Pennine Way. And while they neither know (nor care) what the Pennine Way is, my spirits lift a little.'

Like others, I had found that tackling the Pennine Way meets a very basic desire that we have for personal challenge, fulfilment and self-understanding – getting to know who we really are, what we're about and how far we can go. It works for all ages, too, whether you're a young person trying to prove you have what it takes, or (in my case) someone older looking to pass their midlife MOT. The Pennine Way as a long-distance footpath is as tough as they come, but given decent preparation, fair weather and a little bit of luck, it's perfectly achievable. Tom Stephenson and the Pennine Way's other early architects realised this; and the likes of Kenneth Oldham and Alan Binns put it into practice with their school parties – 'character-building' was the term in their day.

Near this spot, many years ago, Mike Imrie had a particularly memorable encounter with a fellow Pennine Way walker. Writing in the Pennine Way Association's summer 1996 newsletter, he described how he was descending the Cheviots and making for Kirk Yetholm. Ahead, almost crawling along, was another walker. 'As I approached him my first thought was that he was a novice just out for the day, but then I realised that his large pack contradicted that impression. He had on a pair of ordinary trousers, albeit a bit the worse for wear, and had a jersey tied around his waist. He was a bit above average height with the sort of generous and shapeless figure more often found in a public bar than on the hills … His shoulders were slumped in weary despair and as I stopped beside him I noticed his eyes were tired and dispirited. I gave him the usual greeting of "Pennine Way?" although I didn't think it likely.'

In fact, it transpired he *was* just about to complete the Pennine Way. He had been made redundant and, with no prospect of getting another job, had been encouraged by three mates to walk the Pennine Way with them, even though he had never been hillwalking in his life before. He bought some boots, borrowed some gear and set off from Edale. One of his pals had given up after three days, a second at Horton and the third called it a day at Dufton. But this chap just kept going.

'With a sigh he said that it had taken him about 22 days so he reckoned that it wouldn't really count as "Doing the Pennine Way". I couldn't contain myself. "Mate, you are a bloody marvel!" I exclaimed. "No experience, no fitness, your friends drop out but you keep going. You are just about to finish the hardest long-distance walk in Britain and the number of days is totally irrelevant. You should be proud of yourself and remember what you have achieved for the rest of your life, because you are the most remarkable guy I've met on my whole trip!"

'His back straightened and some life came back into his eyes. He put his pack on and we agreed to meet up that evening in the Border Hotel. As I strode off down to Kirk Yetholm I forgot my own, negligible concern and wondered how many more unsung heroes there were who having committed themselves to something far harder than they could possibly have managed and have stuck it out.'

So much for what I felt inside, but how was I shaping up physically, nearing the end of almost two and a half weeks of walking? The guidebook suggested that by now I should be a well-oiled walking machine and ready for the final push to Scotland. In truth, I didn't feel particularly honed. Although my feet were generally fine, save for one small blister, my toes had started grumbling after two days of wet socks and were beginning to feel a little delicate. Both knees continued to ache, my shoulders still protested when I heaved my pack on and off, and at times I felt incredibly weary. I'd taken advice from a Land's End to John o'Groats walker, who happened to be staying at Byrness for the night. He had been walking most of the Pennine Way as part of a rather circuitous end-to-end route that had notched up almost 1000 miles already – and he hadn't quite reached the Scottish border. Unsurprisingly, he looked lean and fit, although in a reassuringly normal way. I asked him how his feet and legs were faring. He said he had lots of problems to start with, including blisters on both feet, but they soon disappeared after about 300 miles and since then he had been absolutely fine. Oh, great. So I continue walking beyond Kirk Yetholm for another 30 miles or so to Edinburgh and my legs will stop hurting?

In particular, my left knee continued to ache, something I had put down to a rather clumsy scramble up the rougher part of Pen-y-ghent when I jarred the inside of it on a rocky slab. But after I got back home I came across a reference to a purported medical condition called 'Pennine Way Knee'. The author described it as the path's 'bespoke injury', and apparently it mainly affects the left leg because (the theory goes) much of the Pennine Way is along the western edge of the Pennines, so that the left leg is continually stretched more than the right. I searched in vain for reference to the condition in respectable medical textbooks, as well as in slightly less reliable internet walking forums and blogs; but although there were plenty of stomach-turning accounts of Pennine Way walkers suffering damaged knee ligaments and twisted knees, hobbling in agony down long slopes at the end of the day, I couldn't find any corroboration of Pennine Way Knee.

In the end, I came to the simple conclusion that it was perfectly normal for a 50-year-old man's body to start complaining a bit towards the end of a 268-mile hillwalk, and in particular those beleaguered lower joints that had taken the brunt of the ups and downs. As anticipated, the Pennine Way had provided me with a stern physical challenge, putting my body through a test like it had seldom experienced before, and although it had been tough and I was sore, I had made it. I had put one foot in front of the other for 17 continuous days and had walked all the way from Derbyshire to Scotland. And now my knees, I liked to think, were simply volunteering a view probably held by the rest of my body parts that it was time to take a rest.

From the refuge hut, at the top of the College valley, it was clear that my hope of it being downhill all the way to the end was over-optimistic. There was a final long slope ahead, a climb to the top of the last major hill of the Pennine Way, called the Schil. It was another sizeable, shapely lump, big but not too big; but unlike most other smooth Cheviot tops, this one had a small rocky pinnacle. It was mid afternoon, the weather was clear and improving further, and I was almost there. I rested for some time at the top and gazed in a rather unfocused way at the panorama northwards into the heart of Scotland.

I was reminded of the concluding lines of Kenneth Oldham's book, the very first walkers' guide to the route: 'There lie the Cheviots crowned purple and gold, and not only the Cheviots, but the whole of the Pennines laid out below. And all this is yours for you have walked over it, and now it is part of you. Nothing will ever take it away, for this is your heritage. *This* is the Pennine Way.'

I glanced round for a moment to gaze at the hills I had just crossed. The main Cheviot range seemed more green and brown than purple and gold, but it looked strikingly beautiful either way, a series of soft ripples extending southwards as far as I could see. Turning back, the last outliers were now ahead of me, small and gentle bumps gradually petering out into a flat patchwork of fields. For the last few miles down to the lane into Kirk Yetholm, there's a choice of two routes. The lower route used to be the main one, but problems with erosion led to an alternative via Steer Rig and White Law for an elevated conclusion to the walk that is half a mile longer. (The latter is now the main route but both are walkable and officially part of the Pennine Way.)

In the very far distance, the North Sea glittered, while across to my left I could see deep into the rolling countryside of the Borders, towards the Lammermuir and Eildon Hills. It was incredibly peaceful as I sat entirely on my own, not a soul in sight, deep in a contented reverie. A sudden surge of self-achievement at finishing the walk washed over me; this is what they say hits you at the end of the Pennine Way, I thought; this is the raw emotion and almost indescribable sense of fulfilment that comes with both completing this remarkable challenge and concluding a long and intensive journey on foot through the lonely hills of the north.

Kirk Yetholm was a couple of miles below, hidden behind one of those soft hillocks. I had walked two hundred and however many miles – the total really didn't matter any more – and the Pennine hills were mine, because I had walked over them, and they were now part of me and nothing could ever take that away.

Afterword

Alfred Wainwright was quite right about my entry into Kirk Yetholm. There was no brass band to meet me, no one waiting to pin a medal on my breast. A few people were around on that tranquil late afternoon, but no one took any notice of me, except one local man outside the pub who obligingly took my photo beneath the famous sign ('The Border Hotel – end of the Pennine Way') and who, I think, wouldn't have refused a pint in return if I'd offered.

Most long-distance walkers will be familiar with the sense of anticlimax at the end of an epic journey on foot – 'Is that it? So what do I do now?' – but perhaps in my case it was magnified by an added and self-imposed intensity. There was a momentary feeling of emptiness, as if the adrenaline rush had come to an abrupt end; and stranger still, it almost seemed as if I hadn't bargained for the moment when it would all be over and I would stop walking.

I sat in the bar of the Border Hotel, with my free half pint and certificate, good-natured chit-chat going on all around. No one seemed bothered that I had just walked over 250 miles to reach their pub, realising a lifetime's ambition in the process. In truth, I didn't really mind as I needed a few moments to adjust to a bustling indoor environment after many hours alone on the bare hilltops; but it was a reminder that the satisfaction and achievement were entirely my own and of little interest to those around me.

It also gave me the chance to reflect that, after almost three weeks' walking up the backbone of England, I had come to understand the Pennine Way much better. I had grasped how a footpath, a line on a map, had managed to weave together a story that began with early 20th-century class struggle and hard-fought access freedoms, and continued through to the mainstreaming of outdoor recreation and changing leisure habits in 21st-century Britain. I had learnt how the creation of the Pennine Way was inextricably linked to the birth of our national parks and a new look at nature conservation and our public footpath network – truly groundbreaking moments, if in hindsight with the odd flaw. From environmental destruction to pioneering moorland

225

restoration, the Pennine Way took the blame but also provided a way forward. And, of course, it provided the script for the life and times of the extraordinary Tom Stephenson.

All this might be jolly interesting and certainly helped explain how a path could forge its own place in history, but I could have walked all the way to Kirk Yetholm without giving most of it a moment's thought. I recalled the start of my walk at Edale, when I'd wondered why this exhilarating upland path evoked such profound feelings. Was I a different person in any way and had I enriched myself?

I had quite a long time to think about this, not least because returning from the Scottish Borders to rural Derbyshire by public transport the next day (two buses, one train, one lift) took the best part of eight hours. But I was in no rush; I had become accustomed to Pennine Way time. As I gazed out across rural Northumberland, I thought back over the last few weeks and about what the Pennine Way meant to me, now that I had finally walked it all. Being out there – among the open hills and moors – for a long period, combined with the rhythm of the long journey on foot repeated day after day, had encouraged a profound level of retrospection. For a short while, I had excused myself from the hurly-burly of daily life, switched to a different gear, and it was really rather nice. I wasn't returning home with any startling new ideas or planning to make any radical changes; I hadn't worked out the secret of life or anything like that, but I had found moments of inner calm and contemplation and worked a few things out in my head. Plus, I had also started making plans to walk the Pennine Way in the other direction.

However, there was no denying that it was about the personal challenge, too, both physical and mental, and the need for self-reliance and digging deep to find inner strength. The Pennine Way had provided me with the opportunity and motivation to achieve, to have an experience and to say afterwards, with quiet satisfaction, 'I did that'. I think it would still have been the same if I had walked it at 18 years of age instead of at 50 – perhaps then it would have been weighted more towards bursts of frontier adventure than to periods of mature reflection, but it would have been no less memorable.

It was, for me, an unquestionably enriching experience, despite (or possibly because of) the effort and personal challenge involved.

As so many others have evidently also found, walking this exciting, commanding and at times exasperating long-distance path allows us to raise our horizons and tells us a great deal about *ourselves*, which is why the Pennine Way is likely to endure.

That the Pennine Way is a survivor is clear for all to see. After years of planning and a long gestation, there was the first flush of youth in the 1960s and 70s, when anyone who was anyone walked the trail; then came the growing pains of the 1980s and 90s, when the adventurous hike became a gruelling slog and people took against it. Entering middle age, it was crisis time, visibly thinning on top and losing a grip on its shape, so the Pennine Way went into therapy – but the medicine seems to have worked. Arguably, there is no better time to walk the Pennine Way than the present. Most of the worst eroded sections have been repaired, and the crowds that once thronged the path are a thing of the past. The trail and its infrastructure are evolving to meet changing demand, with modern lifestyles dictating shorter outings rather than full-distance hikes, but the wild landscapes are as breathtaking as ever and the horizon-raising experience is as intense as it was half a century ago.

I'm confident that the Pennine Way will continue to sit at the apex of our trail hierarchy for many years to come, regardless of how many people actually set foot on it. It will always be the oldest, the first, the one that the others followed. There is too much bound up in its long and complex history for it to be ignored or forgotten. For us as a nation, the Pennine Way is in our long-distance walking DNA.

In 1937, two years after Tom Stephenson wrote his famous 'long green trail' article, he published another eloquent piece in the *Daily Herald* about his vision for this 'Great North Trail', as it was called, and about his hope – in those frustrating, uncertain and difficult years – that the Pennine Way could be a force for good and inspire the next generation. 'We shall give them a new life and a new philosophy,' he wrote. 'We shall endow them with a better physique and open their minds to the beauty, the peace and the soul-satisfying gifts of high and lonely places.' All this, from a simple footpath.

Bibliography and sources

Pennine Way guidebooks and general walking literature

Armitage, Simon: *Walking Home* (Faber & Faber, 2012)

Atkins, William: *The Moor* (Faber & Faber, 2014)

Berry, Geoffrey: *Across Northern Hills* (Westmorland Gazette, 1975)

Bibby, Andrew: *Backbone of England: Life and Landscape on the Pennine Watershed* (Frances Lincoln, 2008)

Binns, Alan: *Alan's Story: A Barrowload of Happiness and a Few Tears* (Nu-Age Print & Copy, 2014)

Binns, Alan: *Walking the Pennine Way* (Frederick Warne, 1966)

Bogg, Pete: *Laughs along the Pennine Way* (Cicerone Press, 1987)

Coburn, Oliver: *Youth Hostel Story* (National Council of Social Service, 1950)

Davies, Hunter: *Wainwright: The Biography* (Michael Joseph, 1995)

De Waal, Gerard: *Going Dutch: The Pennine Way* (GéDéWé, 1987)

Dillon, Paddy: *The Pennine Way* (Cicerone Press, 2010)

Grogan, Tony and Chris: *Heart of the Pennine Way* (Skyware, 2015)

Hall, Damian: *Pennine Way* (National Trail Guide) (Aurum Press, 2012)

Hankinson, Bob: 'The Pennine Way in Winter', in Roger Smith (ed.) *The Winding Trail* (Diadem Books, 1981)

Hillaby, John: *Journey Through Britain* (Constable, 1968)

Hillaby, John (ed.): *Walking in Britain* (Collins, 1988)

Hopkins, Tony: *The Pennine Way* (Zymurgy Publishing, 2005)

Hopkins, Tony: *Pennine Way North* (National Trail Guide) (Aurum Press, 1989)

Hopkins, Tony: *Pennine Way South* (National Trail Guide) (Aurum Press, 1990)

Hughes, Ted: 'Hill-Stone was Content', in Ted Hughes *Remains of Elmet* (Faber & Faber, 1979)

Hughes, Ted: 'Pennines in April', in Ted Hughes *Lupercal* (Faber & Faber, 1960)

Marriott, Michael: *The Shell Book of the Pennine Way* (Queen Anne Press, 1968)

Mortlock, Colin: *The Adventure Alternative* (Cicerone Press, 1984)

Oldham, Kenneth: *The Pennine Way* (Dalesman, 1960)

Parker, Mike: *The Wild Rover* (HarperCollins, 2011)

Peel, JHB: *Along the Pennine Way* (Cassell & Co, 1969/David & Charles, 1972)

Pilton, Barry: *One Man and His Bog* (Corgi, 1986)

Ramblers' Association: *The Long Green Trail: The first fifty years of Tom Stephenson's Pennine Way* (Ramblers' Association booklet, 1985)

Ramblers' Association: *Tom Stephenson* (Ramblers' Association booklet, 1976)

Sainty, Chris: *The Pennine Way: A Walker's Guide* (DB Publishing, 2014)

Shoard, Marion: 'Tom on Tom', *The Rambler* (February/March 1989), p19

Smith, Roger (ed.): *The Winding Trail* (Diadem Books, 1981)

Speakman, Colin: *Walk!* (Great Northern Books, 2011)

Speakman, Colin: *Walking in the Yorkshire Dales* (Robert Hale, 1982)

Stephenson, Tom: *Forbidden Land: The Struggle for Access to Mountain and Moorland*, ed. Ann Holt (Manchester University Press, 1989)

Stephenson, Tom: *The Pennine Way* (HMSO, 1969/1980)

Stephenson, Tom: *The Pennine Way* (Ramblers' Association booklet, undated)

Wainwright, A: *A Coast to Coast Walk* (Westmorland Gazette, 1973/ Frances Lincoln, 2010)

Wainwright, A: *Pennine Way Companion* (Westmorland Gazette, 1968/ Michael Joseph, 1994/Frances Lincoln, 2004)

Wallington, Mark: *Pennine Walkies* (Arrow Books, 1997)

Westacott, Hugh: 'The Pennine Way', in John Hillaby (ed.) *Walking in Britain* (Collins, 1988)

Wickers, David and Pedersen, Art: *Britain at Your Feet* (Hamlyn, 1980)

Wood, John: *Mountain Trail* (George Allen & Unwin, 1947)

Wright, Christopher John: *A Guide to the Pennine Way* (Constable, 1967)

Surveys and documents

The Local Pennine Way Conference (typed verbatim report) (Council for the Preservation of Rural England, 15 September 1951)

MoorLIFE: Layman's Report 2010–2015 (Moors for the Future Partnership, 2015); see www.moorsforthefuture.org.uk for more information

Pennine Way Association/Council newsletters (1976–2015); available via www.pennineheritage.org.uk

Pennine Way Condition Survey 1989 (Pennine Way Co-ordination Project, 1990)

The Pennine Way Management Project (Countryside Commission, 1991)

Pennine Way Management Project Review 1991–2001 (Peak District National Park Authority & Countryside Agency, 2001)

Pennine Way Survey 1971 (Countryside Commission, 1971)

Pennine Way Survey 1990: Use and Economic Impact (Countryside Commission, 1992)

Ramblers' Association archives (various reports, booklets, correspondence and cuttings) held at the London Metropolitan Archives

Results of the National Trail User Survey 2007 (Natural England & Countryside Council for Wales, 2007)

Index

LISTING OF CICERONE GUIDES

The Cathar Way
The GR20 Corsica
The GR5 Trail
The Robert Louis Stevenson Trail
Tour of the Oisans: The GR54
Tour of the Queyras
Tour of the Vanoise
Vanoise Ski Touring
Via Ferratas of the French Alps
Walking in Corsica
Walking in Provence – East
Walking in Provence – West
Walking in the Auvergne
Walking in the Cevennes
Walking in the Dordogne
Walking in the Haute Savoie –
    North & South
Walks in the Cathar Region

GERMANY
Hiking and Biking in the
    Black Forest
Walking in the Bavarian Alps

HIMALAYA
Annapurna
Bhutan
Everest
The Mount Kailash Trek
Trekking in Ladakh
Trekking in the Himalaya

ICELAND & GREENLAND
Trekking in Greenland
Walking and Trekking
    in Iceland

IRELAND
The Irish Coast to Coast Walk
The Mountains of Ireland

ITALY
Gran Paradiso
Sibillini National Park
Shorter Walks in the Dolomites
The Way of St Francis
Through the Italian Alps
Trekking in the Apennines
Trekking in the Dolomites
Via Ferratas of the Italian
    Dolomites: 1&2
Walking in Abruzzo
Walking in Italy's Stelvio
    National Park
Walking in Sardinia
Walking in Sicily
Walking in the Central
    Italian Alps
Walking in the Dolomites
Walking in Tuscany

Walking in Umbria
Walking on the Amalfi Coast
Walking the Italian Lakes
Walks and Treks in the Maritime
    Alps

MEDITERRANEAN
Jordan – Walks, Treks, Caves,
    Climbs and Canyons
The High Mountains of Crete
The Mountains of Greece
Treks and Climbs in Wadi Rum
Walking and Trekking on Corfu
Walking on Malta
Western Crete

NORTH AMERICA
British Columbia
The Grand Canyon
The John Muir Trail
The Pacific Crest Trail

SOUTH AMERICA
Aconcagua and the
    Southern Andes
Hiking and Biking Peru's
    Inca Trails
Torres del Paine

SCANDINAVIA
Walking in Norway

**SLOVENIA, CROATIA
AND MONTENEGRO**
The Islands of Croatia
The Julian Alps of Slovenia
The Mountains of Montenegro
Trekking in Slovenia
Walking in Croatia
Walking in Slovenia:
    The Karavanke

SPAIN AND PORTUGAL
Coastal Walks in Andalucia
Mountain Walking in
    Southern Catalunya
Spain's Sendero Histórico:
    The GR1
The Mountains of Nerja
The Northern Caminos
Trekking through Mallorca
Walking in Andalucia
Walking in Madeira
Walking in Mallorca
Walking in Menorca
Walking in the Algarve
Walking in the Cordillera
    Cantabrica
Walking in the Sierra Nevada
Walking on Gran Canaria
Walking on La Palma

Walking on Lanzarote and
    Fuerteventura
Walking on Tenerife
Walking on the Costa Blanca
Walking the GR7 in Andalucia
Walks and Climbs in the
    Picos de Europa

SWITZERLAND
Alpine Pass Route
The Swiss Alps
Tour of the Jungfrau Region
Walking in the Bernese Oberland
Walking in the Valais
Walks in the Engadine

TECHNIQUES
Geocaching in the UK
Indoor Climbing
Lightweight Camping
Map and Compass
Mountain Weather
Outdoor Photography
Polar Exploration
Rock Climbing
Sport Climbing
The Hillwalker's Manual

MINI GUIDES
Alpine Flowers
Avalanche!
Navigation
Pocket First Aid and
    Wilderness Medicine
Snow

MOUNTAIN LITERATURE
8000 metres
A Walk in the Clouds
Abode of the Gods
Unjustifiable Risk?

For full information on all our
guides, books and eBooks,
visit our website:
www.cicerone.co.uk.

Walking – Trekking – Mountaineering – Climbing – Cycling

Over 40 years, Cicerone have built up an outstanding collection of over 300 guides, inspiring all sorts of amazing adventures.

Every guide comes from extensive exploration and research by our expert authors, all with a passion for their subjects. They are frequently praised, endorsed and used by clubs, instructors and outdoor organisations.

All our titles can now be bought as e-books, ePubs and Kindle files and we also have an online magazine – Cicerone Extra – with features to help cyclists, climbers, walkers and trekkers choose their next adventure, at home or abroad.

Our website shows any new information we've had in since a book was published. Please do let us know if you find anything has changed, so that we can publish the latest details. On our website you'll also find great ideas and lots of detailed information about what's inside every guide and you can buy individual routes from many of them online.

It's easy to keep in touch with what's going on at Cicerone by getting our monthly free e-newsletter, which is full of offers, competitions, up-to-date information and topical articles. You can subscribe on our home page and also follow us on **twitter** Facebook and Twitter or dip into our blog.

Cicerone – the very best guides for exploring the world.

CICERONE

2 Police Square Milnthorpe Cumbria LA7 7PY
Tel: 015395 62069 info@cicerone.co.uk
www.cicerone.co.uk and www.cicerone-extra.com